Almost unnoticed before the 2007 subprime crisis, credit rating agencies have since become the focus of much attention: who are they? How do they operate? Should we regulate them? ... and so on. Ahmed Naciri provides answers. His book explains their activities and how they discretely shape the world capital markets. This book is a must for anyone involved with finance.

Julien Bilodeau, *Professor, Université de Sherbrooke, Canada*

A solid and timely contribution to a fundamental issue within corporate and global finance. Features in depth analysis of the industry in terms of scope, structure, contribution, cross country performance, weaknesses and, finally, dark sides. It also provides viable future scenarios and possible approaches for reform. A must read for all involved in international business and finance.

M.S.S. el Namaki, *Dean, Victoria University, Switzerland*

Credit Rating Governance

Credit rating agencies play an essential role in the modern financial system and are relied on by creditors and investors on the market. In the recent financial crisis, their power and reliability were often questioned, yet a simple rating downgrade could threaten to bankrupt a whole country.

This book examines the governance of credit rating agencies, as expressed by their ability to fairly, ethically and consistently assign higher rates to issuers having lesser default risks. However, factors such as the drive for increased revenue and market share, the inadequate business model, the inadequate methodology of assessing risk, opacity and inadequate internal monitoring have all been identified as critical governance failures for credit agencies. This book explores these issues, and proposes some potential solutions and improvements.

This book will be of interest to researchers and advanced students of corporate finance, finance, financial economics, risk management, investment management and banking.

Ahmed Naciri is Professor at the School of Business at UQAM, Canada. His work has earned him the Award of Excellence from the Canadian Association of Administrative Sciences.

Routledge studies in corporate governance

1 **Corporate Governance Around the World**
Ahmed Naciri

2 **Behaviour and Rationality in Corporate Governance**
Oliver Marnet

3 **The Value Creating Board**
Corporate governance and organizational behaviour
Edited by Morten Huse

4 **Corporate Governance and Resource Security in China**
The transformation of China's global resources companies
Xinting Jia and Roman Tomasic

5 **Internal and External Aspects of Corporate Governance**
Ahmed Naciri

6 **Green Business, Green Values, and Sustainability**
Edited by Christos N. Pitelis, Jack Keenan and Vicky Pryce

7 **Credit Rating Governance**
Global credit gatekeepers
Ahmed Naciri

Credit Rating Governance

Global credit gatekeepers

Ahmed Naciri

Routledge
Taylor & Francis Group
LONDON AND NEW YORK

First published 2015
by Routledge
2 Park Square, Milton Park, Abingdon, Oxon OX14 4RN

and by Routledge
711 Third Avenue, New York, NY 10017

Routledge is an imprint of the Taylor & Francis Group, an informa business

British Library Cataloguing in Publication Data
A catalogue record for this book is available from the British Library

Library of Congress Cataloging in Publication Data
Naciri, Ahmed
Credit rating governance: global credit gatekeepers / Ahmed Naciri. – 1 Edition.
pages cm. – (Routledge studies in corporate governance)
Includes bibliographical references and index.
1. Rating agencies (Finance) 2. Credit ratings. 3. Financial services industry. I. Title.
HG3751.5.N33 2015
332.1'78–dc23 2014029703

ISBN: 978-1-138-79654-6 (hbk)
ISBN: 978-1-315-75783-4 (ebk)

Typeset in Sabon
by Wearset Ltd, Boldon, Tyne and Wear

This book is dedicated to all those who, because of others' greed, have lost life savings or retirement plans, in transactions in which they had no understanding or saying.

With business margins exceeding 40 per cent and secured by a quasi-legal oligopoly, credit rating agencies were granted so great power of wealth creation that had never been granted before and that only central banks can challenge.

Ahmed Naciri

Contents

Figures

Tables

Appendices

Preface

The 2007 financial and economic crisis has gripped the world financial system, and although many market participants have played an effective role in the development of the financial slump that wreaked havoc in communities and neighbourhoods across the world and had horrible social consequence, credit rating agencies (CRAs) appeared the most to be blamed. They were accused of mistakes, misjudgements and misdeeds. Although, incisive erosion of business standards of responsibility and ethics is to be underlined and had irreversibly damaged the trust in the whole financial system.

Financial system integrity and the public's trust in those markets are, however, essential to economic wellbeing. Indeed, the soundness and the sustainability of the prosperity of the financial system rely on notions like fair dealing, responsibility and transparency. Businesses and individuals are expected to pursue profits, conditional that they produce quality products and services and conduct themselves well (Financial Crisis Inquiry Commission Report, 2011). One reason credit rating agencies appeared to be most blamed, among the pillars of the business world for their rating role, despite that breaches to ethic and corporate governance in business activity seem to stretch from the ground level to the corporate suites, resides in the fact that major regulators have forced issuers and investors to blindly rely on credit ratings for their assessment of risk. This book endeavours to help gaining insight in credit rating activity and to unearth weakness that seemed to have ruined its governance.

Three main agencies control over 95 per cent of the world market and decades before the subprime crisis already witnessed excessive reliance on credit rating agencies for credit default assessment and for regulatory puposes. The aftermath of the subrime crisis has, however, ushered in a period of protest and questioning of the role of the major rating agencies culminating in new regulatory reforms requiring credit agencies to have more competition and tranparency and requiring national regulatory financial authorities to review their rules and guidelines for the sake of removing any reference to credit ratings in financial regulations.

Assessing creditworthiness of clients was always at the heart of business activities, even before the seventeenth century, but was essentially based on clients' wealth and morality and no reference was made to future economical prospects, turndowns or strategic development they may face or choose. Systematic classification of debtors by their level of default risk is, however, relatively new. Although, financial institutions of the seventeenth century had already clients' in-house classification systems allowing them to assess debtors' creditworthiness. What is new, however, is trusting third parties, neither debitors nor creditors, with the task. What is even more intriguing is to see governments going even further and trusting such third parties by a legislative power. Till recently, for instance, financial market authorities have been increasingly relying, for their regulatory activities, on private rating agencies, making nation states and their institutions dependent on them for their financing. Fitch Ratings, Moody's and Standard & Poor's, the Big 3 became therefore the real gate keepers of the world credit. These three biggest agencies have become, by the beginning of the twenty-first century, the most powerful and influential single private group ever on the global financial system. They were trusted with world capital allocation and wealth distribution. The Big 3's critical role and their powerful position, were unearthed by the 2007 global financial crisis that showed they had gained power over governments and investors, a power that far outranks any group that influential voters might have (Chakrabortty, 2012) and nowhere such power can be more obvious than in the case of the downgrade of countries, sending them to pasture for speculators and completely destabilizing to the breaking edge their economies. In 2009, for instance, Moody's issued a report entitled 'Investor fears over Greek government liquidity misplaced', and guess what happened? Within six months Greece was seeking a bailout (Kingsley, 2012). The Big 3 are able to make kneel governments: recall this sentence from a French Prime Minister following France's AAA downgrade: 'We will do everything to get [the triple A] back' (Chakrabortty, 2012). Recall also the S&P warning made in the middle of last turmoil in Tunisia to neighbouring governments that if they tried to calm social unrest with 'populist' tax cuts or spending increases, they may face a downgrade (Chakrabortty, 2012). Although a downgrade need not spell disaster, it still makes lenders likely to be more nervous about getting their money back and makes them inclined to charge issuers higher interest rates. It will also render government's debt repayments steeper, and more likely to default. Such an infernal cycle seemed to have given agencies contentious negotiating power they never dreamed of. It is indeed claimed that agencies do not deal robustly enough with the issuers who pay them, while on the other hand, they seem to be very aggressive with those who don't (Kingsley, 2012), up to practising arm twisting policy to get them asking for ratings and pay for. The case of the German insurer Hannover is often advanced; it seems that the insurer saw its debt downgraded to junk status, because of its refusal to pay for an unsolicited rating (Klein, 2004). Agencies are commonly blamed for the inaccuracy of their ratings (more than half of all corporate debt ever rated AAA by S&P has been downgraded within seven years, Engelen *et al.*, 2012); they are also blamed for their lack of tranparency and their feable integrity,

> since they can't rest on their records, the discredit agencies prefer to drape themselves in the cloak of science, claiming the work they do is highly technical and independent and were declining any voluntary reporting regarding their approaches and methodologies of rating assessment.
>
> (Chakrabortty, 2012)

Agencies are also blamed for their astronomically high fees they bill issuers with, which have nothing to do with 'their oracular genius' (Chakrabortty, 2012).

Nation states are today the first to challenge the superpower status that they have granted, in a very short period of time, to the Big 3 and are angrily reprimanding them for all the sins that have happened to the ill financial system. Especially that it is believed what gives agencies such immense power is not so much their 'brilliant analysis', but simply the function they perform (Chakrabortty, 2012). Regulatory power has proven to be a poisoned chalice for agencies, although many jurisdictions may have continued to trust them if it was not for America's AAA downgrade and the threat to downgrade the 15 EU countries. 'S&P has shown really terrible judgment and they've handled themselves very poorly.... They've shown a stunning lack of knowledge about basic US fiscal maths', argued the US treasury secretary Timothy Geithner commenting on America's downgrading (BBC News Business, 2011) and this will cost S&P a landmark suit of $5 billion by the US government. Agencies still wield tremendous power that many believe needs more regulation, and ambitious steps were taken by the international financial community to curb agencies' hegemony and to bring them under stricter monitoring and control. Consequently, agencies are now submitted to tough regulations aiming to enhance their transparency and to prohibit the use of ratings for regulatory purposes.

Given such an important role that credit agencies play in the financial system, it is paramount to understand their structure and their interaction with their environment. This book highlights the driving reasons behind the global rating oligopoly, built under the consenting eye and the complicity of the financial standard setter. Since the subprime financial crisis, however, there have been considerable efforts on behalf of the world financial community, not only in developed countries but also in a number of other jurisdictions, to find a way out of credit agencies' grip. For this reason the book also focuses on the regulatory reversal constituted by recent supervision measures of CRAs undertaken by the international financial community aiming to curb agencies' opacity and appetite and assesses their chance of success. The book suggests methods of measuring governance improvement for CRAs that can help users to gain insight in credit rating activity and into the regulatory process at work and assessing the progress made in CRAs' governance. The book reaches the conclusion that the Big 3 have in a clever way built up their system in such a way that it seems difficult, if not impossible, to do anything against it, applauds the extent and the courage of new regulations for CRAs, but remains pessimistic about their realistic effect, despite the earliness of regulations. The book draws attention to a more fundamental question regarding the accuracy of the risk-modelling techniques used by CRAs that may lead to some lack of foresight and keep them from having all the needed insurance for timely reacting and making them appear shy in some rating circumstances and overreacting in others. Indeed, the problem posed by credit ratings agencies seems to lie not solely in their alleged malpractice or negligence, but also in the inability of the methodologies they use to assess default which do not allow 'ordinality' in risk of default classification.

Despite the expressed view that the rating crisis could not have been foreseen or avoided, this book argues that there were warning signs, well rooted in the rating system, but were ignored or discounted, and focuses on ways of correcting them. The book, therefore, suggests alternatives and comes at a very sensitive moment and provides an assessment of the progress made by agencies on the road of transparency and more competition and of the chance of small agencies of benefiting from whatever is left over in the market share. It therefore contributes to a better understanding of the changing rating environment.

References

BBC News Business (2011), 'Geithner on "terrible judgement" of Standard and Poor', at: www.bbc.co.uk/news/business-14445912, retrieved 24 May 2014.

Chakraborty, A. (2012), 'Time to take control of the credit rating agencies', at: www.theguardian.com/commentisfree/2012/jan/16/time-control-credit-ratings-agencies, retrieved 3 May 2014.

Financial Crisis Inquiry Commission (2011), '*Financial Crisis Inquiry Commission report: final report of the National Commission on the causes of the financial and economic crisis in the United States*', ISBN 978-0-16-087727-8.

Engelen, E., I. Ertürk, J. Froud, S. Johal, A. Leaver, M. Moran and K. Williams (2012), 'Misrule of experts? The financial crisis as elite debacle', *Economy and Society*, Vol. 41, No. 3, pp. 360–381.

Kingsley, P. (2012), 'How credit ratings agencies rule the world', at: www.theguardian.com/profile/patrick-kingsley, retrieved 12 June 2014.

Klein, A. (2004), 'Credit raters' power leads to abuses, some borrowers say', at: www.washingtonpost.com/wp-dyn/articles/A8032-2004Nov23.html, retrieved 22 June 2014.

Abbreviations

ABS	asset-backed securities
AC	audit committee of the board
AFS	Australian financial services
A.M. Best	Alfred M. Best Ratings
APEC	Asia-Pacific Economic Cooperation
AR	accuracy ratio
ASIC	Australian Securities and Investments Commission
BCBS	Basel Committee on Banking Supervision
Big 3	Fitch Rating, Moody's and Standard & Poor's
BIS	Bank of International Settlement
CAP	cumulative accuracy profile
CAPM	Capital Assets Pricing Model
CDO	collateralized debt obligation
CEO	chief executive of operations
CEREP	central repository (of the European Securities and Markets Authority, ESMA)
CFR	Council of Foreign Relations
CGFS	Committee on the Global Financial System
CMBS	commercial mortgage-backed security
CPG	Credit Policy Group
CPSS	Committee on Payment and Settlement Systems
CR	credit rating
CRA	credit rating agency
CRP	credit rating provider
Dagong	Chinese rating agency
DBRS	Dominion Bond Rating Service.
DFATA	Department of Foreign Affairs and Trade, Australia, 2009
EC	European Commission
ECB	European Central Bank
EDF	expected default frequency
EJR	Elgon-Jones Ratings Company
ESMA	European Securities and Markets Authority
EU	European Union

FASB	Financial Accounting Standards Board
FCIC	US Financial Crisis Inquiry Commission
FIDC	Federal Deposit Insurance Corporation
FINMA	Swiss Market authority
FSB	Financial Stability Board
GDP	gross national product
HR Ratings	HR Ratings, Mexico
IA	internal audit
IAIS	International Association of Insurance Supervisors
IAS	International Accounting Standard
IASB	International Accounting Standards Board
ICRA	Investment Information and Credit Rating Agency
IFRS	International Financial Reporting Standards
IIA	Institute of Internal Auditors
IMF	International Monetary Fund
IOSCO	International Organization of Securities Commissions
JCR	Japanese credit rating agency
KBRA	Kroll
MAS	Monetary Authority of Singapore
NAIC	National Association of Insurance Commissioners
NAFTA	North American Free Trade Agreement
NRSRO	Nationally Recognized Statistical Rating Organization
OECD	Organisation for Economic Co-operation and Development
RMBS	residential mortgage-backed security
SEC	Securities and Exchange Commission (USA)
SIV	structured investment vehicles
SPE	special purpose entity
SPV	special purpose vehicle
SRCB	Standing Rating Committee of the Board
TRC	technical rating committee
UK	United Kingdom
US, USA	United States of America

1 Introduction to the world of credit rating

A credit rating (CR) is meant to be an opinion on the creditworthiness of an issuing entity (e.g. an issuer of bonds or a contractor of debt), on a debt instrument (e.g. bonds, loans or asset-backed securities)[1] or, for some agencies, on the financial strength of an insurer (for life and property-casualty insurers). Credit ratings may allow uninformed investors to quickly assess the broad risk properties of tens of thousands of individual securities using a single and well-known scale (Becker and Milbourn, 2009). Credit ratings also can play much more fundamental roles in enhancing market efficiency: (i) they can, for instance, reduce information asymmetries by providing information on the rated security. (ii) They can contribute to solve certain principal–agent problems, such as fixing the level of risk that an agent can take on behalf of his principal. (iii) 'They can solve collective action problems of dispersed debt investors by helping them to monitor performance, with downgrades serving as a signal to take action' (World Bank, 2009). Credit ratings are supposed to be based on formal, as well as rational, activity and presented according to an agreed ranking system or scale in the form of 'AAA', 'AA', 'A' to 'CCC'. Till the 1980s, the demand for credit ratings was not substantial, economic entities were still filling most of their financial needs by resourcing to banks and credit unions, and endeavouring to concentrate on things in which they were feeling to have advanced knowledge and intimate confidence. From the 1980s onwards, however, as the financial system became more and more deregulated and an enforcement mechanism reduced, companies started increasingly borrowing from the globalized debt markets, and consequently credit ratings agencies became more and more relevant and valuable (Kingsley, 2012). Credit rating activity also developed tremendously, and became part of a vast area of finance and accounting research called 'default prediction', which includes application of numerous statistical tools and other prediction means and involving deepening appreciation of various credit weaknesses. Default prediction has been a subject of formal analysis since at least the 1930s and has been imposed as a very lucrative industry by the world three largest credit rating agencies. Although the importance of a viable rating industry seems clear, the accuracy of the ratings is yet to be established.

A credit rating agency (CRA) is a service provider specializing in the supply of credit ratings, on a professional basis. When a CRA assesses default risk efficiently it can reduce costs whenever safety is essential. Although there are, at least, over 150 known rating agencies all over the planet, the global credit rating market remains characterized by an oligopoly, where three major rating agencies control the world rating market (SEC, 2011) and where all medium and smaller credit rating agencies are confined to very particular market and/or particular niche needs, despite the fact that some small agencies like Dominion Bond Rating Service (DBRS), Japan Credit Rating Agency, Ltd, Dagong Global Credit Rating, and Rating and Investment Information, Inc., seem to be well established regional players (in Canada/US, Japan and China respectively) with ambitions of further developing their international market share. There are also a number of local rating agencies that are active in different countries, issuing ratings locally both for general purposes and for specialized uses; their impact on the global financial markets remains nonetheless very marginal.

In recent years the demand for debt ratings has increased dramatically and this has caused the CRAs to 'steal the show' and increase dramatically their influence, as more and more governments and financial institutions borrow on the international bond markets. Agency ratings have gained much acceptance during the last few decades, for diverse reasons:

- i Ratings are expected to make securities markets more efficient by reducing information costs for investors and creditors.
- ii Financial regulators in many national jurisdictions were relying extensively on credit ratings; for instance, most members of the Basel Committee on Banking Supervision (BCBS) were using agency ratings in financial regulatory supervision. Members of the European Union were also relying on the ratings of agencies that were recognized as External Credit Assessment Institutions (ECAI), allowing them to assess bank capital requirements within the European standardized approach for credit risk measurement (SEC, 2011). As a rule, national financial regulations used to give a quasi-institutional role to rating, but there were/are also references to credit ratings in many private contractual agreements. Consequently, ratings end up having an impacting effect on the stability of financial markets. Currently, however, new rules forbidding the use of credit rating for regulatory purposes are enacted and risk upsetting the rating activity: they will be discussed in next chapters.
- iii Investors use ratings as key information in reaching their investment decisions. They are usually dependent on the degree of risk they are willing to accept (EC, 2013). The Securities and Exchange Commission of the US added:

> demand for credit ratings exists from investors, both individual and institutional, who value an independent assessment of the relative or absolute credit risk of a particular debt obligation or obligor. As such, credit ratings serve a certification function in the marketplace, providing rated issuers with less costly access to debt markets.
>
> (SEC, 2011)

iv Ratings triggers are commonly used in bank loan agreements and often investment managers and financial institutions are commonly required by charter or regulations to use credit ratings to establish investment risk standards for their investment holdings (SEC, 2011).[2] Here a rating downgrade can have a direct impact on issuer indebtedness capacity and on financial institutions' capital levels.

v The rating assigned to an issuer or security affects the issuer's cost of raising capital and often any downgrade in its rating may announce indebtedness problems and may initiate immediate debt repayment.

vi Sovereign ratings play a crucial role for the rated country and an upgrade may signify easier financing and downgrading may have the immediate effect of rendering a country's borrowing more difficult/expensive.

As can be seen, credit ratings matter and they may impact tremendously on investors, borrowers, issuers and governments, as they may have an important signalling effect. While a rating upgrade may signal easier (cheaper) financing, a rating downgrade can have reverse impact and may even lead to 'spill over effects',[3] with a destabilizing impact on financial markets. The oligopolistic nature of the rating agency industry combined with financial crisis and the greater efficiency of markets in determining bond yields, has provoked questions about the use of ratings.

Different views of the role of credit agencies can, therefore, be encountered: on the one hand, there are those who view agencies as mere cost reducing and summarizing mechanisms of publically disclosed information. Consequently, they are convinced that agencies add no new content to such publically reported information and consequently they do not make markets more efficient by providing information that is hard to obtain, they may just mimic existing public information. There are, by contrast, those who believe that agencies are delivering inside information, through the lowering of ratings (Liu *et al.*, 1999); whether agencies provide inside information on their own, or if they just use a more sophisticated process of divulging them remains to be explored (Ederington *et al.*, 1987). There are also those who believe that issuers are interested in agencies' ratings, not so much for their real informational content, but rather because of regulatory requirements and for competitive reasons (Langohr, 2006). Among them are those who applaud agency rating only in cases of favourable outcome. The European Commissioner for Economic and

Financial Affairs, Olli Rehn, for instance, qualified the 2013 France downgrade as erroneous (Adam and Deen, 2013). There are, finally, those exceeded by the rating situation, who think that

> whether the ratings agencies get this or that decision right or wrong [...] is not the point. They have become the buck-passing agencies for weakened states. The most important public judgements of creditworthiness ought to be made in public institutions, not behind corporate doors.
>
> (Price, 2012)

For almost a decade now, financial markets worldwide are battling from a major confidence crisis, that they are still struggling to overcome, and CRAs are considered by market participants to be close to the origin of the problems that have arisen with subprime. Actually, 'without the active participation of the rating agencies, the market for mortgage-related securities could not have been what it became' argued the Financial Crisis Inquiry Commission of the United States (FCIC, 2011). Literature would traditionally report other important critics to rating agencies, particularly to the three largest. Critiques like heavy concentration characterizing the rating industry and opacity were often mentioned, but also the issuer-pay model of remuneration, the usual overreaction of agencies in adjusting ratings to crisis and therefore contributing to their aggravation, and inaccuracy of ratings.

i With regard to market concentration, credit rating agencies are blamed for the rating oligopoly they instituted in the credit market. 'Oligopoly' is actually the term usually used for qualifying the rating market that has historically been dominated by three globally active credit rating agencies, Fitch Ratings Ltd (Fitch), Moody's Investors Service, Inc. (Moody's) and Standard & Poor's Rating Services (S&P), together named the Big 3. They accounted for approximately 95 per cent of the outstanding credit ratings insured by all CRAs all over the world. All the Big 3 are headquartered in the US, although they have also offices in hundreds of countries. Government regulators are believed to be the main reason behind credit rating agencies' vertiginous ascension, but also the wide range of private contractual agreements that were referenced to ratings.

ii It is commonly argued that CRAs are insufficiently transparent about the reasons behind their attribution of ratings to issuers/investors. Users of rating don't seem to have access to enough information or to the reasons that motivate them, and this keeps them from conducting their own credit risk assessments or just insuring the accuracy of the ratings in hand. The opacity policy of the ratings followed by agencies has the vicious effect of keeping issuers from assessing efficiently the accuracy of the rating assigned.

iii CRAs were blamed for their issuer-pay model of remuneration where issuers select which agency will be entrusted with the rating and pay for it. It is believed that such a dynamic may have led to conflict of interest on the part of agencies. It may also have encouraged issuers to shop for ratings; this is seen as perhaps the biggest and most impacting problem in the current ratings system, since rating agencies have financial interests in generating business from issuers that seek the rating (EC, 2013). Agencies are, therefore, perceived as lacking independence from the rated entities that hire them and pay for the ratings.

iv Agencies are blamed for the overreaction with which they usually face crisis. CRAs not only are believed to have failed to reflect early enough in their ratings the worsening of market conditions, but they are also seen as overreacting to those changes in issuer conditions. As a rule, investors often took little or no interest in the deepening of their understanding of agencies' rating methodologies, assumptions or underlined fundamentals, trusting blindly CRAs' expertise. It is viewed 'that the hard wiring and the mechanistic reliance on CRAs materially contributed to instability during the financial crisis' (FSA *et al.*, 2013) and therefore should be a key area of CRA reform.

The accuracy of rating is far from making consensus among users. Concerns about accuracy of the credit ratings, however, are not new and have constantly existed and occasionally resurfaced since the 1980s and even before, but the Big 3 were constantly operating on a blank check formula and were rejecting any invitation for dialogue. All the credit agencies' critics can be reduced to one main element, namely the poor governance of agencies followed in producing ratings, mainly deterred by subprime debacle and suggesting that the existing governance framework for the operation of CRAs needs to be significantly reinforced, as it may not produce accurate ratings (EC, 2013). Consequently, governments have recently changed their stand, especially those who have experienced unexpected sovereign downgrades; this prompts them to finally seriously consider CRAs' critics and to question the consistency of the ratings they produce. In February 2013, for instance, the US government filed a civil suit against S&P, seeking damages of $5 billion for the agency's alleged role in misleading investors during the run-up to the financial crisis. This suit may mean the end of S&P, if found guilty. More importantly, this suit also sounds the 'death knell' for the usual invocation of the First Amendment by agencies to subtract themselves from any liability and opens the door to further civil action against them by investors, especially for those who bought presumably safe triple-A financial products before the crisis (CFR, 2014).

The aforementioned features of the rating industry have raised questions about the quality of the ratings provided and dissatisfaction with CRAs has reached unprecedented heights, leading to lively discussions on regulating

CRAs, at the international scene. In October 2010, the Financial Stability Board (FSB) endorsed principles to reduce financial authorities' and institutions' reliance on ratings. This has been approved by the G20 (G20, 2010a, 2010b). In response to the G20 statements and the FSB principles, the Basel Committee on Banking Supervision (BCBS) is currently working on specific policy actions to reduce reliance on ratings in the regulatory framework and make several recommendations that will be included in the Basel III rules. Dodd–Frank and other rules in the US and Europe are trying to reform the process, requiring removing references to rating agencies from rules, while others suggest regulating CRAs more heavily. The former leaves uncovered and unregulated a large portion of credit activity, while the latter may give the perception that ratings have official approval. No good solutions have yet emerged but market discipline should always be given priority. This book, however, adopts the view that 'the greatest tragedy would be to accept the refrain that no one could have seen credit crisis coming and thus nothing could have been done. If we accept this notion, it will happen again' (FCIC, 2011), For this reason the main objective of this book is to introduce credit rating activity, examine the reasons behind credit agencies' alleged governance failures and rating inaccuracy. The book underlines the reactions these governance failures might have initiated, by relating the regulatory answers they have engendered, in order to test the veracity of the former and to assess the success of the latter. It presents alternative views on disputed issues and such logic has also suggested the following overview of the chapters composing the book.

Chapter 1, 'Introduction to the world of credit rating', gives a summary picture of the world of credit ratings, underlines how credit ratings as mere opinions based on established criteria and methodologies matter a lot, how investors and regulators expect them to be objective, emphasizes the tremendous harm that can result from any breach to governance on the part of credit rating agencies and, finally, summarizes the other chapters of the book.

Chapter 2, 'Credit rating agencies, who are they and what they do?' explains who are credit agencies, what is their activity, how credit ratings are expressed and are used by creditors and investors on the market to assess debt risk and, consequently, setting their cost, and stresses the fact that although there are over 140 credit agencies on the global market, three major players (the Big 3) hold more than 95 per cent of its activity.

Chapter 3, 'The Big 3, the global credit market gatekeepers', proceeds with an in-depth analysis of the Big 3 to show how every piece of information on the global credit rating industry points to the supremacy of Fitch, Moody's and S&P (the Big 3) over the global rating market. It identifies the path followed by them to dominate the global rating market and, using Herfindahl-Hirschman (HHI) methodology, the chapter tests whether such rating market concentration and control are actually on the rise or decreasing.

Chapter 4, 'Credit rating agencies' methodologies, metrics and rating accuracy', presents the more popular default prediction models and shows how default prediction has been imposed by CRAs as an extremely lucrative industry, under the consenting eye of the financial regulator and within a relatively short period of time. The chapter tests the accuracy of credit agencies' methodologies and challenges CRAs' findings.

Chapter 5, 'Ordinal credit ratings: the threat to rating accuracy', explains why indicating to investors that 'lower ratings correspond to higher default rates', as do rating agencies is just not enough and suggests the possibility that the rating methodology followed by CRAs may have kept them from assessing risk accurately, because of its failure to weight default by level of risk. The chapter tests CRAs' methodologies and offers an alternative approach.

Chapter 6, 'Credit ratings critics, telling it like it is', discusses the tremendous amount of blame expressed towards CRAs, mainly for their constant breaches to good governance principles (conflicts of interest, opacity, etc.) and assesses the rationality of the critics.

Chapter 7, 'Credit rating agencies external monitoring', shows how, till very recently, credit rating agencies were submitted to hardly any regulatory framework and how a strong consensus has recently emerged in favour of stricter regulatory intervention to curb their perceived excesses. The chapter also focuses on CRAs' recent regulatory and supervision frameworks aiming to reduce reliance on CRAs' ratings for regulatory purposes and increasing their transparency and independence.

Chapter 8, 'Credit rating agencies internal monitoring', wonders whether CRAs have the appropriate organizational structure to allow them to produce accurate ratings. It discusses agencies' ownership, the functioning of the board, agencies' independence, etc., and underlines the fact that CRAs' Boards of Directors are called to play a more impacting role than in normal organizations. Many weaknesses were discovered; therefore the chapter suggests the empowering of credit rating committees of the board as a mean of addressing rating weaknesses.

Chapter 9, 'Agencies rating quality control systems', wonders whether CRAs' internal auditing practice can be expected to enhance the quality of ratings. It analyses how agencies' auditing practices conform to current international standards (IIA, 2009) and ensure rating accuracy, and many weaknesses are encountered.

Chapter 10, 'The Cha6, shall they present a serious challenge to the Big 3?' underlines why for the sake of better governance, the market dependence on the Big 3 must be reduced, describes the credit rating market outside the Big 3 and assesses small agencies' market share. The chapter relates six, although benign, breaches to Big 3 credit rating market supremacy and assesses their chance of success in taking advantage of this new regulatory era. It explains why the rating market is and will for long time be a North American market first.

Chapter 11, 'Critical perspective and concluding remarks', indicates that although most people would agree on the need for supervising CRAs for the sake of improving their governance and decreasing their hegemony on the world credit rating market, most continue desperately to rely on them for credit risk assessment;[4] it discusses the reasons for such addiction and risks some suggestions.

As can be seen, some chapters are theoretical and/or descriptive: chapters 2, 6, 7 and 8. Other chapters are empirical and analyse some facets of agencies' governance. Chapter 3, for instance, tests of agencies' oligopoly using Herfindahl-Hirschman (HHI) methodology, Chapter 4 assesses the accuracy of the ratings, Chapter 5 tests the accuracy of ordinal credit ratings, Chapter 9 tests the quality of agencies' internal control systems and Chapter 10 assesses the chances of small agencies of competing with the Big 3.

Conclusion

Rarely has a private human business organization been granted so much power as credit rating agencies; their credit ratings play an incredibly important role in modern financial systems, by telling investors what debt securities to acquire and how much to pay for. Unfortunately, many concerns about CRA governance are routinely echoed. They are largely interrelated and are surely amplifying each other's effects. A strong consensus has recently emerged for reducing references to ratings, at least, as legislative references. But caution is warned in rapid replacement of CRAs, since problems are also expected from using replacement measures. Change has to be negotiated gradually, so as to avoid ambushes, shocks and surprises.

Notes

1 An asset-backed security (ABS), is a financial security backed by a loan, lease or receivables against assets other than real estate and mortgage-backed securities. For investors, asset-backed securities are an alternative to investing in corporate debt (Investopedia website).
2 Ratings triggers give lenders the right to require collateral or the repayment of a loan, in case of non-respect of contractual provisions.
3 Spillover effects are externalities of economic activity or processes that affect those who are not directly involved.
4 For instance, US regulators depend on credit grades to monitor the safety of $450 billion of bonds held by US insurance companies. Even the plans crafted by the Federal Reserve Bank and the US Treasury to stimulate the economy count on rating firms to determine how the money will be spent.

Bibliography

Adam, S. and M. Deen (2013), 'France credit rating cut to AA by S&P on growth outlook', Bloomberg, 8 November, at www.bloomberg.com/news/2013-11-08/

france-credit-rating-cut-to-aa-by-s-p-on-weak-growth-prospects.html, retrieved 3 March 2014.

Becker, B. and T. Milbourn (2009), 'How did increased competition affect credit ratings?' Harvard Business School Working Paper, No. 09-051.

Council of Foreign Relations (CFR) (2014), 'The credit rating controversy', at: www.cfr.org/financial-crises/credit-rating-controversy/p22328, retrieved 3 March 2014.

Ederington, L., J. Yawitz and B. Roberts (1987), 'The informational content of bond ratings', *Journal of Financial Research*, Fall, Vol. 10, pp. 211–226.

European Commission (EC) (2013), 'New rules on credit rating agencies (CRAs): frequently asked questions', Memo 13/13.

Financial Crisis Inquiry Commission (FCIC) (2011), 'Final report of the National Commission on the causes of the financial economic crisis in the United States', ISBN 978-0-16-087727-8.

FSA, HM Treasury and Bank of England (2013), 'The United Kingdom authorities response to the European Commission internal market and services consultation document on Credit Rating Agencies', at: https://circabc.europa.eu/d/d/workspace/SpacesStore/0d1ea101-b6d0-470b-b8b3-e28e4c1cba30/BoE-FSA-Treasury_EN.pdf, retrieved 2 June 2014.

G20 (2010a), 'Toronto G20 summit declaration, 26–27 June', at: www.g20.org/Documents/g20_declaration_en.pdf, retrieved 10 July 2014.

G20 (2010b), 'Seoul summit leaders' declaration, 11–12 November', at: www.g20.org/Documents2010/11/seoulsummit_declaration.pdf, retrieved 10 July 2014.

Institute of Internal Auditors (IIA) (2009), 'Standard 1300', effective 1 January 2009.

Kingsley, P. (2012), 'How credit ratings agencies rule the world', at: www.theguardian.com/business/2012/feb/15/credit-ratings-agencies-moodys, retrieved 21 April 2014.

Langohr, H. (2006), 'The credit rating agencies and their credit ratings', Presentation to the Bond Market Association's 'Rating Industry Day Conference', 23 February 2006.

Liu P., F.J. Seyyed and S.D. Smith (1999), 'The independent impact of credit rating changes: the case of Moody's rating refinement on yield premiums', *Journal of Business Finance and Accounting*, April/May, Vol. 26(3), pp. 337–363.

Price, C.T. (2012), 'Credit rating agencies: the wrong institutions for public judgement', at: www.opendemocracy.net/openeconomy/tony-curzon-price/credit-rating-agencies-wrong-institutions-for-public-judgement, retrieved 15 November 2013.

Securities and Exchange Commission (SEC) (2011) 'Annual report on nationally recognized statistical rating organizations', December, at: www.sec.gov/divisions/marketreg/ratingagency/nrsroannrep1212.pdf, retrieved 10 July 2014.

USA Today (2014), 'Citigroup has agreed to pay $7 billion', 14 July, at: www.usatoday.com/story/money/business/2014/07/14/justice-citi-7-billion-dollar-settlement/12616741/, retrieved 15 July 2014.

World Bank (2009), 'Credit rating agencies', crisisresponse, October, at: http://siteresources.worldbank.org/EXTFINANCIALSECTOR/Resources/282884-1303327122200/Note8.pdf, retrieved 10 July 2014.

2 Credit rating agencies

Who they are and what they do

Introduction

Concerns about the implications of business default for economic development are not new; they have been the focus of investors since the early 1800s, and this could have marked the beginning of credit rating activity. It was, however, the 1837 financial crisis (that lasted until the mid-1840s) that seemed to have extensively fuelled the pertinence of such activity. Most CRAs were initiated during the aftermath of this crisis era. Even, if at first glance, these agency launchings appear unconnected, they all share the common need of assessing credit quality of debt issuers to make it easier for investors to take their decisions. In a relatively short period of time, credit ratings have become the international standard by which investors can compare and assess the creditworthiness of different debt issuers and rate their debt securities. Consequently, issuers are finding it even harder to issue debts without obtaining in advance credit ratings from CRAs, but critics of credit rating are also on the menu.

This chapter explains who are the rating agencies and what they do. Additional to an introduction, the second section of the chapter gives a historical overview of credit ratings, the third section gives an international overview of credit rating, section four discusses the rating fees, the fifth discusses rating agencies staffing, the sixth discusses agencies' revenue, the seventh section explains what agencies do, the eighth explains the rating process and the ninth section concludes the chapter.

Credit ratings

Theoretically, credit ratings measure the ability of debt issuers to fulfil their financial obligations towards their creditors. Rating can be either a corporate rating or a sovereign rating. Corporate rating assesses whether a prospective corporate debt issuer will be able to meet its obligations, while a sovereign credit rating determines the overall ability of a country to provide a safe investment environment to foreign investors, based on macroeconomic factors such as a country's economic strength, levels of investment flows, fiscal policy, balance of payment, etc.; they can also be financial strength ratings for insurers. Originally introduced as guides for unsophisticated investors, credit ratings have later acquired several unsuspected new utilizations. Many mutual funds and pension funds, for instance, usually imposed limits on the amount of portfolio that can be invested in lower rating securities and most issuers of debt and investors introduced explicitly in their financial contracts covenants that refer to credit ratings (SEC, 2013b) and seek guidance from agencies on the structuring of their structured financial transactions (Gailliard, 2010). Progressively, credit ratings gained wide acceptance from financial market regulators that saw in them a means of simplifying their prudential supervision task, as a measurable means of assessing the respect of the rules they promulgated. Although the regulatory use of credit ratings was initially limited to draw a boundary line between 'investment grade' and 'speculative grade' debts ('investment grade' and 'speculative grade' to be discussed in a later chapter), in the end, everyone ended using them; this includes public authorities in charge of financial institutions' supervision and the banking authorities that specifically limited banking institutions in their investments in securities classified by the rating agencies as speculative. In some cases, banks are even prohibited from investing in such securities. Consequently, credit ratings saw their use extended to the whole debt sector.

A short history of credit rating agencies

The activity of assessing clients' creditworthiness must be as old as business activity itself, but it was only at the beginning of the nineteenth century that it emerged as a structured business activity. Clients' creditworthiness was previously mainly established by looking at the religious morality of the issuer and/or by considering his family ranking in society. It was only in the 1820s that the English bank Barings trusted a retired businessman with the task of classifying risk based on several thousands of its Bostonian clients (Hidy, 1939 as reported by Gaillard, 2010). Clients were then classified in a system that is close to today's agency classifications, and composed of five categories:

- i category one, comprising clients with a certain risk of default but whose solvency is not jeopardized in the short run;
- ii category two, comprising solvent clients whose activity has a limited interest for the bank;
- iii category three, comprising clients with high risk of default;
- iv category four, comprising debtors having ties with competitors; and
- v category five, composed of defaulted debtors.

Similarly, in the aftermath of the 1837 financial crisis, one of the visionaries in the field of credit quality assessment, of the name of Louis Tappan, had the brilliant idea of creating his own and probably the first mercantile credit bureau in the world; that had as its objective the assessment of merchant ability to meet their indebtedness obligations. Later Tappan's business was acquired by Robert Dun and it released its first credit rating guide in 1859 (Gaillard, 2010). Ten years later, precisely in 1849, John Bradstreet created a business similar to a mercantile credit agency that published its first ranking of debtors in 1857. Nearly a century later, in 1933, the two agencies (Robert Dun and John Bradstreet) consolidated their businesses under the banner of Dun & Bradstreet that later became the owner of Moody's Investor Services in 1962. Although, Poor's Publishing Company issued its first ratings in 1916 – so did Standard Statistics Company in 1922 and the Fitch Publishing Company in 1924 – the real take-off of credit rating activity seemed, however, to have been consolidated by the publication of the 'Moody's analyses of railroad investments' manual (Investopedia, n.d.).

The year 1941 marked a turning point in rating business; this is the year when Standard Statistics and Poor's Publishing Company joined activities to form Standard & Poor's (S&P). Since then newcomers to the rating market are few. The Duff and Phelps entry to the rating market, in 1982, is noticeable by its bond ratings publication, but we can also mention newcomers like McCarthy, Crisanti and Maffer, which was founded in 1975 and later acquired by Xerox Financial Services, a while before its fixed income research and rating service was merged into Duff and Phelps in 1991. Similarly, John Knowles Fitch launched the smallest of the three largest agencies, Fitch Ratings, in 1913. He founded the US Fitch Publishing Company that later in 1997 merged with the London-based IBCA Limited. Although Fitch Rating enjoys a smaller market share than S&P and Moody's, it has grown substantially through acquisitions of smaller agencies; it has, for instance, acquired both Chicago-based Duff & Phelps Credit Rating Co. and Thomson Financial BankWatch as well as several other small agencies (Investopedia, n.d.).

As global capital flows shifted from banking sector to capital markets, and thanks to complaisant regulators and generous globalization, large CRAs have found themselves rating debt in financial markets all over the world, in developed, developing and emerging economies alike.

International overview of credit rating agencies

The market for credit ratings has grown spectacularly since the 1960s; before then, investors tended to neglect credit quality and risk in their decision-making, assuming that debt issuers were equivalent. It is only the 1970 recession that shocked investor memories and made them begin to worry about the financial condition of indebted issuers; they, therefore, started challenging the then traditional quasi-mechanical roll over of their debts. This new behaviour by investors would have unpredictable consequences on the whole financial system for:

i it would result in a sudden liquidity shortage;
ii it would force many of these issuers to default effectively;
iii it would force many issuers to actively recourse to credit ratings for the sake of reassuring newly nervous investors;
iv it would render CRAs a 'one-stop' destination for issuing debt; and
v it became a well-established practice that new debt issue must have been rated by at least one credit rating agency, if not two, preferably among the largest, in order to gain market acceptance.

We provide in Appendix 2.1 to this chapter the list of most known agencies around the globe. This will help us to grasp the extent of the global rating market. This list is constructed based on three different sources of information, believed to be the most representative of CRAs with significant activity:

i The list of the agencies registered with the Securities and Exchange Commission as a Nationally Recognized Statistical Rating Organization as of 31 December 2013, Item 7A.
ii The list of agencies registered with the European Securities and Markets Authority (ESMA), in accordance with Article 18(3) of the Credit Rating Agencies Regulation, as of 3 June 2013.
iii The listing provided by the default risk website.[1]

All together, there are 121 agencies originating from these three sources and will constitute our main study population for the rest of the book. The list is composed of:

i Thirty-three CRAs that are either major agencies (Moody's, S&P or Fitch) or one of their affiliates. S&P, Moody's and Fitch have their head offices and main management, administrative and supervisory bodies in the US (Fitch Ratings is actually dual headquartered in New York and London). They operate in the EU through subsidiaries established in several countries. Their activity does not have a territorial character.
ii Eighty-nine CRAs that are very small agencies that are confined to poorly lucrative niches or to difficult environments, usually neglected by large agencies.

Table 2.1 provides the world credit agencies' repartition by regions and countries. Agencies actually come from all continents and regions.

A number of interesting observations can be made out of the reading of Table 2.1:

i Of the 121 identified agencies around the world, only 12 agencies come from the United States, 1 from Canada and 1 from Mexico.

Table 2.1 World credit agencies by regions and/or countries

Region or country	*Number of agencies*	*%*
North America: (United States 12, Canada 1, Mexico 1)	14	12
Europe: (Germany 9, UK 9, France 4, Italy 9, Spain 2, Bulgaria 1, Portugal 1, Cyprus 2, Ukraine 1, Russia 4, Switzerland 2, Poland 1, Greece 1, Slovak Republic 1, Turkey 6)	54	45
Central America: (Costa Rica 1, Caribbean 1)	2	2
South America: (Brazil 1, Peru 4, Chile 2, Ecuador 2, Colombia 2, Uruguay 1)	12	10
Asia and Pacific: (Australia 2, Japan 2, China 5, Uzbekistan 1, Kuwait 1, India 1, Bangladesh 6, Thailand 3, Taiwan 1, Korea 1, Malaysia 4, Philippines 2, Bahrain 1, Sri Lanka 1, Singapore 1, Pakistan 1, Indonesia 2)	35	29
Africa: (South Africa 1, Nigeria 2, Zambia 1)	4	3
Total agencies	121	100

Altogether, the North American region has 14 agencies out of the 121 composing the list.

ii Of the 54 agencies coming from the European region: UK, Italy and Germany count for nine agencies each, Turkey six, France and Russia four, Spain, Cyprus and Switzerland two, and one from Greece, Slovak Republic, Ukraine, Bulgaria and Portugal.

iii Of the 35 agencies coming from Asia and Pacific region, six come from Bangladesh, five from China, four from Malaysia, three from Thailand, two from Japan, Australia, Indonesia and the Philippines, and one from Bahrain, Kuwait, Taiwan, Sri Lanka, Pakistan and Singapore.

iv Of the 14 agencies from Central and South America, Peru four, Chile, Ecuador and Colombia two, Uruguay, Costa Rica, Caribbean and *Brazil* one.

v Of the four agencies coming from Africa, two come from Nigeria and one from South Africa and Zambia.

The study of Table 2.1, also allows us to withdraw some interesting conclusions, for instance:

i We can note the feeble proportion of agencies coming from the North American region (12 per cent); this may actually obscure the decisive role played by them (except for the Mexican HR), not only are the 13 North American agencies the biggest in the world, but they also own more than 30 other agencies, scattered all over the planet.

ii The fact that of the 54 European agencies figuring in the list are representing 45 per cent of all the listed agencies around the world, does not underline that a significant number of them is actually composed of agencies that are affiliated to American agencies, precisely most of those that are located in the UK (nine agencies).

iii The impressive number of European agencies can be misleading for another reason. Indeed, except for agencies coming from Germany and that are American affiliates, most European agencies come from environments with little or no background in credit rating activities. They come from countries like Bulgaria, Slovenia, Czech Republic, to the point where they represent no challenge to the large agencies and cannot, at least for the forseeable future, be considered as serious pretenders to the status of global rating agency.

iv The 63 agencies coming from emerging and developing economies (Africa, Asia Pacific, Central and South America), although counting for more than 50 per cent of the world list, they also appear, except for very few, of very feeble calibre: most of them are of a very limited scope and have little rating capacity.

Overall and the way the situation is currently evolving, credit rating activity appears to be quasi-exclusively a US activity. The three major American agencies, Moody's, S&P and Fitch, together the Big 3, control over 95 per cent of the world rating activities and are realizing around 71 per cent of their revenue in the US. However, in spite of or perhaps because of the rating crisis, some of the small European, developing and emerging economies' agencies are offered a unique historical opportunity of growth, because of a general tendency that is taking off, in favour of eliminating the requirement of Big 3 ratings for regulatory purposes. Some small agencies are showing frustration with the current global credit rating system and are effectively trying to organize themselves in the hope of competing more efficiently with large international agencies (see Chapter 10).

As we saw, credit agencies do not lend themselves to uniform definition, deciding which agency can be part of the study is difficult: for this reason, this book analysis will mainly concentrate on two groups of rating agencies, whose data may be accessible due to:

i Their registration as Nationally Recognized Statistical Rating Organization, (NRSRO) in accordance with the United States Securities and Exchange Commission (SEC) rules and regulations (NRSRO status). An NRSRO is therefore a credit rating agency permitted to issue credit ratings that the US SEC permits other financial firms to use for certain regulatory purposes.

ii Their registration with the European Securities and Markets Authority registration (ESMA) (ESMA status),[2] in accordance with the European Commission Regulation No. 1060/2009 of the European Parliament. Similarly, an ESMA status allows an agency to issue credit ratings that ESMA permits other European financial institutions to use for certain regulatory purposes.

Rating fees

Initially, agencies used to finance their operations through sales of publications and related materials; they were providing ratings free of charge. Once circulated, however, publications and related materials were easily replicated and extensively Xeroxed and consequently did not yield sufficient returns to justify the continuation of their distribution (Partnoy, 2006). However, as agencies discovered they were able to impose charges on issuers for the ratings, they saw their revenue suddenly shifting to meet the rising demand for credit ratings: Standard & Poor's was the first to charge issuers, by starting to bill municipal bond issuers for ratings since 1968 and Fitch and Moody's followed and started to charge corporate issuers for ratings, starting 1970 (agencies annual reports). Currently, most credit rating agencies operate primarily under the 'issuer-pay' model, where issuers pay agencies to have their own debts rated. These issuers' fees vary depending on the size and type of issue and may include both a floor and a ceiling. In addition, negotiated rates are available for regular issuers. For commercial papers issuers Moody's and S&P maintain quarterly charges, based on amount oustanding (up to 7 basis points) plus an annual fee. Usually, in 2007, a representative fee for long-term corporate bond issue ranged from 2 to 4.5 basis points of the principal for each year the rating is maintained,[3] and 12 basis points for collateralized debt obligations (CDOs) (Gaillard, 2010). It means that for a structure finance issue of $1 billion, an agency can cash up to $1.2 million. Fees charged by agencies for sovereign issues seem to be less spectacular: they range from $2,500 to $350,000 for local public institutions and $60,000 to $100,000 for goverments (S&P as reported by Gaillard, 2010).

Credit ratings agencies staffing

Given the specialization character of the rating activity and the specific 'know how' it usually requires, the trend in the number of analytical staff employed by each agency can be a significant indicator of the strength of its business. Consequently, agencies that have continuously increased their analytical staff may have also experienced (or anticipated) an increase in their volumes of ratings. Staffing levels may also indicate if an agency is entering new markets or consolidation an existing one. Since we could not have access to all agencies' data on analytical staffing, our analysis of

Table 2.2 Number of rating analysts employed by NRSROs, as of 31 December of each calendar year

	2010	*2011*	*2012*
A.M. Best	120	123	126
DBRS	75	97	93
EJR	5	5	5
Fitch	1,049	1,096	1,092
HR Ratings*	n.a.	n.a.	29
JCR	57	57	59
KBRA	9	22	37
Moody's	1,088	1,124	1,123
Morningstar	17	26	22
S&P	1,345	1,416	1,436
Total	3,765	3,966	4,022

Source: SEC, 2013 Forms NRSRO, Exhibit 8.

Note
* Since HR Ratings became an NRSRO in November 2012, the relevant information was not reported prior to that date.

staffing will be limited to agencies having NRSRO registration, requiring them to report annually such information to the SEC. Table 2.2 shows the number of rating analysts at each agency having NRSRO registration over the period 2010–2012.

The number of analysts that were employed by all agencies composing the NRSRO sample for the period 2010–2012, has increased by about 6.8 per cent. This relative increase has, however, been much more sizeable at some of the smaller agencies during this period. Comparing 2012 to 2010, for example, we discover that KBRA's analytical staff has more than quadrupled, Morningstar's staff has increased by almost 30 per cent and DBRS' has increased by 24 per cent (SEC, 2012). The aggregate number of analysts employed by agencies other than at S&P, Moody's and Fitch has increased by 31.1 per cent since 2010, i.e. from 283 analysts, its level in 2010, to 371, its level in 2012. In total, analytical staff at agencies other than at the Big 3 accounted for only about 9.2 per cent of all agencies' rating analysts reported at the end of 2012, up from 7.5 per cent in 2010. Although significant, the increase of the number of the rating analysts within small agencies may also be only a matter of catch-up delay in hiring analysts. Note also the effect on small agencies' staffing that new NRSRO status granted to HR Ratings in 2012 may have.

Rating agencies' revenue

Similarly, the trend in agencies' revenue can also represent a significant indicator of the state of the business development of agencies. Table 2.3

Table 2.3 Number of outstanding credit ratings of the year ended 31 December 2012

Agency	*Total number of ratings*	*%*
A.M. Best	6,452	0.26
DBRS	46,112	1.84
EJR	1,161	0.05
Fitch	350,370	13.99
HR Ratings	184	0.01
JCR	714	0.03
KBRA	18,993	0.76
Moody's	923,323	36.87
Morningstar	13,935	0.56
S&P	1,143,300	45.65
Total	2,504,584	100.00

Source: adapted from SEC, 'NRSRO Annual Certifications for the Year Ended December 31, 2012', Item 7A.

provides information regarding the number and the percentages of credit ratings insured by each agency, based on information reported by the NRSROs as of 31 December 2012.

Data in Table 2.3 indicate that S&P and Moody's continue to be the two agencies with the highest number of ratings reported to be outstanding as of 31 December 2012, accounting for about 45.65 and 36.87 per cent, respectively, of all outstanding ratings reported by all the agencies of the sample. Fitch comes third, by reporting having the third highest number of outstanding ratings, accounting for about 14 per cent of all the sample outstanding ratings. In total, these three agencies issued about 96.5 per cent of all the ratings that were reported to be outstanding as of that date. Among the smaller agencies, HR Ratings, JCR and EJR reported having issued 0.01, 0.03 and 0.05 per cent, respectively, of all the outstanding ratings (SEC, 2012).

Table 2.4, constructed based on information contained in the financial reports provided to the US Securities and Exchange Commission under Rule 17g-3, for the year 2013, indicates that the total revenue reported by all the agencies of the sample for their 2012 fiscal year was approximately $5.1 billion, which represented an increase of about 19.4 per cent from its level of the fiscal year 2011. Since 2010, total revenues have grown by 22.4 per cent. Most of the growth since 2010 was registered by large agencies.

Over the years, agencies were able to negotiate shifts in the structure of their revenue: until the mid-1990s, CRAs were specializing in and also deriving most of their revenues from the rating of corporate or sovereign debt. With the growth of structured markets, however, they are increasingly engaged in the highly lucrative activity of rating the new structured

Table 2.4 NRSROs' revenue information, for fiscal years 2012, 2011 and 2010

	2012		*2011*		*2010*	
	$	*% of total*	*$*	*% of total*	*$*	*% of total*
Total	$5.1 billion	100	$4.11 billion	100	$3.96 billion	100
Yearly variation	19.4%		4.0%		–	

Source: adapted from financial reports provided to the Commission under Rule 17g-3, and author calculations.

finance transactions. It is even argued that the success of big agencies is largely based on fee income from regulatory-dependent structured finance rating (Partnoy, 2006).

No matter which way we look at credit rating agencies, whether from the point of view of analytical staffing or revenues, the three major agencies, S&P, Moody's and Fitch, dominate their market and there seems to be no respite and this may justify the wave monitoring initiatives (see Chapter 7) that followed the huge protest in the aftermath of the 2007 crisis.

Credit rating agencies, what do they do?

Credit rating agencies collect and integrate a complex interplay of default risk factors, whether quantitative, qualitative or even subjective, and present it in single ranking scale (AAA, AA+, etc., or Aaa, Aa, etc., depending on the agency). In theory, issuers can be rated on a scale of 0 to 100, for instance, but investors cannot make such fine distinctions. Indeed, it would be hard for any investor to distinguish a rating of 90 vs a rating of 81, and for this reason symbols are used. Investors and debt issuers both use ratings, the first to assess debt's risk and the latter to assess its cost. Credit rating mainly 'focuses on the fundamental relevant factors characterizing an issuer's long-term and short-term risk profile and its ability to generate cash in the future' (Moody's, 2001a) and rests on two basic questions:

1 What is the risk to the debt holder of not receiving timely payment of principal and interest on specific debt security?
2 How does this level of risk compare with that of all other debt securities?

The ratings assigned by agencies are meant to be indicators of the likelihood of default or/and the risk of delayed payment of debt securities. Most rating agencies have their own system of symbols for ranking the risk of default that goes from 'extremely safe', to 'highly speculative'. Each rating agency also applies its own methodology in measuring issuers' creditworthiness and uses a specific rating scale to publish its ratings opinions. Table 2.5 provides rating symbols used by major credit rating agencies registered with the US Securities and Exchange Commission: they are almost identical, except for the number of notches that differs marginally: 22 ratings for S&P, 21 for Moody's and 19 for Fitch.

Major credit agencies may use similar scales and symbols to denote long-term credit ratings, but for other types of credit ratings, the number of rating scales and the rating symbols used vary widely among them. Appendix 2.2 gives Fitch, Moody's and S&P major symbols and definitions for global long-term rating scale. The definitions commonly encountered and the uses of the symbols are:

- i AAA/Aaa symbol is used to express extreme capacity of an issuer to meet its financial commitments.
- ii AA/Aa symbol is used to express very strong capacity of an issuer to meet its financial commitments, although with very low credit risk.
- iii A is used to indicate a strong capacity of an issuer to meet its financial commitments but is somewhat more susceptible to the adverse effects of changes.
- iv BBB/Baa symbol is used to indicate adequate capacity of an issuer to meet its financial commitments. These capacities can, however, be weakened by difficult economic conditions.
- v BB/Ba symbol is used to describe speculative issues to be judged subject to substantial credit risk.
- vi B symbol is used to describe speculative issue subject to high credit risk.
- vii CCC/Caa symbol describes an issuer currently vulnerable, and indicates that he is dependent upon favourable conditions to meet his financial commitments.
- viii CC/C symbol is used to express current vulnerability of an issuer.
- ix C symbol is used to indicate an issuer is in default, with little prospect for recovery of principal or interest.
- x D symbol is used to indicate that an issuer is in default on all of its financial obligations.

Note that the ratings 'AA' to 'CCC' may be modified by adding a plus (+) or minus (–) sign to the symbol, to incorporate relative standing within the major rating categories. Similarly 1, 2 and 3 can be added to modify ratings 'Aaa' to 'Caa', when this scale is used. The modifier 1 indicates that the obligation ranks in the higher end of its generic rating category, the modifier 2 indicates a mid-range ranking and the modifier 3 indicates a ranking in the lower end of that generic rating category (Fitch, S&P and Moody's). Historically, the 'AAA' rating was conceded to only a selected

Table 2.5 Rating symbols by major credit agencies

Credit agencies								
A.M. Best	*DBRS*	*EJR*	*Fitch*	*JCR*	*KBRA*	*Moody's*	*Morningstar*	*S&P*
Aaa	AAA	AAA	AAA	AAA	AAA	Aaa	AAA	AAA
Aa	AA	AA	AA	AA	AA	Aa	AA	AA
A	A	A	A	A	A	A	A	A
Bbb	BBB	BBB	BBB	BBB	BBB	Baa	BBB	BBB
Bb	BB	BB	BB	BB	BB	Ba	BB	BB
B	B	B	B	B	B	B	B	B
Ccc	CCC	CCC	CCC	CCC	CCC	Caa	CCC	CCC
Cc	CC	CC	CC	CC	CC	Ca	CC	CC
C	C	C	C	C	C	C	C	
D	D	D	–	D	D	–	D	SD/D
Rs	–	–	–	–	–	–	–	R
Total number of notches	10	10	9	10	10	9	10	11

Source: adapted from SEC (2012).

club of developed country governments and a few dozen corporations, with strong balance sheets and a minimal risk of default. The number of AAA-rated US corporates, for instance, actually dropped from 60 or so in the 1960s to nine in 2005, as there was a general decline in creditworthiness (Kisgen and Strahan, 2010).

Long-term and short-term ratings scales

Corporate and sovereign ratings are usually classified by agencies as either long-term or short-term ratings. Credit ratings are called long-term ratings, when assigned to most issuers, while when they cover a time horizon of less than 13 months, credit ratings are considered as short-term ratings; they are focusing on the amount of liquidity required from an issuer placing him in a position to meet his financial commitments, in a timely manner. Moody's also assigns long-term ratings to individual debt securities issued from medium-term notes (MTN) programmes, in addition to indicating ratings to MTN programmes themselves. Appendix 2.3 provides short-term symbols used by the three main agencies, Fitch, Moody's and S&P.

Given that the key rating considerations on which short- and long-term ratings are based, and that are almost identical, a strong relationship is usually linking them. At first glance, risks such as employees' mobility and suchlike would appear to be long-term risk components that are expected to have little impact on an issuer's ability to roll over its short-term maturing debt, although the issue of any long-term risk should be expected to immediately impact an issuer's ability to repay or roll over its short-term debt. Consequently, most agencies consider it extremely appropriate to place a higher value on cash flow for short-term ratings, 'creating one meaningful difference in the evaluation of short-term ratings, determined more by the level and the stability of cash flow expected through a full economic cycle' (Moody's, 2001a). This makes necessary the study of all factors that could impact future cash flow of any issuer under consideration, and

> while all ratings, whether short or long-term, exhibit significant similarities, as they essentially reflect the same credit risk, some factors should be weighted differently in determining short versus long-term ratings and this may justify the use of separate scale for them.
>
> (DBRS, n.d.)

Insurers' financial strength ratings

Although other firms need ratings if they issue debt securities or are publicly traded, most insurers, however, have no debt and are not publicly traded, yet most of them seek to be rated, for three reasons: (i) agents are wary of unrated insurers, since they might be financially distressed, (ii) third parties rely on outside assessments of insurer solvency, and (iii) rating agencies are efficient at assessing financial strength, and it is less expensive to pay for a rating than to demonstrate financial strength individually to others (Feldblum, 2011). Financial strength ratings for insurers are different from debt ratings. One small agency takes the lead in the assessment of financial strength ratings for insurers, namely A.M. Best's. According to Feldblum (2011), insurers are divided between secure and vulnerable. Secure insurers are grouped into three categories with two levels in each (excellent ('A++', 'A+'), good ('A', 'A–') and highly fair ('B++', 'B+'). Vulnerable insurers are grouped into seven categories ranging from fair to in liquidation with ten levels in total (fair ('B', 'B–'), marginal ('C++', 'C+'), weak ('C', 'C–'), poor ('D'), under supervision ('E'), in liquidation ('F') and rating suspended ('S'). The last entry, a suspended rating, might occur after a major event, such as an earthquake, whose effects on the insurer are great but still uncertain.

Investment grades vs speculative grades

Ratings are designed exclusively for the purpose of grading issues according to their credit quality (risk) and agencies usually categorize ratings in two broad classes,[4] as indicated in Table 2.6: investment grade 'AAA' to 'BBB', and speculative grade 'BB+' to 'CCC/C'. The investment class expresses the relatively low risk of default of an issue, while issues of the speculative class, i.e. credit ratings for issues below the investment class, express low credit quality, and are commonly called 'junk' issues. Note that some agencies may segment ratings in three broad classes instead of two: (i) investment class: 'AAA' to 'AA', (ii) medium class: 'A' to 'BBB', and (iii) speculative class: 'BB+' to 'CCC/C', with the medium class qualifying issues with low risk of default.

Line 1 in Table 2.6 corresponds to S&P's and Fitch's symbol classifications and line 2 corresponds to Moody's classification. One of the problems related to the dichotomy 'investment grade vs speculative grade', resides in its inconsistency. Indeed, the simple crossing in Table 2.6 from 'BBB–' category to 'BB+' category, for instance, would transform the status of a debt issuer from an investment grade to a 'junk' grade, although such a move will only represent a single notch downgrade in quality. The repercussions of such a dichotomy can be highly problematic for issuers and it is therefore essential for them to remain within the investment area for several specific reasons:

- i for the benefit of the much more advantageous lower indebtedness cost it entails;
- ii because investment grade status constitutes a psychological frontier not to be crossed or located under, given that many institutional investors are usually forbidden by bylaws from investing in speculative grade securities;

Table 2.6 Investment and speculative classes

Investment										*Speculative*						
AAA	AA+	AA	AA–	A+	A	A3	BBB+	BBB	BBB–	BB+	BB	BB–	B+	B	B–	CCC to C
0	1	2	3	4	5	6	7	8	9	10	11	12	13	14	15	16
Aaa	Aa1	Aa2	Aa3	A1	A2	A3	Baa1	Baa2	Baa3	Ba1	Ba2	Ba3	B1	B2	B3	Caa1

iii because agencies usually make each downgrade/upgrade a special events: downgrades from investment category to speculative are so publicized and can be seen as a failure, and therefore susceptible of focusing attention on the financial difficulties of the concerned issuer;
iv similarly, transition from speculative to investment grade is often presented as a management success and gives rise to laudatory reviews.

As a reaction to the negative repercussions of the dichotomy 'investment grade vs junk grade', calls for the standardizing of credit rating terminology and symbols are sometimes echoed, arguing that standardization may, for instance, facilitate comparing credit ratings across rating agencies and industries; and also may result in fewer opportunities for manipulating credit rating scales to give the impression of accuracy (SEC, 2012). It is feared, however, that the wished standardization may not be feasible, given the number and the uniqueness of rating scales and differences in credit rating methodologies used by different credit rating agencies. Further, it is feared that required standardized credit rating terminology may also reduce CRAs' incentives for improving their methodologies and surveillance procedures. CRAs anyway see no need for further ratings standardization.

The accuracy of ratings was, however, often challenged and agencies were often blamed for many a wrong doing: not only are they believed to be at the origin of a major financial crisis, but are also suspected of upgrading some issuers allowing abnormal returns to be made, and eventually unduly downgrading other issuers, making them have to pay more than necessary for their funding. Consequently agencies are accused of mingling with the market efficiency they are supposed to enhance and this is something agencies are always refuting, arguing and warning that ratings represent their mere opinions as to the relative creditworthiness of securities. Agencies, for instance, warn that 'credit ratings are, and must be construed solely as, statements of opinion and not statements of fact or recommendations to purchase, sell or hold any securities' (Moody's, 2009). It is, however, often wondered how simple opinions, as those of agencies ratings may be, can have such an impacting effect on issuers and investors and the global financial system as whole? According to agencies, ratings can be impacting and beneficial to users in many ways (Moody's, 2001):

i since ratings can be crucial elements in pricing debt securities for most market players, and often they are used as a benchmark for setting investment guidelines;
ii as ratings are widely disseminated, they allow issuers easier access to capital;
iii credit ratings also ensure improved flexibility to financing;
iv the credibility of ratings also increases the frequency and the economy of entering capital markets;

v the credibility of ratings allows larger offerings to be sold at longer maturities; and
vi ratings help maintaining and stabilizing confidence in the markets.

Many, however, persist in believing that the main reason for agencies' impacting effect on the market resides in the tremendous regulatory power conceded to them over the years. Indeed, 'Over the years regulators globally have incorporated credit ratings into laws and regulations to set capital requirements for regulated entities, provide a disclosure framework, and restrict investments' (Baklanova 2012). Very recently, however, such privilege has started to fade.

The rating process

Basically, ratings involve making judgements about the future financial prospects of issuers and when assigning ratings agencies usually tend to look at 'worst' possibilities in the predictable future (Moody's, 2002a). Depending on the debt issue, the process of determining a rating can be lengthy and requiring significant time and effort on many parts: the debt issuer, the debt underwriter and the rating agency. Agencies usually base ratings on both quantitative and qualitative conditions of the debt issuer, but also on the specific provisions of each debt issue under study. In most agencies a technical rating committee (TRC) is set up and entrusted with the rating process. After presentation, study and debate the TRC votes on the rating recommendation. The assigned rating to an issue is usually accompanied by an explanatory analysis note, and it is first communicated to the issuer and the issue underwriter, and then rendered accessible to the general public. In case of dissatisfaction, the issuer is usually given the opportunity to appeal a rating. The TRC functioning will be discussed in Chapter 9.

While minor differences in the rating processes across different jurisdictions can be encountered, agencies commonly use two different approaches to rate issues and issuers: one for corporate finance rating and another for structure finance rating.

The corporate finance rating process

The rating process can take several months; at Moody's, for instance, the rating process takes approximately 60–90 days, from the time of the preliminary discussion to the public release of the rating (Moody's, 2001a). The process outlined in Figure 2.1, describes the general principles and the steps usually taken during the corporate finance rating process that may differ slightly for sovereign rating. A credit rating is called sovereign when the rating concerns a sovereign entity, i.e. a government; it indicates the risk level of the investing environment of a country under examination. Credit ratings cover a large spectrum of economic activities. These include

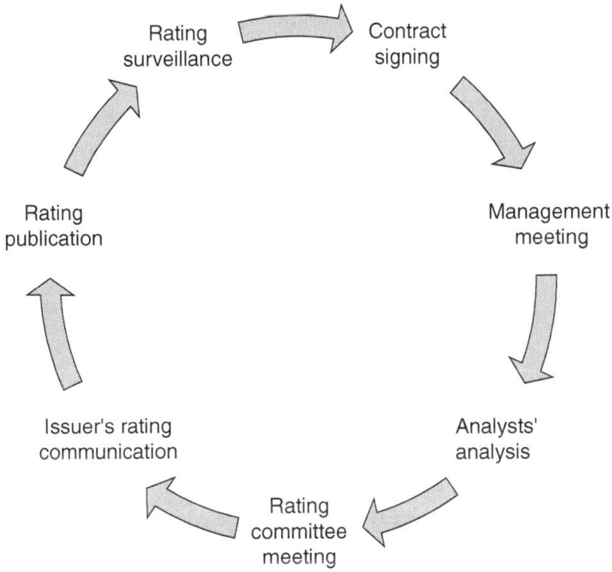

Figure 2.1 The corporate finance ratings process (source: adapted from Standard and Poor's at: https://ratings.standardandpoors.com/about/about-credit-ratings/ratings-process.html).

'corporate, sovereign (including supranational and sub-national), financial, bank, insurance, municipal and other public finance entities and the securities or other obligations they issue, as well as structured finance securities backed by receivables or other financial assets' (Banker Almanac website).

As indicated in Figure 2.1, the rating process is accomplished in eight successive steps (S&P): the rating process always starts by a request for rating to be received from the signing of the rating agreement, usually the agency is contacted directly by the issuer requesting the rating; but the agency can also be contacted by the issuer's investment banker or dealer (Step 1).

Once a letter of agreement has been signed, the agency will initiate the process by putting in charge an analyst (or a team) whose first task is to review the pertinent information. In the case of a new issuer, the rating process takes off with an introductory meeting with the issuer, whose purpose is to introduce and explain to the new issuer the agency's rating policies, approach, process and methodology, and to provide him with additional information regarding the specific sorts of data that will be most necessary in developing a good understanding of the issuer, by the agency (Step 2). In some agencies the analyst discusses the meeting agenda with the issuer in advance of the meeting, to ensure the issuer is aware of the type of information required. The discussion at the rating meeting generally focuses on the following issues:

i background and history of the company/entity;
ii industry/sector trends;
iii national political and regulatory environment;
iv management quality, experience, track record and attitude towards risk taking;
v management structure;
vi basic operating and competitive position;
vii corporate strategy and philosophy;
viii debt structure, including structural subordination and priority of claim; and
ix financial position and sources of liquidity.

Following the meeting, the agency's analyst(s) will proceed with the study, and will generally conduct further discussions with the issuer in order to obtain follow-up information and eventually further clarifications (Step 3).

Upon completion of the analysis, the analyst in charge will make a recommendation to the agency's rating committee (Step 4).

The lead analyst studies the suggested rating recommendation and agrees it, in order to present it along with its rationale to the rating committee. He also makes sure that all relevant issues related to the credit rating are presented and discussed. The lead analyst will also make sure that the role of the rating committee of introducing as much objectivity into the process as possible, is well understood and respected by every member (Step 5).

Once the rating committee has made its decision, the issuer will be informed of the rating and its rationale (Step 6).

For public ratings,[5] new ratings are communicated by press release simultaneously to the major financial media worldwide. These press releases will also appear on agencies' websites (Step 7).

After rating is assigned and published, agencies usually maintain ongoing monitoring of issuer outstanding ratings and usually fully review the rating and conduct yearly meeting with senior management of the issuer. Further, action is taken, as necessary, to update the ratings, whenever significant events occur that directly impact the credit quality of the issuer (Step 8).

The described rating process is characterized by its due process, where the TRC plays the central role. The appointment of the members of the TRC, their required experience, their independence, the way conflicts of interest are managed by them, are all elements that will make a difference between an accurate and a non-accurate rating.

The main role of the credit rating committee is 'to introduce as much objectivity into the process as possible by bringing an understanding of the relevant risk factors and viewpoints to each and every analysis' (Moody's, 2001c). By its very nature, credit rating is subjective and the rating process is usually oriented by a set of common analytical principles. For this reason the TRC should include as many credit risk professionals as necessary, having the appropriate knowledge and experience to consider and address all of the analytical perspectives that may be relevant to the issuer. According to Moody's, the factors to be considered in determining the make up of a rating committee may include:

i the size of the issue;
ii the complexity of the credit;
iii the introduction of a new instrument ; and
iv relevant issues that may have ramifications in the market.

The rating committee presents the rating recommendation and rationale, after ensuring that all relevant issues related to the credit were effectively presented and discussed.

The structure finance rating process

The process outlined in Figure 2.2 describes the general principles and the steps usually taken during the structure finance rating process. Structure finance (to be discussed more deeply in Chapter 6) is an activity where issuers are separate legal entities, created and operated by a relatively concentrated group of sponsors, underwriters and managers (collectively 'arrangers'). Structure finance instruments include residential mortgage-backed securities (RMBS), asset-backed securities (ABS) and collateralized debt obligations (CDOs).

The three large agencies generally followed similar procedures to develop ratings for subprime RMBS and CDOs. The rating of structure finance instruments by agencies is undertaken in four successive steps (NRSRO reports).

The arranger of the structure finance instrument (RMBS, CDOs) initiates the rating process by approaching the rating agency and supplying it with the required data on each of the subprime loans to be held. Then a lead analyst is assigned by the agency, upon data receipt (Step 1).

The lead analyst's first task is to develop loss predictions that are based on quantitative and qualitative factors (Step 2).

Then comes time for the lead analyst to check the proposed capital structure of the suggested structure finance instrument against the requirements for a particular rating (Step 3).

The lead analyst will then conduct an analysis on the cash flow (interest and principal expected) to be received from the pool of subprime loans. The objective is to determine whether it will be sufficient to pay the interest and principal due on each structure finance instrument tranche issued by the trust (Step 4).

Following these steps, the lead analyst develops a rating recommendation for each structure finance instrument tranche and then presents it to a rating committee. The rating committee votes on the ratings for each tranche and usually communicates its decision to the arranger.

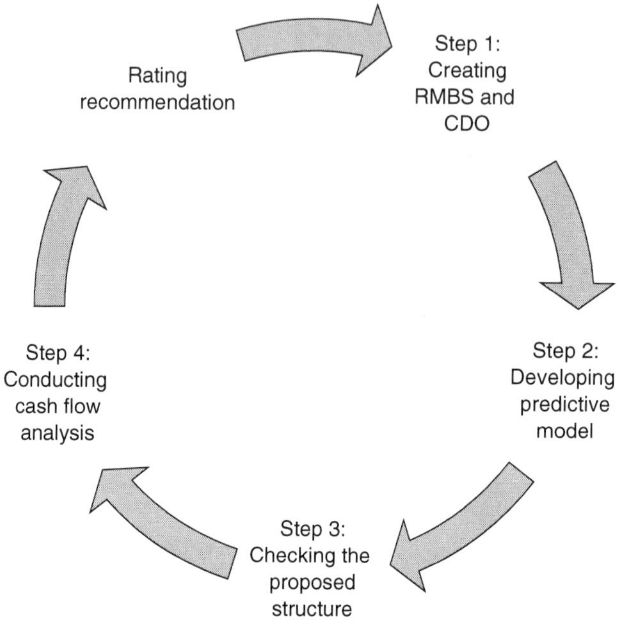

Figure 2.2 The rating of RMBS and CDO (source: adapted from Standard and Poor's at: https://ratings.standardandpoors.com/about/about-credit-ratings/ratings-process.html).

Conclusion

Theoretically, credit ratings are supposed to represent a non-biased, quantifiable and reliable assessment of the creditworthiness of debt issuers. According to *The Economist* (2012), 'credit ratings matter, many big investors incorporate them into their investment guidelines, restricting which assets they may buy and prescribing how much collateral is required in derivatives transactions, for instance. In either case, a weak rating costs money.' Although there are over 140 credit agencies on the global market, few of them hold more than 95 per cent of the world rating market. They have unshared control over access to the debt market and have their say in the determination of the cost of debt. If rationally and accurately developed, CRA ratings would represent the more efficient way of assessing the financial risk of issuers but, are ratings accurately assessed? Much doubt exists. Indeed the role of credit rating agencies was recently virulently decried all over the world and their quality challenged, especially after agencies' liability was clearly established in the 'subprime' crisis.

Appendix 2.1 International list of known credit rating agencies (107 agencies)

Agency	*Country*	*Agency*	*Country*
A.M. Best Company, Inc. Insurance industry emphasis	US, ESMA, NRSRO	Investment Information and Credit Rating Agency (ICRA)	India
A.M. Best Europe, Rating Services Ltd (AMBERS)	UK, ESMA	Islamic International Rating Agency, B.S.C. (IIRA)	Bahrain
Agusto & Co. Ltd	Nigeria	Istanbul International Rating Services, Inc., a.k.a. TurkRating	Turkey
Ahbor Rating	Uzbekistan	Japan Credit Rating Agency, Ltd (JCR)	Japan, ESMA, NRSRO
Apoyo & Asociados Internacionales SAC – Fitch Associate	Peru	JCR Avrasya Derecelendime AS, a.k.a. JCR Eurasia Rating – JCR affiliate	Turkey
ASSEKURATA Assekuranz Rating-Agentur GmbH	Germany, ESMA	JCR-VIS Credit Rating Co. Ltd, JCR affiliate	Pakistan
Axesor SA	Spain, ESMA	Kobirate Uluslararası Kredi Derecelendirme ve Kurumsal Yönetim Hizmetleri A.S., a.k.a. Kobirate	Turkey
Bank Watch Ratings SA Fitch affiliate	Ecuador	Korea Investors Service, Inc. (KIS) –Moody's affiliate	Korea
BRC Investor Services SA	Colombia	Korea Ratings Corporation, f.k.a. Korea Management Consulting and Credit Rating Corp. (KMCC) – Fitch affiliate	Korea
Bulgarian Credit Rating Agency AD	Bulgaria, ESMA	JCR Avrasya Derecelendime A.S., a.k.a. JCR Eurasia Rating – JCR affiliate	Turkey
Capital Standards Rating (CSR)	Kuwait	Kroll Bond Rating Agency, Inc. Wholly acquiring LACE Financial Corp. in August 2010	US, ESMA, NRSRO
Calificadora de Riesgo, PCA	Uruguay	Lanka Rating Agency, Ltd (LRA) Subsidiary of RAM	Sri Lanka
Capital Intelligence, Ltd	Cyprus, ESMA	Levin and Goldstein	Zambia

continued

Appendix 2.1 Continued

Agency	*Country*	*Agency*	*Country*
Caribbean Information & Credit Rating Services Ltd (CariCRIS)	Caribbean	Malaysian Rating Corporation Berhad (MARC) – Fitch affiliate	Malaysia
CERVED Group SpA	Italy, ESMA	Mikuni & Co., Ltd	Japan
Central European Rating Agency (CERA), a.k.a. Fitch Polska, SA – Fitch affiliate	Poland	Moody's Investors Service	US
CERVED Group SpA	Italy, ESMA	Moody's Investors Service Cyprus Ltd	Cyprus, ESMA
Chengxin International Credit Rating Co., Ltd, Moody's affiliate	China	Moody's France SAS	France
China Lianhe Credit Rating, Co. Ltd	China	Moody's Deutschland GmbH	Germany
Clasificadora de Riesgo Humphreys, Ltd – Moody's affiliate	Chile	Moody's Italia S.r.l.	Italy
Class y Asociados SA Clasificadora de Riesgo	Peru	Moody's Investors Service España SA	Spain
CMC International, Ltd	Nigeria	Moody's Investors Service Ltd	UK
Companhia Portuguesa de Rating, SA (CPR) ARC	Portugal	Morningstar, Inc.	USA
Credit Analysis & Research Ltd (CARE)	India	Muros Ratings	Russia
Creditreform Rating AG	Germany	National Information & Credit Evaluation, Inc. (NICE)	Korea
'Credit-Rating': A Ukrainian rating agency. Рейтинговое Агентство 'Кредит-Рейтинг	Ukraine	NUS Risk Management Institute (not for profit)	Singapore
Credit Rating Agency of Bangladesh, Ltd (CRAB)	Bangladesh	ONICRA Credit Rating Agency of India, Ltd	India
Creditreform Rating AG	Germany	Ontonix	Italy
Credit Rating Information and Services, Ltd (CRISL)	Bangladesh	P.T. Kasnic Credit Rating Indonesia –Moody's affiliate	Indonesia
CRIF SpA	Italy	P.T. PEFINDO Credit Rating Indonesia, a.k.a. PT Pemeringkat Efek Indonesia	Indonesia

CRISIL, Ltd, f.k.a. Credit Rating Information Services of India – S&P affiliate	India
Dagong Global Credit Rating Co., Ltd	China
Dagong Europe Credit Rating Srl (Dagong Europe)	Italy
Demotech, Inc.	US
Dominion Bond Rating Service (DBRS)	Canada,
DBRS Ratings Limited	UK
Duff & Phelps de Colombia, SA, SCV – Fitch affiliate	Colombia
Ecuability, SA	Ecuador
Egan-Jones Rating Company	US
Emerging Credit Rating Ltd (ECRL) Collaboration with MARC	Bengladesh
Equilibrium Clasificadora de Riesgo – Moody's affiliate	Peru
Expert RA	Russia
Euler Hermes Rating GmbH	Germany
European Rating Agency (ERA)	UK
European Rating Agency AS	Slovakia
Pacific Credit Rating (PCR), a.k.a. Clasificadora de Riesgo Pacific Credit Rating SAC	Peru
Pakistan Credit Rating Agency, Ltd (PACRA) – Fitch former affiliate	Pakistan
Philippine Rating Services, Corp.	Philippines
Public Sector Credit Solutions (not for profit)	USA
RAM Rating Services Berhad (RAM), f.k.a. Rating Agency Malaysia Berhad, S&P affiliate	Malaysia
Rapid Ratings International, Inc.	Australia/NZ
Rating and Investment Information, Inc., (R&I)	Japan
Realpoint, LLC	US
RusRating	Russia
Saha Kurumsal Yönetim ve Kredi Derecelendirme Hizmetleri A	Turkey
Scope Credit Rating GmbH	Germany
Seoul Credit Rating & Information, Inc. – JCR affiliate	Korea
Shanghai Credit Information Services Co., Ltd	China
Shanghai Far East Credit Rating Co., Ltd, a.k.a. Xinhua Far East Credit Ratings	China
Slovak Rating Agency, AS (SRA), a.k.a. Slovenská ratingová agentúra, AS Balkans – ERA affiliate	Slovak Republic

continued

Appendix 2.1 Continued

Agency	*Country*	*Agency*	*Country*
Feller Rate Clasificadora de Riesgo – S&P affiliate	Chile	SME Rating Agency of India Ltd (SMERA)	India
Fedafin	Switzerland	Sociedad Calificadora de Riesgo Centroamericana, SA (SCRiesgo)	Costa Rica
Feri EuroRating Services AG	Germany	Spread Research	France
Fitch Ratings, Ltd	US/UK	SR Rating Prestação de Serviços Ltd	Brazil
Fitch France SAS	France	Standard and Poors (S&P)	US
Fitch Deutschland GmbH	Germany	Standard & Poor's Credit Market Services France SAS	France
Fitch Italia SpA	Italy	Standard & Poor's Credit Market Services Italy Srl	Italy
Fitch Polska SA	Poland	Standard & Poor's Credit Market Services Europe Ltd	UK
Fitch Ratings España SAU	Spain	Taiwan Ratings, Corp. (TCR) – S&P affiliate	Taiwan
Fitch Ratings Ltd	UK	Economist Intelligence Unit, Ltd	UK
Fitch Ratings CIS Ltd	UK	TheStreet.com Ratings, Inc., f.k.a. Weiss Ratings, Inc.	US
GBB-Rating Gesellschaft für Bonitätsbeurteilung mbH	Germany	Thai Rating and Information Services Co., Ltd (TRIS)	Thailand
Global Credit Rating Co.	S.Africa	TCR Kurumsal Yonetim ve Kredi Derecelendirme Hizmetleri AS, a.k.a.: Türk KrediRating (TCRating)	Turkey
CRIF SpA	Italy	Veda	Australia
HR Ratings de Mexico, SA de CV	Mexico	Veribanc, Inc.	US
Interfax Rating Agency (IRA)	Russia	Wikirating (not for profit)	Switzerland
ICAP Group SA	Greece		
Investment Information and Credit Rating Agency (ICRA)	India		

Source: NRSRO, ESMA and Defaultrisk, at: www.defaultrisk.com/rating_agencies.htm.

Appendix 2.2 Credit rating definitions of major rating categories[1]

Rating symbols	*Rating definition*		*Rating symbols*	*Rating definition*
	Fitch2	*S&P3*		*Moody's4*
Investment grade				
AAA	Highest credit quality and the lowest expectation of credit risk; assigned only in case of exceptionally strong capacity for payment of financial commitments. This capacity is highly unlikely to be adversely affected by foreseeable events.	The highest rating. The obligor's capacity to meet its financial commitment on the obligation is extremely strong	Aaa	Obligations rated Aaa are judged to be of the highest quality, with minimal credit risk.
AA+,AA,AA–	Very high credit quality and expectations of very low credit risk. Indicate very strong capacity for payment of financial commitments. This capacity is not significantly vulnerable to foreseeable events.	Differs from the highest-rated obligations only to a small degree. The obligor's capacity to meet its financial commitment on the obligation is very strong.	Aa1, Aa2, Aa3	Obligations rated Aa are judged to be of high quality and are subject to very low credit risk.
A+, A, A–	High credit quality and expectations of low credit risk. The capacity for payment of financial commitments is considered strong. This capacity may, nevertheless, be more vulnerable to changes in circumstances or in economic conditions than is the case for higher ratings.	High credit quality and expectations of low credit risk. The capacity for payment of financial commitments is considered strong. This capacity may, nevertheless, be more vulnerable to changes in circumstances or in economic conditions than is the case when obligation is still strong.	A1, A2, A3	Obligations rated A are considered upper-medium grade and are subject to low credit risk.

continued

Appendix 2.2 Continued

Rating symbols	*Rating definition*		*Rating symbols*	*Rating definition*
	Fitch2	*S&P3*		*Moody's4*
BBB+, BBB, BBB–	Good credit quality. There are currently expectations of low credit risk. The capacity for payment of financial commitments is considered adequate but adverse changes in circumstances and economic conditions are more likely to impair this capacity.	Exhibits adequate protection parameters. However, adverse economic conditions or changing circumstances are more likely to lead to a weakened capacity of the obligor to meet its financial commitment.	Baa1, Baa2, Baa3	Obligations rated Baa are subject to moderate credit risk. They are considered medium-grade and as such may possess certain speculative characteristics.
Speculative grade				
BB+, BB, BB–	Speculative. There is a possibility of credit risk developing, particularly as the result of adverse economic change over time; however, business or financial alternatives may be available to allow financial commitments to be met.	Less vulnerable to non-payment than other speculative issues. However, it faces major ongoing uncertainties or exposure to adverse business, financial or economic conditions which could lead to the obligor's inadequate capacity to meet its financial commitment.	Ba1, Ba2, Ba3	Obligations rated Ba are judged to have speculative elements and are subject to substantial credit risk.
B+, B, B–	Highly speculative; significant credit risk is present, but a limited margin of safety remains. Financial commitments are currently being met; however, capacity for continued payment is contingent upon a sustained, favourable business and economic environment. For individual obligations, may indicate distressed or defaulted obligations with potential for extremely high recoveries.	More vulnerable to non-payment than obligations rated 'BB', but the obligor currently has the capacity to meet its financial commitment on the obligation. Adverse business, financial or economic conditions will likely impair the obligor's capacity or willingness to meet its financial commitment.	B1, B2, B3	Obligations rated B are considered speculative and are subject to high credit risk.

CCC+, CCC,CCC–	Default is a real possibility. Capacity for meeting financial commitments is solely reliant upon sustained, favourable business or economic conditions. For individual obligations, may indicate distressed or defaulted obligations with potential for average to superior levels of recovery.	Vulnerable to non-payment, and is dependent upon favourable business, financial and economic conditions for the obligor to meet its financial commitment. In the event of adverse business, financial or economic conditions, the obligor is not likely to have the capacity to meet its financial commitment.	Caa1, Caa2, Caa3	Obligations rated Caa are judged to be of poor standing and are subject to very high credit risk.
CC	Default of some kind appears probable.	Currently highly vulnerable to non-payment.	Ca	Obligations rated Ca are highly speculative and are likely in, or very near, default, with some prospect of recovery of principal and interest.
C	Default is imminent. For individual obligations, may indicate distressed or defaulted obligations with potential for below-average to poor recoveries.	Currently highly vulnerable to non-payment, obligations that have payment arrears allowed by the terms of the documents or obligations of an issuer that is the subject of a bankruptcy petition or similar action which have not experienced a payment default.	C	Obligations rated C are the lowest rated class of bonds and are typically in default, with little prospect for recovery of principal or interest.

continued

Appendix 2.2 Continued

Rating symbols	*Rating definition*		*Rating symbols*	*Rating definition*
	Fitch2	*S&P3*		*Moody's4*
RD	Restricted Default indicates an entity that has failed to make due payments (within the applicable grace period) on some but not all material financial obligations, but continues to honour other classes of obligations.	n.a.		
D	Indicates an entity or sovereign that has defaulted on all of its financial obligations.	Non-payment default.		

Notes

1 www.academia.edu/177848/Regulatory_Use_of_Credit_Ratings_How_it_Impacts_the_Behaviour_of_Market_Constituents.

2 The modifiers '+' or '–' may be appended to a rating to denote relative status within major rating categories. Such suffixes are not added to the 'AAA' long-term rating category, or to categories below 'CCC'.

3 The ratings from 'AA' to 'CCC' may be modified by the addition of a plus (+) or minus (–) sign to show relative standing within the major rating category.

4 Moody's appends numerical modifiers 1, 2 and 3 to each generic rating classification from Aa through Caa. The modifier 1 indicates that the obligation ranks in the higher end of its generic rating category, the modifier 2 indicates a mid-range ranking and the modifier 3 indicates a ranking in the lower end of that generic rating category.

Appendix 2.3 Fitch, Moody's and S&P's short-term symbols

Fitch		*Moody's*		*S&P*	
Symbol	*Definition*	*Symbol*	*Definition*	*Symbol*	*Definition*
F1	Highest credit quality. Indicates the strongest capacity for timely payment of financial commitments.	P-1	Has a superior ability to repay short-term debt obligations.	A-1	Has *strong* capacity to meet its financial commitments.
F2	Good credit quality. A satisfactory capacity for timely payment of financial commitments.	P-2	Has a strong ability to repay short-term debt obligations.	A-2	Has *satisfactory* capacity to meet its financial commitments.
F3	Fair credit quality. The capacity for timely payment of financial commitments is adequate.	P-3	Has an acceptable ability to repay short-term obligations.	A-3	Has *adequate* capacity to meet its financial obligations.
B	Speculative. Minimal capacity for timely payment of financial commitments.	NP	Does not fall within any of the prime rating categories.	B	Is regarded as *vulnerable* and has significant speculative characteristics.
C	High default risk. Default is a real possibility depending upon a sustained, favourable business and economic environment.	–	–	B-1	Have an average speculative grade capacity to meet their financial commitments over the short term compared to other speculative grade obligors.
RD	Defaulting only on one or more of its financial commitments.	–	–	B-2	Have an average speculative grade capacity to meet their financial commitments over the short term compared to other speculative grade obligors.

continued

Appendix 2.3 Continued

Fitch		*Moody's*		*S&P*	
Symbol	*Definition*	*Symbol*	*Definition*	*Symbol*	*Definition*
D	Defaulted on all of its financial obligations	–	–	B-3	Have a relatively weaker capacity to meet their financial commitments over the short term compared to other speculative grade obligors.
–	–	–	–	C	Is *currently vulnerable* to non-payment and is dependent upon favourable economic conditions.
–	–	–	–	R	Is under regulatory supervision owing to its financial condition.
–	–	–	–	NR	Not rated.

Source: adapted from Fitch, Moody's and S&P, at: http://creditrisk.bankersalmanac.com/info/help/credit-ratings/.

Notes

1 Credit rating agencies, from www.defaultrisk.com/rating_agencies.htm, retrieved 2 June 2014.
2 The European Securities and Markets Authority (ESMA) is exclusively responsible for the registration and supervision of credit rating agencies (CRA) in the European Union.
3 One basis point represents 0.01 per cent of the issue total amount.
4 Some agencies may segment ratings in three broad classes: (i) investment class: 'AAA' to 'AA', (ii) medium class: 'A' to 'BBB' and (ii) speculative class: 'BB+' to 'CCC/C', with the medium class qualifiying issues with low risk of default.
5 Ratings can also be private, when the issuer does not want them to be published and rather kept confidential.

References

Baklanova, V. (2012) 'Regulatory use of credit ratings: how it impacts the behaviour of market constituents', at: www.academia.edu/177848/Regulatory_Use_of_Credit_Ratings_How_it_Impacts_the_Behaviourof_Market_Constituents, retrieved 19 March 2014.

Banker Almanac, 'Fitch credit rating definitions', at: http://creditrisk.bankersalmanac.com/info/help/credit-ratings/fitch, retrieved 28 March 2013.

Dominion Bond Rating Service (DBRS) (n.d.), 'Short-term and long-term rating relationships', rating scales, at: www.dbrs.com/research/236758/short-term-and-long-term-rating-relationships.pdf, retrieved 7 October 2013.

Economist, The (2012), Bank downgrades: 'Berated: a ratings agency is poised to pounce', 16 June, at: www.economist.com/node/21556939, retrieved 15 June 2012.

Feldblum, S. (2011), 'Rating agencies', at: www.casact.org/library/studynotes/Feldblum_Rating_Oct%202011.pdf, retrieved 2 March 2014.

Gailliard, N. (2010), 'Les agences de notation', Repères Économie, Paris.

Investopedia (n.d.), 'A brief history of credit rating agencies', at: www.investopedia.com/articles/bonds/09/history-credit-rating-agencies.asp, retrieved 5 June 2014.

Kisgen, D. and P. Strahan (2010), 'Do regulations based on credit ratings affect a firm's cost of capital?' *Review of Financial Studies*, Vol. 23, pp. 4325–4347.

Moody's (2001a), 'How to get rated', at: www.moodys.com/Pages/amr002001.aspx#process, retrieved 5 October 2013.

Moody's (2001b), 'The benefit of ratings', at: www.moodys.com/Pages/amr002001.aspx, retrieved 23 March 2014.

Moody's (2001c), 'Rating committee', at: www.moodys.com/Pages/amr002001.aspx#process, retrieved 20 March 2014.

Moody's (2009), 'Moody's: ratings definitions', at: www.moodys.com/sites/products/AboutMoodysRatingsAttachments/MoodysRatingsSymbolsand%20Definitions.pdf, retrieved 23 March 2014.

Partnoy, F. (2006), 'How and why credit rating agencies are not like other gatekeepers'. In R.E. Litan and Y. Fuchita, *Financial gatekeepers: Can they protect investors?* Washington, DC: Brookings Institution, p. 13.

Securities and Exchange Commission (SEC) (2012), 'Summary report of commission staff's examination of each nationally recognized statistical rating organization', at: www.sec.gov/reportspubs/special-studies/nrsro-summary-report-2012.pdf, retrieved 10 October 2013.

Securities and Exchange Commission (SEC) (2013a), 'Annual report to the congress on nationally recognized statistical rating organizations', at: www.sec.gov/divisions/marketreg/ratingagency/nrsroannrep1213.pdf, retrieved 10 October 2013.

Securities and Exchange Commission (SEC) (2013b), 'Summary report of commission staff's examination of each nationally recognized statistical rating organization', at: www.sec.gov/reportspubs/special-studies/nrsro-summary-report-2013.pdf, retrieved 10 October 2013.

3 The Big 3

The global credit market gatekeepers

As mentioned in Chapter 2, the very few largest credit rating agencies control over 95 per cent of the world credit market. It is, however, commonly admitted that competition in the rating market was necessary and can lead to credit ratings that are of higher quality and good reputation to investors and at a lower price (SEC, 2011). For this reason much legislation has, since 2006 (Rating Agency Act, 2006) and particularly after the 2007 crisis, tried to decrease concentration in the global rating market and, in 2008, the SEC proposed amendments designed to achieve the goals of the Rating Agency Act; namely to attain greater accountability, transparency and competition in the credit rating industry (SEC, 2011). The control of the Big 3 over the global rating market may not need to be proven; every piece of information on the global credit rating industry points in that direction. What is sought in this chapter is to determine whether such market concentration and control are actually on the rise or decreasing. For this reason, the chapter is dedicated to the identification of the path followed by the Big 3 to gain the quasi-total control on the global rating market, and assesses the impact of the recent regulations aiming to reduce concentration in the rating industry, based on Herfindahl-Hirschman (HHI) methodology.

Additional to this introduction and the conclusion, the second section of the chapter describes the path of the Big 3 in gaining control of the global rating market; the third section deals with rating agencies' ownership; the fourth analyses the reasons behind the credit rating market concentration; the fifth tests the dynamic of the concentration within the credit rating industry; the sixth explores other means of assessing increased rating market concentration; the seventh discusses Big 3 manoeuvres of enforcing concentration; the eighth discusses the test results; and the final section concludes.

The path of concentration followed by the Big 3

Although around 121 credit agencies were identified on the global market (Chapter 2, Appendix 2.1) only 25 of them are registered with the Securities and Exchange Commission (SEC), as NRSRO, or with the European Commission (EC), as ESMA, or with both. Among the registered agencies two players, Moody's and Standard & Poor's hold more than 80 per cent of the world rating market followed by Fitch with about 15 per cent, placing it third. These Big 3 also control more than 30 agencies among 121 listed, scattered around the world. They have an oligopolistic say in the allocation of global credit, therefore impacting its cost. Indeed an upgrade of an issuer can facilitate his indebtedness, while a downgrading can significantly increase his capital costs and negatively affect his stock price (if not completely denying him indebtedness). In reaction to the oligopoly built over the years by the Big 3, tremendous efforts have been made by national and international regulatory agencies to curb their appetite for global rating market total control; the American regulator, for instance, introduced for this purpose its Credit Rating Agency Reform Act since 2006 ('Rating Agency Act') that became effective on 26 June 2007 and many other national jurisdictions have followed (see CRA regulations in Chapter 7).

A market is called oligopolistic when it is shared by a limited number of players and can be described as having weak competition. In order to test the evolution of market concentration in the rating industry, Herfindahl-Hirschman (HHI) methodology will be used on data available since 2007, for the population of Nationally Recognized Statistical Rating Organizations (NRSRO). Although, NRSRO registration was initiated in 1973, the year 2007 is actually the first year the SEC started publishing its NRSRO report in accordance with the Credit Rating Agency Reform Act. During 2007, the SEC received applications for registration as NRSROs from ten operating credit rating agencies and all applications were granted registration. Except, on 24 December 2009, when Dagong Global Credit Rating Co., Ltd (Dagong), from China, submitted its application for registration as an NRSRO to the SEC and its request was denied for insufficient information. The NRSRO list underwent important changes in 2010 and 2011: in 2010 LACE Financial Corp. was purchased by KBRA Holdings; Realpoint LLC was purchased by Morningstar Inc.; and, in 2011, Rating and Investment Information, Inc., registered as an NRSRO since 24 September 2007, withdrew from registration and HR Ratings (Mexico) was registered (SEC, 2012).

The use by the SEC of the term NRSRO goes back to 1975, in the Net Capital Rule for broker-dealers, as an objective benchmark prescribing capital charges for different types of debt securities. Since then, the term NRSRO has been used in a number of regulations all over the planet. Although NRSRO was conceived for a narrow purpose, NRSROs ratings were 'used widely as benchmarks in federal and state legislation as well as in rules issued by other financial regulators, the US Congress has also incorporated the NRSRO concept into other pieces of financial legislation' (SEC, 2011). The ten credit rating agencies registered as NRSROs, as of the date of this work, represent over 97 per cent of the global rating market and form the sample for the study; they are: A.M. Best Company, Inc. (AMB), DBRS, Inc. (DBRS), Egan-Jones Ratings Company (EJR), Fitch Ratings, Inc. (Fitch), HR Ratings de México, SA de CV (HR), Japan

Credit Rating Agency, Ltd (JCR), Kroll Bond Rating Agency, Inc. (KBRA), Moody's Investors Service, Inc. (Moody's), Morningstar Credit Ratings, LLC (Morningstar), Standard & Poor's Ratings Services (S&P).

A brief review of the history of major agencies composing the sample will, we hope, help understanding the reasons behind credit rating market concentration. A.M. Best was founded in 1899 and has grown steadily over the past century. It first started operating out of a single room in New York's financial district, to be today engaged into a worldwide operation. AMB established offices in London in 1997, Hong Kong in 2000 and Dubai in 2012.[1] DBRS is a Canadian credit agency, formed in 1976 in Toronto but also having offices in New York, Chicago and London. DBRS is currently providing ratings across a broad range of financial institutions, corporate entities, government bodies and various structured finance product groups in North America, Europe, Australasia and South America.[2] Egan-Jones is an American rating agency founded in 1995: it has two rating practices, one for 'buyside' managers and another for issuers. EJR also rates private placements, bank loans, bonds, notes and other debt instruments and gets paid by the users.[3] The adventure of Fitch Rating (the third largest global rating player) started in 1913, with the founding of the Fitch Publishing Company that specialized in the publication of financial statistics for use in the investment industry via 'The Fitch Stock and Bond Manual' and 'The Fitch Bond Book'. The AAA through D rating system in use today was actually introduced since 1924 thanks to Fitch. Early in the 1990s Fitch decided to become a full-service global rating agency: it merged with IBCA of London, a subsidiary of the French holding company Fimalac S.A. in the late 1990s and also acquired market Thomson Bank-Watch, Duff & Phelps Credit Ratings Co. and Algorithmic. Fitch also created two subsidiaries: Fitch Solutions and Fitch Training.[4] HR Ratings is a Mexican agency mainly operating in Mexico and rates governmental entities, corporates, financial institutions and infrastructure. HR is the first Latin American ratings agency registered as an NRSRO.[5] The Japan Credit Rating Agency was established in 1985. It mainly publishes ratings to Japanese companies, local governments and other Japanese entities. It is registered with both NRSRO and ESMA. It is also eligible for rating Japanese local banks under the Basel framework.[6] Kroll Bond Rating Agency is an American agency,[7] established in 2010 and quickly got NRSRO registration on top of being recognized by the National Association of Insurance Commissioners (NAIC) as a credit rating provider (CRP). Moody's origins can be traced back to the beginning of the 1900s, when John Moody and Company first published its 'Moody's Manual' containing basic statistics and general information about stocks and bonds of various industries. 'Moody's Manual' remained a national publication from 1903 until the stock market crash of 1907. In 1909, however, Moody began publishing 'Moody's Analysis of Railroad Investments' adding analytical information about the value of securities to basic statistics. The expansion of this idea led to the creation of Moody's Investors Service in 1914, which in the ten years that followed would provide ratings for nearly all of the government bond markets at the time. By the 1970s Moody's began rating commercial paper and bank deposits and became the full-scale rating agency that it is today.[8] Morningstar is an American credit rating agency specializing in identifying credit risk in structured finance investments mainly for institutional investors. Morningstar also offers investment management services through its registered investment adviser subsidiaries. The company currently has operations in 27 countries.[9] Henry Varnum Poor is certainly the forerunner of securities analysis and reporting to be developed over the next century. He inaugurated the saga of Standard & Poor's. In 1860, he first published the 'History of Railroads and Canals in the United States'. In 1906 Standard Statistics was formed which published corporate bond, sovereign debt and municipal bond ratings and merged with Poor's Publishing in 1941 to form Standard & Poor's corporation which was acquired by the McGraw Hill Companies Inc. in 1966. S&P has become best known by indexes such as the S&P 500, a stock market index that is both a tool for investor analysis and a means for decision-making.[10]

According to the SEC (2011), several factors have made the demand for Big 3 credit ratings to explode in recent years:

i First, during the second half of the twentieth century, the financial market underwent profound structural changes 'that have ultimately increased the number of participants, their anonymity, and the complexity of their investment strategies'.

ii Second, the financial disintermediation which marked the second half of the twentieth century also caused a shift in issuers' borrowing behaviour to capital markets at the expense of bank credit, leading to securitization, and this has created increasing investors' reliance on credit ratings.

iii Third, even for non-regulatory purposes, users of credit ratings often privileged Big 3 ratings, due to the good image they were projecting. Some banks, for instance, may recall debt if its rating falls below investment grade status and some insurance departments require an insurer to have an A– or better rating to write surety business.

iv Fourth, economies of scale and sunk costs may have favoured the largest and more established rating agencies that could usually allocate their costs across a wider range of ratings, and this provided them with a more efficient cost base.

v Fifth, the quality of credit ratings is difficult to assess at the time of issue. Investors therefore often use the quality of prior ratings as a benchmark and an agency that has a long history of quality ratings also develops a reputational asset.

vi Sixth, credit assessment may be even more difficult if an agency is a newcomer to the market, lacking long time establishment and reputation.

vii Seventh, in 1940–1970, only 0.1 per cent of corporate debt defaulted therefore creditors did not require ratings to provide capital. By 2010, much corporate debt was below investment grade. Some countries and large firms defaulted on their debt, and ratings became essential to secure new issues (Feldblum, 2011).

viii Finally, the extreme sophistication of financial instruments and the difficulty faced by regulatory authorities to monitor them, made them opt for Big 3 ratings (assumed to be of higher accuracy) for regulatory purposes. In the 1970s, for instance, the SEC imposed capital and liquidity requirements on securities owned by banks and other financial institutions. The major rating agencies were designated Nationally Recognized Statistical Ratings Organizations (NRSRO) by the SEC, and financial institutions could satisfy their capital requirements by investing in securities with favourable ratings by an NRSRO (Feldblum, 2011).

Rating agencies' ownership

Ownership of agencies can have an impacting effect on ratings accuracy and in Table 3.1 has an overview of the ownership structure within the major credit rating agencies.

Table 3.1 Major credit rating agencies and owners

Agency	*Ownership*
A.M. Best Company, Inc. (AMB)	Independent
DBRS Ltd (DBRS) (Canada)	Independent
Egan-Jones Rating Company (EJR)	Independent
Fitch, Inc. (Fitch)	French Fimalac (50%) US Hearst Corporation (50%)
HR Ratings (Mexico)	?
Japan Credit Rating Agency, Ltd (JCR) (Japan)	Financial institutions
Kroll Bond Rating Agency, Inc. (KBRA)	Marsh & McLennan Companies[1]
Moody's Investor Services, Inc. (Moody's)	Dun and Braadstreet
Morningstar	As of December 2008, Joe Mansueto owned approximately 57% of the outstanding shares in Morningstar[2] and a Japanese bank, Softbank 20%
Standard & Poor's Rating Services (S&P)	McGraw-Hill

Source: adapted, Yahoo Finance.

Notes
1 Marsh & McLennan Companies is a global professional services firm offering clients with advice and solutions in the areas of risk, strategy and human capital.
2 http://en.wikipedia.org/wiki/Morningstar,_Inc.

Ownership structures of small NRSROs do not seem to present any serious problem of conflicts of interest. This, however, does not seem the case for the Big 3. Two of them are owned by financial institutions: Moody's, for instance, was acquired by Dun & Bradstreet[11] in 1962 and was spun off as a separate entity and listed on the NYSE in 2000. Standard & Poor's, on the other hand, is a division of McGraw Hill, and only Fitch Ratings seems to be owned by independent interests. It is, indeed, 50 per cent owned by Hearst Corporation, one of the largest diversified media companies of the United States, and 50 per cent owned by financial services Females, a French holding company listed on the Paris stock exchange. Given that Moody's and S&P represent over 80 per cent of the global rating market, their affiliation to financial institutions can pose a serious threat of independence and may raise serious possibility of conflicts of interest. The risk, for instance, is that a large investor may try to press a credit agency to allocate lower initial ratings than required, for the sake for higher yields, while another institution that can only invest in highly rated instruments, due to regulatory requirements, might pressure CRAs to assign favourable initial ratings on particular securities.

Reasons behind the credit rating market concentration build up

Several reasons are usually advanced as explanations for the extreme concentration encountered in the global credit rating market:

i It is believed for instance that the Big 3 have benefited from the special financial market situation that prevailed some 80 years ago when

> equities were thought to be complicated and bonds were thought to be simple so it appeared to make sense to have a few rating agencies set up to tell us all what bonds to buy. But flash forward to the slicing and dicing of credit today and it's really a pretty wacky concept.
>
> (Partnoy, 2006)

ii While the Big 3 were usually stressing the fact that their ratings constitute mere opinions to be taken as such, they were at the same time, constantly lobbying for the status of 'Nationally Recognized Statistical Ratings Organizations' and, ever since they were awarded such privilege by the Securities and Exchange Commission of the United States in 1973, their hegemony over the world rating market has become unchallenged and has been endorsed all over the world, thus creating an artificial and impassable entry barrier to the credit rating market.

iii Big 3 control over the credit market has received its biggest boost from Basel II, the second of the Basel Accords now extended and effectively superseded by Basel III that used to and still does give a ruling power to Big 3 ratings. As ratings were gaining greater acceptance in the marketplace regulators of the financial market and institutions were till recently increasingly using them to enforce and simplify their prudential oversight task.

iv The long-established Big 3 have benefited from a learning curve on how to attract new customers successfully.

v Ratings reflect the sunk labour costs of producing them and that are non-coverable once ratings have been issued. Therefore the providing of adequate coverage of a particular debt by new CRAs would require them first to make substantial investment in sunk costs. This is more the case in unsolicited ratings (Langohr, 2006).

vi Each new entrant agency runs the risk of facing scarcity of human and analytic resources than an established CRA (IOSCO, 2004). The new entrant will therefore be always disadvantaged, as established CRAs will often be able to hire any required additional and more experienced staff, for analysing larger and more sophisticated issues.

vii Issuers are usually motivated to have their debts rated by one of the Big 3, not so much because of the intrinsic value of the rating itself, but rather because other participants do so. 'As others seek Big 3 ratings, it becomes necessary for an issuer to seek a rating from a credible CRA to be seen to fit in with other issuers. Therefore existing CRAs benefit from having network externalities' (Langohr, 2006).

viii Mutual and pension funds are usually imposed limits on the portfolio amount that they can hold in non-investment grade securities. Further, debt issuers and investors frequently explicitly specify ratings into covenants of their financial agreements.

ix In complex transactions like in structure finance, issuers usually seek guidance from agencies on the structuring of their financial transactions.

x Wide ranges of private contractual agreements, which make reference to ratings, actually create a potential barrier to entry for newcomers to the rating market. Their effect can be an increase in demand and liquidity for the securities of the concerned issuers (SEC, 2012).

xi Ratings triggers are also commonly encountered in bank loan agreements and guaranteed investment contracts and, whenever this is the case, any decline in the rating, below a certain level, can alter parties to an agreement (SEC, 2012).

xii Other statutory and regulatory limitations may create a potential barrier to entry for new entrants (SEC, 2012).

Among the advanced reasons for the extreme concentration in the credit rating market, the use of rating for regulatory requirement comes first. Indeed, the Joint Forum of 2009, identified the followings uses (Joint Forum, 2009):

i in determining capital adequacy requirements for financial institutions (such as securitization exposures for banks in Basel II);
ii in identifying or classifying assets, such as for eligible investments (for example, of mutual funds) or permissible concentrations (for example, of asset managers);
iii in evaluating the credit risk of assets in securitization or covered bond offerings;
iv in determining disclosure requirements (such as for rated entities); and
v in determining prospectus eligibility (for example, whether investment-grade-rated debt is eligible for expedited or automatic regulatory review before its offering).

Further, it is argued that the 'hardwiring' of rating agencies in regulation 'both forces market participants to use their services and protects the rating agencies from outside competition and liability' (Partnoy, 2006). The 1970s and 1980s witnessed a few new entrants to the rating market that, for a very short time, dreamed of surviving the Big 3 oligopoly, by specializing and concentrating on specific rating niches. To mention the case of Duff & Phelps, for instance, which specializes in sovereign rating, Thomson Financial Bank Watch for credit institutions, A.M. Best for insurance companies, MacCarthy, Crisanti & Maffei for risky issuers: most of them were quickly seeped/acquired by the Big 3 (Gailliard, 2010). Although, acquisition strategy seems to constitute one of the Big 3's main tools of establishing and strengthening their dominance over the global rating market, among the advanced reasons for global credit rating market concentration, the reliance on ratings for legislative purposes comes first. Such reliance was extended to virtually every corner of the financial system and the finance industry. International organizations and governments used to pay little attention to ratings that were not emanating from the Big 3 and often required them. Recently, however, following the Financial Stability Board (FSB, 2013) recommendation, to be discussed in the regulatory chapter, major global regulators have adopted new legislation forbidding the use of credit rating for regulatory purposes. Our hypothesis, however, is that, given the Big 3's structural rooting in the global rating market, recent CRA regulations should not have any significant effect on rating market concentration, although the primacy of some regulations may not yet allow a permanent testing of their effects.

Testing the concentration dynamic within the credit rating industry

In order to test the trend in the level of concentration within the credit rating market, during the period 2008–2012, the Herfindahl–Hirschman Index (HHI) is used. The HHI is commonly considered a valid measure of market concentration (Investopedia website). It is used to assess credit market concentration using the available data on NRSRO, as reported by the SEC in the 2012 NRSRO report to the Congress (SEC, 2012). The HHI is expressed as the ratio of the size of firms within a given market in relation to the whole market and can be considered as an effective indicator of the level of concentration within such a market. Further, its behaviour over time can be used to assess the changes in levels of concentration within a given market. It is commonly admitted that 'as a general rule mergers that increase the HHI by more than 100 points in concentrated markets raise antitrust concerns' (Investopedia website). The way of determining the HHI is simple and takes form in steps:

1 first, consider the market share of each competitor ($M_1\%$, $M_2\%,\ldots,$ $M_n\%$);
2 second, multiply the result in (1) by 100;
3 third, squaring the result in (2); and
4 finally, add up the figures.

So:

$$\text{HHI} = (M_1\% \times 100)^2 + (M_2\% \times 100)^2 + \ldots + (M_n\% \times 100)^2 \quad (3.1)$$

Where:

$M_1\%, M_2\%,\ldots, M_n\%$, represent market share one, two,…, n $(M_1\% + M_2\% + \ldots + M_n\% = 100\%)$.

The HHI methodology can be illustrated quantitatively by using a simple arithmetic example. Suppose we want to determine the degree of concentration in a rating market where only three agencies A1, A2 and A3, operate and provide their ratings. Assume further that agency A1 holds a 50 per cent share of the whole market, while A2 and A3 hold 40 and 10 per cent each respectively. The degree of concentration in the described market can be assessed using the HHI as follows:

$$\text{HHI} = (0.50 \times 100)^2 + (0.40 \times 100)^2 + (0.10 \times 100)^2$$
$$= 2{,}500 + 1{,}600 + 100 = 4{,}200$$

The measurement of the HHI is performed on a scale of 0 to 10,000 points and is interpreted as follows:

i When the HHI approaches zero this would mean that the market consists of a large number of players of relatively similar size. This is usually the case when we are dealing with a perfectly competitive market. Thus if a market is composed of 100 agencies each holding 1 per cent share, then the HHI would be 100 or:

$$HHI = (0.01 \times 100)^2 \times 100 = 100$$

ii When the HHI is approaching 10,000 it would mean that the market is dominated by a small number of larger size firms. The more the HHI approaches 10,000, the more the market is considered monopolistic. Thus in a market where one company owns a 100 per cent share the HHI would equal 10,000, or:

$$HHI = (100\% \times 100)^2 = 10,000$$

The HHI is largely used to determine whether real competition prevails in a given sector or whether a suggested merger of companies can be approved by monetary authorities. The decision rules are the following:

i $HHI \leq 1,000$ = perfect competition, and
ii $HHI \geq 1,800$ = lack of competition.

In this regard, the Department of Justice of the United States seems to consider a market producing an HHI of less than 1,000 to be a competitive marketplace, a market producing an HHI of 1,000 to 1,800 to be a moderately concentrated market and, finally, a market producing an HHI of 1,800 or greater to be a highly concentrated market. These decision rules indicate that only markets with an HHI of 1,000 or less are to be considered competitive, and markets with an HHI of 1,800 or more are to be considered non-competitive.

HHI results analysis and discussion

Given the non-availability of public data we recourse to the SEC HHI Inverse (HHII) data to construct our own. The SEC computes the HHII, in the following way: HHII = 10,000/HHI, we can therefore compute the HHI by posing: HHI = 10,000/HHII.

The results of the application of the HHI methodology to agencies for the period 2008–2012, is provided in Appendix 3.1 which is therefore constructed by just dividing 10,000 by HHII reported by the SEC for the years 2007 through 2012 for the ratings outstanding in each class of ratings and, overall, for the following rating categories considered: financial institutions, insurance institutions, corporate issuers, asset-backed securities, government securities, total ratings and total excluding government securities. Asserting that the global credit rating market is concentrated is self-evident, but the HHIs computed during the period 2007–2012 may also contain additional information:

i For example, credit market concentration is far beyond the ceiling threshold of 1,800.

ii Also as indicated by Figure 3.1, when the behaviour of the HHI for all rating categories is expressed including and excluding the government securities category, some overall deterioration in market concentration is to be mentioned.

The HHI for all rating categories (including government securities category) (the upper curve in Figure 3.1), has decreased during the period 2007–2012 from 3,774 (its 2007 level) to 3,636 (its level of 2012) and this may be considered as an improvement. This can, however, be a misleading conclusion, because if the year 2007 (the year of crisis) is excluded, then we find that the HHI has actually increased by 10 per cent; it has increased during the period 2008–2012 from 3,344, its 2008 level to 3,636, its 2012 level. It becomes therefore obvious that the concentration in the rating market has actually been reinforced from 2008 and beyond, despite some stability in 2011 and 2012. Note, however, that when the government rating category is excluded, the lower curve in Figure 3.1, the HHI for all other rating categories (excluding government securities category), would rather have experienced a decrease in concentration of 28 per cent since 2007, and this is quite substantial. We should, however, keep in mind that such a decrease is mainly due to the year 2007. The situation has stayed essentially flat during the period 2008–2012, except for the year 2010 where a decrease of 4 per cent took place. Combining the information conveyed by the two curves in Figure 3.1, we can assert that market concentration within the rating market has actually been reinforced during the period 2008–2012 and that the pace of such concentration would have been even greater if it was not for the government securities rating category, where more competition was introduced in 2008, due the financial crisis.

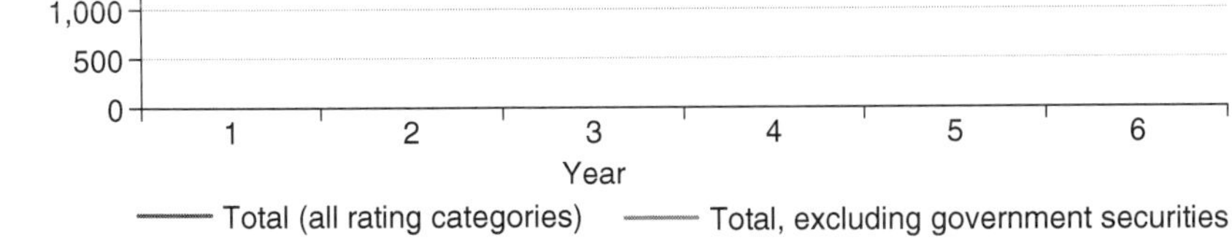

Figure 3.1 HHI for all rating categories including and excluding government securities category (source: HHIs were computed by the author based on SEC HHI Inverses).

Note also that the increase in HHI was not equally shared by all rating categories. In 2012, for instance, the class of financial institutions and insurance companies were relatively the least concentrated categories of rating, with HHIs of 2,488 and 2,688 respectively, while government securities and corporate issuers were the most concentrated categories of rating, with HHIs of 4,000 and 3,333 respectively. The classes of financial institutions, asset-backed securities, and government securities have experienced decreases in concentration during the period 2007–2012, with a drop in HHIs of 16, 21 and 6 per cent respectively, while financial institutions, asset-backed securities and government categories have experienced increases in concentration during the same period.

Table 3.2 provides the yearly changes in the HHI for the period 2008–2012: the biggest improvement in credit rating competition has occurred between 2007 and 2008. The variation in the HHI for 2008 is negative for each category of ratings and in the whole including and excluding the government securities category.

The largest annual change during the years 2008–2012 occurred in the class of asset-backed securities where the HHI dropped by 26 per cent in 2009, although much of that decrease, 19 per cent, was cancelled in 2010. Financial institutions was the only category of rating that experienced a steady decrease in HHI for the period 2007–2011, indicating a constant improvement in competition within that segment of the credit rating market. Corporate issuers is the category of rating where concentration has being continuously increasing during the period 2009–2012, while the insurance companies category has conveyed a mixed message, leaning towards increase in competition.

Other means of analysing the concentration trend within the rating industry

The weak level of competition in the credit market identified by the HHI analysis can be confirmed by several other means like: (i) agencies' rating activities; (ii) the number of rating analysts employed by agencies; (iii) the trend in agencies' revenue and margins.

Figure 3.2 provides the percentage of credit ratings outstanding reported by each Big 3 and all other agencies together, in annual certification reports, for the calendar years ending 31 December 2009 to 2012.

The reading of Figure 3.2 indicates that S&P continues to be the agency with the highest number of ratings reported to be outstanding as of 31 December of each year from to 2009 to 2012, accounting for about 42.38 per cent in 2009 and 45.65 per cent in 2012, with an increase of 3 per cent during the whole period. Moody's is the second agency with the highest number of ratings reported to be outstanding as of 31 December of each year from to 2009 to 2012, accounting for about 37.23 per cent in 2009 and 36.87 in 2012, with a decrease of 1.5 per cent during the period. Fitch

Table 3.2 HHI yearly changes for the period 2007–2012 (%)

Year	*Financial institutions*	*Insurance companies*	*Corporate issuers*	*Asset-backed securities*	*Government securities*	*Total (all rating categories)*	*Total, excluding government securities*
2008	–0.09	–0.01	–0.14	–0.04	–0.17	–0.11	–0.26
2009	–0.03	0.05	0.19	–0.26	0.07	0.05	–0.01
2010	–0.04	0.14	0.00	0.19	–0.02	–0.01	0.01
2011	–0.04	–0.10	0.05	–0.05	0.09	0.05	–0.04
2012	0.03	0.01	0.01	–0.02	–0.01	0.00	0.01

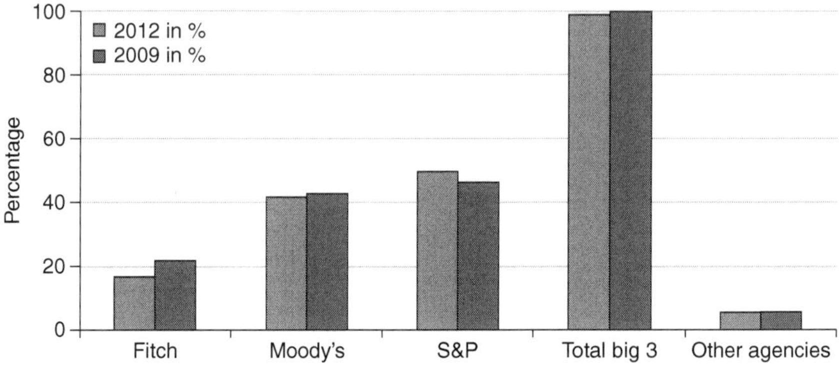

Figure 3.2 Percentage of credit ratings outstanding reported by the Big 3 for years ending 31 December 2009 and 2012 (source: adapted from the SEC Annual Report on Nationally Recognized Statistical Rating Organizations, December 2013).

reported having the third highest number of outstanding ratings, accounting for about 17.61 per cent in 2009 and 14.0 per cent in 2012 with a decrease of 3.60 per cent during the period. In total, the Big 3 issued about 97.22 of all the ratings that were reported to be outstanding as of 31 December 2009 and only 96.5 per cent in 2012 indicating a slight decrease of 0.65 per cent over a period of four years, and leaving all other agencies with only 2.80 per cent in 2009 and 3.5 per cent in 2012.

The percentage of ratings issued by the Big 3 for the year ended 31 December 2012 for each of the five rating classes are presented in Table 3.3. The concentration of ratings exercised by the Big 3 is high across all five categories, but varies across them. Moody's, S&P and Fitch have accounted for at least 75.47 per cent of the outstanding ratings in each rating class in 2012. The percentage of ratings issued by the Big 3 has ranged from a low of 75.47 per cent for insurance ratings to a high of 99.9 per cent government ratings and seems that this was always the case.

Table 3.3 The percentage of ratings issued by the Big 3 for the year ending 31 December 2012 for each class of rating

Agencies	*Financial institutions*	*Insurance institutions*	*Corporate issuers*	*Asset-backed securities*	*Government securities*
Fitch	26.53	19.02	14.88	21.61	11.59
Moody's	26.06	18.28	31.48	31.61	39.15
S&P	30.93	38.18	45.90	37.42	48.32
Total Big 3	83.52	75.47	92.25	90.64	99.06
Other agencies	16.48	24.53	7.75	9.36	0.94

Of the Big 3, S&P is taking the lead in every class of rating with almost 50 per cent of corporate issuers and government securities. Moody's seems to perform better in government securities and Fitch in financial institutions categories. Other agencies perform a little better in insurance institutions and financial institutions, but are completely absent from government securities ratings.

The level of rating market concentration can also be seized, by looking at the number of rating analysts employed by agencies. Table 3.4 provides the percentage of rating analysts employed by agencies for the period 2010–2012. During this period, the number of analysts that were employed by all the NRSROs increased by about 6.8 per cent, from 3,520 rating analysts in 2009, to 4,022 rating analysts in 2012, a 14 per cent increase.

When the year 2009 is excluded, data would show the Big 3 having actually suffered a decrease in their analytical staff by around 2 per cent from its level of 2010. The three largest credit rating agencies report employing 4,022 credit analysts, or approximately 90.78 per cent, of the total number of credit analysts employed by all of the NRSROs. In 2012, the Big 3 employed 90.78 per cent of credit analysts to perform 96.5 per cent of the ratings. Among the Big 3, Fitch seems to employ more analytical staff, in proportion to its market share in 2012. Fitch has indeed the highest ratio ratings to analysts (despite its smaller size, Fitch employs 321 analysts compared to 797 for S&P and 823 for Moody's). On average the Big 3 as a group employs one credit analyst for 662 ratings a year. The relative increase in staffing levels has, however, been much greater at some of the smaller NRSROs during this period. For example, comparing 2012 to 2010, small agencies' analytical staff has gained almost 2 per cent of the agencies staff since 2010, i.e. from 283 analysts in 2010 to 371 in 2012. In total, analytical staff at the NRSROs other than S&P, Moody's and Fitch, accounted for about 9.22 per cent of all NRSRO rating analysts at the end of 2012, up from 7.52 per cent in 2010. Such gain in analytical staffing could, however, be just a recovery phenomenon from previous understaffing.

Table 3.4 Percentage of rating analysts employed by the agencies as of 31 December of each calendar year

Agencies	*2009 in %*	*2010 in %*	*2011 in %*	*2012 in %*
Fitch	29.40	27.86	27.63	27.15
Moody's	31.14	28.9	28.34	27.92
S&P	28.95	35.72	35.7	35.7
Big 3	89.49	92.48	91.68	90.78
Other NRSRO	10.51	7.52	8.32	9.22
Total agencies	100	100	100	100

Source: adapted from SEC, Forms NRSRO, Exhibit 8.

Another way of assessing the change in concentration within the rating market over time is by looking at the trend of agencies' revenue and margins. The high level of concentration detected in the global rating market can also be felt through an analysis of the income and margin distributions among rating agencies. Table 3.5 provides such information for the period 2009–2013.

The total reported revenue to the SEC by agencies for the fiscal year 2013 was approximately $5.24 billion and this represents an increase of 57 per cent compared to its 2009 level. The total revenues of NRSRO has actually increased by 22.4 per cent, since 2010 and most of that growth was assured by the Big 3. In fact since 2010, the Big 3 have cashed over 94 per cent of all income earned by all NRSROs. Figure 3.3 depicting Moody's and S&P revenue behaviour indicates that although both agencies have increased their revenue since 2009, Moody's has increased its revenue by 65 per cent and S&P by 48 per cent, and Moody's revenue enjoyed much more stability.

Most of the growth in revenue registered since 2010 was realized by S&P, Moody's and Fitch. Overall, the Big 3 have accounted for about 94.7 per cent of the 2012 fiscal year revenue of all NRSROs, a slight increase over their 94.0 per cent share of fiscal year 2011 (SEC, 2012). For the year 2010, 70.8 per cent of the total revenue reported to the SEC by all of the NRSROs for that year came from the US, 16.0 per cent from the European region, 8.1 per cent from Asia and 5.1 per cent from the rest of the world. The US share of agencies' revenue decreases by 1.3 per cent from its level of 2008, to the benefit of Asia and the rest of the world.

Table 3.5 Moody's and S&P revenue and operating income ($ millions) and margin for the period 2009–2013

	2013	*2012*	*2011*	*2010*	*2009*
Revenue					
• Moody's	2,973	2,750	2,281	2,032	1,797
• S&P	2,274	2,034	1,767	1,195	1,537
Total revenue	5,247	4,784	4,048	3,227	3,334
Rate of increase	9.68%	18.18%	25.44%	-3.21%	–
Operating income					
• Moody's	1,235	1,007	888	773	688
• S&P Ratings	1,000	849	720	762	712
Total operating revenue	2,235	1,856	1,608	1,535	1,400
Margin					
• Moody's	41%	39%	39%	38%	38%
• S&P Ratings	44%	42%	41%	45%	46%
Weighted margin	42%	40%	40%	41%	42%

Source: adapted from Moody's and McGraw-Hill annual reports 2009–2013.

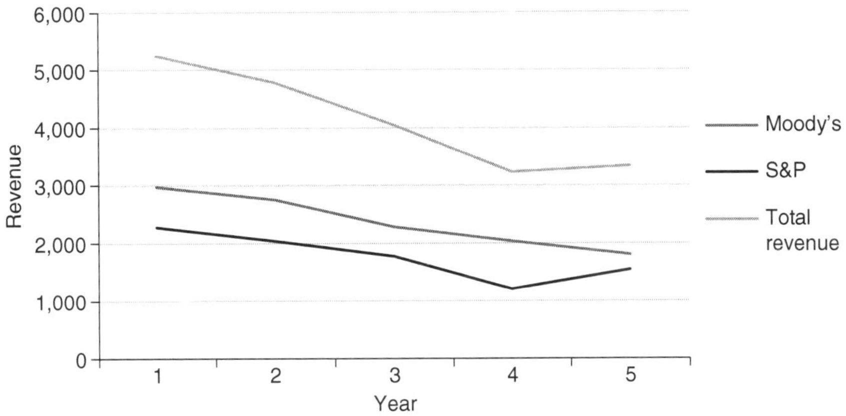

Figure 3.3 Moody's and S&P revenue behaviour (2009–2013) (source: adapted from the SEC Annual Report on Nationally Recognized Statistical Rating Organizations, December 2013).

Major agencies were also enjoying very high profit margins, for the years 2009 to 2013, Moody's Investor Services margins, for instance, were 38 per cent, 38 per cent, 39 per cent, 39 per cent and 41 per cent, respectively, 46.0 per cent, 45 per cent, 41 per cent, 42 per cent and 44 per cent, for S&P and N/A, 39.5 per cent, 38 per cent and 32.7 per cent, for Fitch Ratings. Two-thirds of rating agencies' revenue came actually from activities in the USA; 16 per cent of rating revenues originated from the European region, 8 per cent from Asian continent and 5 per cent from the rest of the world. A transfer between regions seems, however, to take shape, since we are witnessing a degreasing shift of the US share to the benefit of the Asian region; the European share of rating revenue seems to stay flat.

Agencies' revenue and margin analysis bring us also to conclude the extreme concentration of the global rating market, and can be considered as further evidence of the Big 3's undivided control over the rating market.

Big 3 manoeuvres of enforcing concentration

Since the early twentieth century, the Big 3 seemed to have worked successfully to dominate the global rating market and, by the turn of the century, Moody's and S&P already ended up imposing their duopoly to the rest of the world; Fitch later joined them. Since then they have constantly expressed a fierce opposition for any reduction (not to mention elimination) of existing barriers to entry to the rating market, arguing that such reduction/elimination would eventually lead to reduced disclosure of information and to the deterioration of rating quality. As new entrants may engage in 'race to the bottom' strategies in order to sell their services more cheaply (McDaniel, 2002). As an example of the Big 3's race to more market share, Appendix 3.2 gives a summarized picture of Moody's extended global penetration. Moody's has affiliates in all continents and major economies. Although S&P does not give information regarding its affiliates we know that S&P Ratings Services issues ratings from locations as diverse as the US, Canada, Latin America, Europe/Mid-Asia Pacific, Mexico, Argentina, Brazil, East Africa, Australia, Hong Kong, Singapore, Japan, England, France, Germany, Italy, Taiwan, Spain, Sweden, Russia, Israel, UAE, South Africa (S&P 2012). Like Moody's, S&P has a strong global presence covering all continents and developed economies. Table 3.6 gives an unmistakable view of the fierce determination of the Big 3 to

Table 3.6 A non-exhaustive list of acquisitions made by the three largest CRAs during the period 2000–2008

Acquired company	*Acquiring agency*	*Country*	*Year*
Duff & Phelps	Fitch IBCA	US	2000
Thomson Financial BankWatch	Fitch IBCA	Canada	2000
AMR	Fitch IBCA	France	2000
Crowe Chized & Company LLP Mo	Moody's	US	2000
Canadian Bond Rating Service	S&P	Canada	2000
Central European Rating Agency	Fitch	Poland	2001
Magister	Moody's	Argentina	2001
Charter Research	S&P	US	2001
Credit Ratings System	Fitch	US	2002
KMV	Moody's	US	2002
Atlantic Rating	Fitch	Brazil	2003
Interfax Rating Agency	Moody's	Russia	2004
Capital IQ	S&P	US	2004
Algorethmics	Fitch	Canada	2005
ValueSpread	Fitch	UK	2005
Economy.com	Moody's	US	2005
Assirt Research	S&P	Australia	2005
Crisil	S&P	India	2005
Taiwan Ratings	S&P	Taiwan	2005
Reoch Credit Ltd	Fitch	UK	2006
CRA Rating	Moody's	Czech Republic	2006
Wall Street Analytics	Moody's	US	2006
GSCS	Fitch	Dubai	2007
PT Kasnic Credit Ratings Indonesia	Moody's	Indonesia	2007
CA Ratings	Moody's	South Africa	2007
Imake Consulting	S&P	US	2007
ABSXchange	S&P	US	2007
ClaRifi	S&P	US	2008
BQuote	Moody's	US	2008
Fermat International	Moody's	Belgium	2008
Enb Consulting	Moody's	UK	2008

Source: Gailliard (2010).

control the global rating market; it gives an overview of acquisitions made by the Big 3 during the sole period 2000–2008.

Moody's has made 12 acquisitions of several affiliates during the period 2000–2008, four in the US and the rest in countries like Argentina, Russia, Czech Republic, Indonesia, South Africa, Belgium and UK. S&P has made nine acquisitions of affiliates during the same period, five of them in the United States and four in countries like Canada, Australia, India and Taiwan. Fitch has made, during this period, 11 acquisitions of affiliates, two in the US and the rest in countries like Canada, France, Poland, Brazil, UK and Dubai. The control of the global market seems, therefore, to be a constant preoccupation of all the Big 3. Besides acquisitions, agencies sometimes recourse to special methods to increase their market share, thus

> last year after struggling to win business Standard & Poor's changed its criteria for rating bonds backed by residential mortgages. Since the change the company has generally given the most optimistic forecasts for the bonds of any rating agency. That has made S. & P. popular with the banks issuing the bonds.
>
> (*New York Times*, 2013)

Similarly, agencies may have used computer programs assessing risk that were manipulated to ensure high ratings and big profits. The Justice Department of the US, for instance, contends in a civil lawsuit that S&P inflated the ratings on complex mortgage securities, hurting investors. 'Such models, which analyses large amounts of data, frequently crop up in financial scandals' (Eavis, 2013).

Moody's and S&P are also believed to have engaged in heavy-handed 'blackmail' tactics in order to get business from new issuers and even dared lowering their ratings in case of refusal. Moody's, for instance, published an 'unsolicited' rating of Hanover Re with a subsequent letter indicating, 'It looked forward to the day Hannover would be willing to pay.' Faced with a refusal, Moody's kept downgrading the insurer over successive years, while making payment requests that were rebuffed. At the end (in 2004) Moody's cut Hannover's debt to junk status and even though other rating agencies gave it strong ratings, shareholders were confused by the downgrade and this resulted in a loss of US$175 million in the insurer's market capitalization (Klein, 2004).

As result of a well-orchestrated strategy the reach of the three big credit agencies extends into virtually every dimension of the financial system but at the expense of a lot of criticisms regarding their governance.

Results discussion

Oligopoly seems to describe best the global credit market, and the reliance on rating for regulatory purposes has been a strong incentive for market participants to use Big 3 ratings. Consequently, the pressure to break the regulatory rating monopoly of the Big 3 became untenable, especially on the run of the subprime crisis. It finally became obvious that the best way to approach the ratings problem was still to find a way to a situation where no one is legally required to use ratings and to make CRAs compete in a market free of entry barriers. There was therefore a need to remove regulatory and statutory requirements for investors and borrowers to meet CRA ratings. Recently regulators have done just that: new rules that aim to reducing reliance on CRA ratings for regulatory purposes were adopted, despite the Big 3 continuing to protest, arguing that increasing competition within the credit rating industry can be harmful for users. The HHI analysis indicates that market concentration within the rating industry has actually been reinforced during the period 2008–2012. This fact is also confirmed by the study of the number of ratings reported by agencies to be outstanding for the period 2007 to 2012, and by the analysis of agencies' revenues. Our results seem to point to the consolidation of the market concentration in the aftermath of the financial crisis, i.e. during the period 2008–2013 after the grace period of 2007. At this time, 2014, the effect of the new SEC and EC legislation forbidding the use of credit ratings for regulatory purposes, although still difficult to assess, is not expected to see the control of the Big 3 over the credit market to decrease significantly. The Big 3 seem rather to consolidate further their market position, if we consider the behaviour of revenue and the number of outstanding credit ratings. The Big 3 have issued about 96.5 per cent of all the ratings that were reported to be outstanding as of 31 December 2012.

Conclusion

The HHI test for high profit margins reveals, not only an excessive level of concentration is prevailing, implying a limited choice of rating providers for both investors and issuers, it also points out to an increasing trend in margin increases. Consequently, the Big 3 must be continuing to enjoy actually a sizeable economic rent, and continue pricing abnormally higher fees for their services. This also justifies all efforts of larger agencies of setting and defending entry barriers that seem to impede significantly the functioning of the rating market and seriously prevent potential newcomers. Although most people would love to see CRAs be submitted to stricter rules decreasing their hegemony on the world credit rating market, many users continue to rely on them for credit risk assessment. The US regulators, for instance, used to depend on credit ratings to monitor the safety of $450 billion of bonds held by US insurance companies. As the tighter rules for CRAs recently initiated seem to have had little effect, people are wondering what to do about agencies.

Appendix 3.1 HHI for NRSROs for each one of the categories of rating considered for the period 2007–2012

Year	*Financial institutions*	*Insurance companies*	*Corporate issuers*	*Asset-backed securities*	*Government securities*	*Total (all rating categories)*	*Total, excluding government securities*
2007	2,967	2,488	3,058	3,690	4,255	3,774	3,774
2008	2,688	2,469	2,639	3,546	3,534	3,344	2,809
2009	2,597	2,604	3,145	2,632	3,774	3,497	2,793
2010	2,506	2,967	3,155	3,125	3,717	3,472	2,817
2011	2,404	2,660	3,311	2,959	4,049	3,650	2,703
2012	2,488	2,688	3,333	2,907	4,000	3,636	2,717
Variation, 2007–2012	–480	201	275	–783	–255	–137	–1,056
Percentage of variation in a scale of 10,000	–0.16	0.08	0.09	–0.21	–0.06	–0.04	–0.28

Source: computed by the author from data adapted from HHI statistics published by the SEC.

Notes
HHI ≤ 1,000 = perfect competition; HHI ≥ 1,800 = monopoly, and rating categories as defined in article 3(a)(62) of the SEC.

Appendix 3.2 Moody's credit rating affiliates, as of December 2013

Affiliate	*Country*	*Affiliate*	*Country*	*Affiliate*	*Country*
Moody's Investors Service Limited One	United Kingdom	Moody's Canada Inc.	Canada	Moody's Investors Service Pty. Limited	Australia
Moody's Interfax Rating Agency Limited	Russia	Moody's Investors Service South Africa (Pty)	South Africa	Moody's Italia S.r.l.	Italy
Moody's Investors Service Hong Kong Limited	Hong Kong	Moody's Eastern Europe LLC	Russia	Moody's Japan	Japan
Moody's de México SA	México	Moody's America Latina Lt	Brazil	Moody's Investors Service Singapore.	Singapore
Moody's Investors Service España SA	Spain	Moody's America Latina Ltda	Argentina	Moody's Investors Service Cyprus Limited.	Cyprus
Moody's France SAS.	France	Moody's Latin America	Mexico	Moody's Investors Service Middle East Limited	UAE
		Moody's Deutschland GmbH	Germany		

Source: Moody's Investors Service Inc. Annual Certification of Form NRSRO 2012.

Notes

1 See www.ambest.com/about/history.html.
2 See www.dbrs.com/about#sthash.9x2goYFk.dpuf.
3 See www.egan-jones.com/.
4 See www.fitchratings.com.
5 See www.hrratings.com/en/chairmans_message.
6 See www.jcr.co.jp/english/.
7 See www.krollbondratings.com/about.
8 See www.moodys.com/.
9 See ratingagency.morningstar.com/RPLogin.aspx.
10 See www.standardandpoors.com/ru_RU/web/guest/home.
11 Dun & Bradstreet is a company that dominates the global market for business information data.

Bibliography

Eavis, P. (2013), 'U.S. contends S.&P. purposely used faulty models', 5 February, at: http://dealbook.nytimes.com/2013/02/05/financial-models-at-the-heart-of-lawsuit-against-s-p/?_php=true&_type=blogs&_r=0, retrieved 13 June 2014.

Feldblum, S. (2011), 'Rating agencies', at: www.casact.org/library/studynotes/Feldblum_Rating_Oct%202011.pdf, retrieved 2 March 2014.

Financial Stability Board (FSB) (2013), 'Credit rating agencies reducing reliance and strengthening oversight', Progress report to the St Petersburg G20 Summit.

Gailliard, N. (2010), 'Les agences de notation', Repères Économie, Paris.

International Organization of Securities Commissions (IOSCO) (2004), 'Code of conduct fundamental for credit rating agencies', December, at: www.iosco.org/library/pubdocs/pdf/IOSCOPD271.pdf, retrieved 20 May 2013.

Investopedia, at: www.investopedia.com/terms/h/hhi.asp, retrieved 25 March 2014.

Joint Forum (2009), 'Stocktaking on the use of credit ratings', Basel: Bank for International Settlements, at: www.bis.org/publ/joint22.pdf, retrieved 2 March 2014.

Klein, Alec (2004), 'Credit raters' power leads to abuses some borrowers say', *Washington Post*, 24 November, at: www.washingtonpost.com/wp-dyn/articles/A8032-2004Nov23.html, retrieved 26 April 2014.

Langohr, H. (2006), 'The credit rating agencies and their credit ratings', Presentation to the Bond Market Association's 'Rating Industry Day Conference', 23 February.

McDaniel, R.W. (2002), 'Written statement of Raymond W. McDaniel: president Moody's Investors Service. Before the United States Securities and Exchange Commission', 21 November, at : http://www.sec.gov/news/extra/credrate/moodys.htm, retrieved 10 October 2013.

New York Times (2013), 'Ratings shift', 17 September, at: http://topics.nytimes.com/top/reference/timestopics/subjects/c/credit_rating_agencies/index.html, retrieved 2 April 2014.

Partnoy, F. (2006), 'How and why credit rating agencies are not like other gatekeepers'. In R.E. Litan and Y. Fuchita, *Financial gatekeepers: Can they protect investors?* Washington, DC: Brookings Institution, p. 13.

Securities and Exchange Commission (SEC) (2011), 'Annual report to the congress on nationally recognized statistical rating organizations', at: www.sec.gov/divisions/marketreg/ratingagency/nrsroannrep1212.pdf, retrieved 10 October 2013.

Securities and Exchange Commission (SEC) (2012), 'Annual report to the congress on nationally recognized statistical rating organizations', at: www.sec.gov/divisions/marketreg/ratingagency/nrsroannrep1212.pdf, retrieved 12 October 2013.

Securities and Exchange Commission (SEC) (2013a), 'Annual report to the congress on nationally recognized statistical rating organizations', at: www.sec.gov/divisions/marketreg/ratingagency/nrsroannrep1213.pdf, retrieved 12 October 2013.

Securities and Exchange Commission (SEC) (2013b), '2013 summary a of commission staff's examination of each nationally recongized statistical rating organization', at: www.sec.gov/aspubs/special-studies/nrsro-summary-report-2013.pdf, retrieved 12 October 2013.

Standard & Poor's (S&P) (2012), 'Form NRSRO to the security exhange commission'.

United States (2006), 'The Credit Rating Agency Reform Act of 2006 of United States' ('Rating Agency Act'), Pub. L. No. 109–291.

4 Credit rating agencies' methodologies, metrics and rating accuracy

Introduction

Credit ratings are part of the large field of default prediction in finance, englobing a number of statistical methods and tools that are often based on accounting numbers. These tools have been effective in deepening the understanding of credit defaults, whether from corporate or sovereign origins. As discussed in the previous chapter, default prediction has been imposed by the Big 3 as an extremely lucrative industry, under the consenting eye of the financial regulator and within a relatively very short period of time. But are the followed approaches to credit default assessment appropriate for the task? This is the issue discussed in this chapter.

The chapter discusses credit agencies' methodologies of assessing credit default and analyses their level of accuracy. Following this introduction, the second section defines the credit default risk and its analysis; the third introduces some default prediction models; the fourth, discusses credit agencies' default assessment methodologies; the fifth presents agencies' rating metrics and defaults studies; the sixth relates independent assessment of credit ratings accuracy; the seventh concludes the chapter.

What is credit default risk?

Risk in finance and accounting expresses the likelihood that income from an investment may differ from its expected outcome. For debt securities investors and lenders, financial risk expresses the possibility they may lose money when investing in company debt securities, whenever its cash flow proves to be insufficient to meet its debt financial obligations. For its part, the risk of default appears as a restrictive form of the financial risk; it refers mainly to the possibility that an issuer of debt securities may fail meeting its obligations towards its securities holders, and this may inevitably lead to a loss of the interest revenue they were supposed to receive and eventually to a loss of the principal.

The risk of default has undergone, during the last century, several changes in definition. It is reported that in 1909, for instance, John Moody used to underline that credit ratings reflected the safety and the solvency of debt issuers. Today, however, the risk of default definition has been extended to describe situations in which governments, companies or individuals are not in a position of honouring their debt financial commitments, requiring payments of debt interests and/or principal and includes also late payments and any change in the contractual arrangements that may jeopardise payments or may lead to their delay. Indeed, lenders, like other investors, are exposed to default risk in virtually all loan extensions. One very highlighted example of such failure is the recent case of Greece, where private creditors were forced to accept the cancellation of half of what was owed to them (*The Economist*, 2012). To mitigate the impact of default risk, lenders typically charge interest rates that are proportionate to issuer levels of risk of default and the higher the risk, the higher the required rate of interest on the granted loans will be, and vice versa. Default risk can therefore be seen as closely linked to the cash flow generating capacity of the issuer that has become an essential component of fixed income investments. Default risk assessment has therefore become an important financial activity and several approaches of issuer defaults predictions have been suggested and among the most popular are the cash flow analysis, ratio analysis, default prediction models and agencies' credit rating.

Default risk assessment

Cash flow analysis in default assessment

To assess the risk of default, concern has recently shifted from measures based on profitability to measures based on cash flow. Thus the less cash flow an issuer of debt securities can generate, the lower will be its ability to cope with its debt obligations. Therefore the stability and sustainability of the generating capacity of the cash flows of an issuer of debt are the best guarantee an issuer can offer to investors and the best guaranty an investor can get; stability and sustainability of cash flows provide the necessary assurance of issuer ability to face its debt obligation, while ensuring the continuity of its operations and without recoursing to additional external funding. Credit agencies use a variety of quantitative measures based on cash flows to analyse the risk of debt security issuers' default. Figure 4.1 gives an overview of some measures of cash flow, commonly encountered, based on accounting numbers and often used by agencies.

The cash flow measures discussed in this section may present slight differences compared with those encountered in classical finance books. Figure 4.1 relates the cash flow measures commonly used by agencies (Fitch Ratings). Although, in the long run, cash flow and net revenue are intimately related, in the short run, however, an issuer can survive a temporal shortage in net revenue but he cannot survive the same shortage in

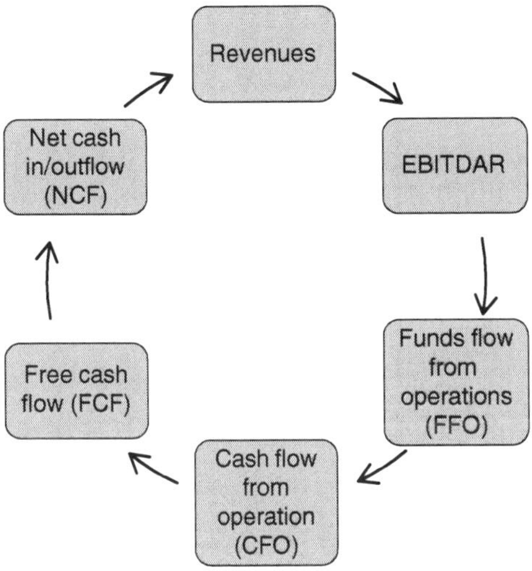

Figure 4.1 Some common cash flow measures.

cash flow. After revenues, the next important element of cash flows is the operating 'earning before interest, taxes, depreciation, amortisation and long-term rentals', EBITDAR given by:

$$\text{EBITDAR} = \text{earning before taxes} + \text{interest expenses} + \text{depreciation and amortization} + \text{long-term rentals} \quad (4.1)$$

The EBITDAR is a cash flow measure commonly used to analyse and compare the performance between issuers and sectors, and as EBITDAR is assessed before the means of financing (interest expenses) and accounting choices effects (accounting for leases) are taken in consideration, it actually expresses the core cash flow generating capacity of issuers. In this sense, the EBITDAR plays a key role in the analysis of the risk of issuers' default. Given, however, the limitations of the EBITDAR, as a pure measure of cash flows, the credit agencies may also recourse to a number of other sub-measures in order to more closely identify the ability of issuers to address their debt obligations; these may include (Fitch Ratings), additional to the traditional ratio analysis:

i funds flow from operations (FFO);
ii cash flow from operations (CFO);
iii free cash flow (FCF); and
iv net cash in/outflow (NCF).

Funds from operations (FFO) generally refers to cash generated by an issuer from its normal operations and therefore does not include cash flows related to financing, such as credit or debit interest, nor does it include gains or losses from the sales of assets or their amortization. Thus, the determination of funds from operations is performed as follows

FFO = EBITDAR – cash interest paid, net of interest received – cash tax paid + associate dividends – long-term rentals +/– other changes before FFO (4.2)

It is important to distinguish FFO from cash flow from operations, CFO, which is a key component of the cash flow statement (prepared using the indirect method) and representing the amount of cash flow available generated by a company's core operations after all payments identified by the issuer for ongoing operational requirements, interest, dividends and tax. The CFO is given by the following expression:

CFO = FFO +/– working capital (4.3)

The expression '+/– working capital' indicates the annual increases/decreases in working capital components, such as the component of current assets (excluding cash) and the component of current liabilities components (excluding bank). The CFO is an important indication of whether a company is in a position to generate sufficient positive cash flow to maintain and grow its operations, or whether it will need additional external funding.

Free cash flow (FCF) represents the cash that an issuer is able to generate after putting aside the required amount of money needed for maintaining or expanding its asset base. The FCF measures an issuer's cash from operations, after substracting capital expenditures, non-recurring or non-operational expenditures and dividends. FCF is calculated as:

FCF = CFO +/– non-operational cash flow – capital expenditure – dividends paid (4.4)

The net cash flow (NCF) refers to the amount of money left after issuer's transactions have been completed and that all charges and any deductions related to them have been subtracted. The NCF is given by:

NCF = FCF + receipts from asset disposals – business acquisitions + business divestments +/– exceptional and other cash flow items (4.5)

Interest has also grown for a particular financial statement that is intended to help assessing a debt issuer cash flow generating ability and issuer global solvency; the cash flow statement as required by International Accounting Standard 7 (IAS 7) and by most accounting jurisdictions. This is a listing of all cash inflows and cash outflows during the reporting period. The CFO discussed before is one of the three main parts constituting this statement. To enhance the informational value of the presentation, the cash flow components are classified according to the nature of the activities that generates them. The three primary categories of cash flows, within the cash flow statement, are:

i cash flows from operating activities, CFO, as expressed by (4.3);
ii cash flows from investing activities, CFI; and
iii cash flows from financing activities, CFF.

Indeed, classifying each cash flow by source (operating, investing or financing activities) is more informative than simply listing the various cash flows.

Ratio analysis

The assessment of risk of default was traditionally based on ratio analysis, i.e. comparing elements of financial statements, in the hope of discovering clues regarding (in the case of agencies) an issuer's solvency capacity or insolvency facts. 'The detection of company operating and financial difficulties is a subject which has been particularly amenable to analysis with financial ratios' (Altman, 2012). This section is devoted to the presentation of the commonly used ratios in solvency analysis and most of their definitions are those usually adopted by rating agencies, particularly Fitch Ratings. These ratios are:

i The debt-to-capital ratio, defined as 'the company's debt divided by its total capital. Debt includes all short-term and long-term obligations. Total capital includes the company's debt and shareholders' equity, which includes common stock, preferred stock, minority interest and net debt' (Investopedia website). It measures the degree of indebtedness of an issuer. A high proportion of debt in the issuer capital structure usually indicates a high risk of default.
ii The capital expenditure ratio is yet another ratio that divides cash flow from operations[1] by capital expenditures.[2] It shows whether an issuer earns more from his main operations or spends more and, therefore, how easy it is for him to service its debt.
iii The debt coverage ratio, that divides cash flow from operations by interest charges on debt and the yearly reimbursement of debt (expressed in equivalent before tax); it indicates if an issuer is able to face its yearly debt obligations.
iv The operating or profitability margin which is EBITDAR divided by revenues; it allows gaining insight into an issuer's profitability from one period to the next, removing gains due entirely to revenue growth.

- v The FFO interest coverage, which is FFO plus gross interest paid plus preferred dividends, divided by gross interest paid plus preferred dividends, can be a central measure of the financial flexibility of an issuer. This measure compares the operational cash-generating ability of an issuer (after tax) to its financing costs.

Depending on the specific situation of the issuer, many other ratios can be added to the analysis to help gaining insight in the issuer's ability to face its debt obligations. It should be underlined, however, that analysis of trends in a number of ratios is more relevant than any individual ratio analysis, which concentrates on one performance measure only at a single point in time. For this reason several default prediction models were suggested and are discussed next.

Default prediction models

We start by the *Z*-Score model, commonly referred to as Altman *Z*-Score (Altman, 1968). Because of the huge volume of research that has been performed on the *Z*-Score, as well as the general academic and practical familiarity that have characterized it, it is still a common component of many credit default systems. The *Z*-Score model is constructed from six basic accounting ratios/variables and one market-based variable. These seven variables are combined into five ratios to constitute the pillars of the *Z*-Score and to be merged in a single figure, as in equation 4.6:

$$Z = 2.1\,X_1 + 4.1\,X_2 + 3.3\,X_3 + 6.0\,X_4 + 0.1\,X_5 \tag{4.6}$$

Where:

X_1 = working capital/total assets;
X_2 = retained earnings/total assets;
X_3 = total assets earnings before interest and taxes EBIT/total assets;
X_4 = market value of equity/book value of total liabilities;
X_5 = sales/total assets;
Z = overall index or score.

The *Z*-Score model is appealing because each independent variable composing its formula describes a different relevant credit aspect of an issuer's operational activities: liquidity (X_1), cumulative profitability (X_2), asset productivity (X_3), market-based financial leverage (X_4) and capital turnover (X_5). All these financial aspects are collectively addressed by the *Z*-Score that presumes that each ratio is linearly related to an issuer's probability of bankruptcy. The *Z*-score effectiveness is, however, dependent on valid and complete information

Merton (1974) found that the consideration of a company's equity as an option on its assets can accurately allow the assessment of its default risk. He suggested what he called the 'Distance to Default Model' (DD) and he used the put-call parity to assess the long option,[3] commonly considered a valid proxy to credit risk of issuers (Stokes, 2013). Merton assumes that the company has contracted a debt to be reimbursed at a future time *t*. In his reasoning any indebted issuer is to be considered to have failed whenever the value of its assets goes under the nominal value of its maturing debt at time *t*; the introduction of the option pricing formula allows the determination of the expected value of the asset at time *t* and compares it to the value of the debt. Formulated as indicated, the organization is therefore seen as a European call option on corporate assets, and, when its assets value is lower than its debt, the issuer is considered as likely to default. The Distance to Default Model is expressed as follows:

$$DD = (\ln(V/F) + (\mu - 0.5 * \sigma_V \hat{} 2)\ T)/(\sigma_V \sqrt{T}) \tag{4.7}$$

Where:

- V = total value of the firm (unobservable, must be inferred);
- μ = expected continuously compounded return on V;
- F = face value of firm's debt;
- T = time to maturity;
- σ_V = volatility of underlying firm, unobservable, calculated using the following relationship between the firm and its equity: $\sigma_E = (V/E)\ N(d_1)\ \sigma_V$, where E is market cap and $N(d_1)$ is the cumulative standard normal distribution function on d_1 (for those really keen, the formula for d_1 is available within the second linked source at the end).

The DD formula basically allows measuring the difference between the value of an issuer's assets and the nominal value of its debt, all scaled by the standard deviation of the value of the assets of the issuer. DD computations provide the value of the standard deviation by which an issuer is far from its default position. The smaller, therefore, the value of DD, the greater will be the probability of default of the issuer. The DD model is certainly less intuitive than the *Z*-score, because it does not specifically address accounting cash values that are generally considered in analysis of default or bankruptcy scenarios. In addition, the DD model neglects financial commitments that are the real determinants of issuer financial difficulties.

Given the critiques expressed towards the *Z*-score model, mainly with regard to its poor performance compared to more modern proposals, Bemmann (2005) suggested a simple model with a single variable called the total liabilities to total assets (TLTA), which is a simple ratio that includes both long-term and short-term debts. The higher the TLTA, the higher also will be the degree of leverage and therefore the level of default risk. The probability of bankruptcy would therefore increase as the TLTA increases.

Ohlson (1980) raised questions about the Multiple Discriminant Analysis (MDA) model, particularly regarding the restrictive statistical requirements imposed to it. In order, according to him, to correct the situation, he recourses to logistic regression to predict company default. Ohlson's logit model is given by:

$$Y = B_0X_0 + B_1\ X_1 + B_2\ X_2 + \ldots + B_n\ X_n \tag{4.8}$$

Failing is 0 for failed firm-years and 1 for other firm-years.

Independent variables are:

X_1: log (total assets/GNP price-level index);
X_2: total liabilities divided by total assets;
X_3: working capital divided by total assets;
X_4: current liabilities divided by current assets;
X_5: 1 if total liabilities exceed total assets, 0 otherwise;
X_6: net income divided by total assets;
X_7: funds provided by operations (income from operation after depreciation) divided by total liabilities;
X_8: 1 if net income was negative for the last two years, 0 otherwise;
X_9: $(Nit - Nit-1)/(|Nit|+|Nit-1|)$, where *Nit* is net income for the most recent period. The denominator acts as a level indicator. The variable is thus intended to measure the relative change in net income.

Ohlson's argument for choosing these variables is hardly based on any rationality. The first six variables were chosen just because he perceived them to be the ones most frequently mentioned in previous literature (Stokes, 2013).

Logistic regression is an odds ratio of success to default risk and which aims to create a prediction function based on a specific sample. This form of regression is typically used when absence of linearity between the independent variables is suspected. It is therefore used as an alternative to linear regression. Despite having no need to use assumptions of linearity, logistic regression presents, however, its own assumptions and characteristics that make it unsatisfactory in many situations.

Credit agencies' default assessment methodologies

Debt securities investors often rely heavily on credit ratings to determine whether to buy a debt security and lenders whether to approve a loan request. 'Prior to the development of quantitative measures of company performance, agencies were established to supply a quantitative type of information assessing the creditworthiness of particular merchants' (Altman, 2012).

Credit agencies use seemingly overall comparable methodologies to assess the risk of default of debt issuers. Most agencies use, for instance, technical credit rating committees (TCRC), previously introduced and to be discussed more in Chapter 9. These are small groups of credit professionals that are entrusted with the appropriate assessment of issuers' default risk, based on the weighting of all their risk factors, taking into account a variety of possible scenarios for the issuers and finally drawing a conclusion on what their ratings should be (Moody's, 2003). Also although quantitative to a large extent, most agencies' approaches strive to ensure that objective and factual analytical discussions constitute the starting point and the basis of rating committees' discussions and deliberations (Fitch Ratings, n.d., criteria). But differences in the assessment of risk of default by the CRAs can be observed among them, and this may actually pose a risk model problem for the whole process of determining default risk. This section describes methods for assessing the risk of default used by the three largest global credit rating agencies, mostly followed by the rest of agencies.

Moody's approach

From Moody's documentation we can learn that Moody's adopts a multidisciplinary analysis of default that is supposed to enable an appropriate understanding of all relevant factors of risk involved and such analysis is rooted on the judgement of technical credit rating committees, TCRC. Several monitoring principles of Moody's approach to rating are summarized in Figure 4.2, adapted from Moody's 'Ratings policy & approach' (Moody's, 2003).

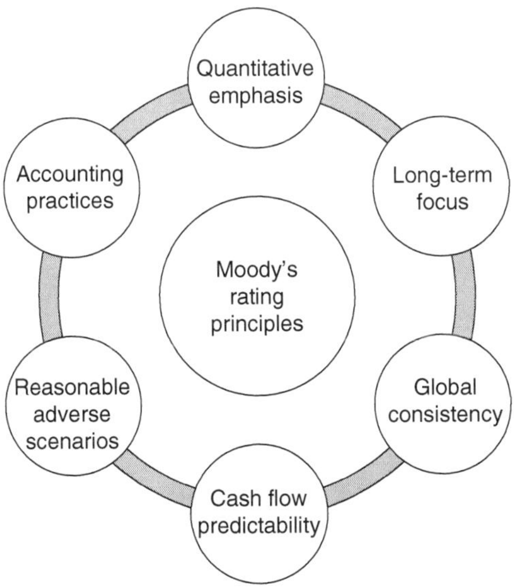

Figure 4.2 Moody's basic principles of rating.

The focus on the fundamental factors seems to be the rule in Moody's approach, because it is believed at Moody's that this is what actually characterizes the long-term ability of each issuer to honour its debt financial obligations. The Moody's approach to rating also includes several checkpoints that ensure a universal comparability and an overall consistency to the credit rating. Overall, Moody's approach is intended to provide an answer to one single question, namely: 'What is the level of risk associated with receiving timely and full payment of principal and interest on this debt obligation specific and how does that risk compares with that of all other debt obligations?' (Moody's, 2003).

Although, Moody's uses different rating methods for different industries, this section will only present Moody's approach to assessing credit default risk for companies in the global chemical industry, as described in Moody's 'Ratings policy & approach' (2003). This, we hope, will help better understand how the qualitative and quantitative characteristics of default risk are combined to classify issuers by levels of their risk, not only in this sector, but also overall. The assessment of the credit default risk is performed at Moody's in two distinct steps:

i first, the rating framework is built; and
ii second, broad rating categories are mapped.

Moody's starts by building the framework for assessing credit default risk for issuers in the global chemical industry and this framework contains five important key factors: (i) scale, (ii) business profile, (iii) profitability, (iv) leverage and coverage and (v) financial policy. Table 4.1 provides key factors and sub-factors that are used by Moody's to construct a grid for assessing credit default risk.

Most main key elements presented in Table 4.1 also include a number of sub-factors, for a total weight of 100 per cent. The 'scale factor', for

Table 4.1 Moody's grid used for assessing credit default risk

Key factors	*Sub-factors*	*Weight*
Scale	(i) Revenue and property (RP),	%
	(ii) Plant and equipment (PP&E net)	%
Business profile		
Profitability	(i) EBITDA margin and	%
	(ii) ROA – EBIT/avg. assets;	%
Leverage and coverage	(i) Debt/EBITDA,	%
	(ii) EBITDA/interest expense, and	%
	retained cash flow/debt;	%
Financial policy		%
Total weight		100%

Source: Moody's (2003).

Table 4.2 Numeric rating value

Aaa	*Aa*	*A*	*Baa*	*Ba*	*B*	*Caa*	*Ca*
1	3	6	9	12	15	18	20

instance, is decomposed into two sub-factors, namely: 'revenue and property' (RP), and 'plant and equipment' (PP&E net) (Moody's, 2003). Factors of the grid can be measured over various periods of time; the TCRCs at Moody's may, for example, find it useful to examine analytically the performance of a given debt issuer, both historically and on a forecasted basis, over a number of years the committee considers as a natural 'business cycle' for a given sector or sub-sector. Since the rating of an issuer factor or/and sub-factors of the grid may not always correspond to its overall credit rating, rating analysis in a given area may cover factors that are common to all sectors 'such as ownership, management, liquidity, corporate legal structure, governance and country related Risks, as well as other factors considered meaningful' (Moody's, 2003). After the determination of each sub-factor, rating results are mapped to the major rating categories to determine the overall rating of the grid. Each sub-factor rating is converted into a numerical value, based on the scale provided in Table 4.2.

Numerical rating for each sub-factor is multiplied by its weight and results are summed up to produce a composite weighted-factor rating which is then converted to alphanumeric form based on rank, as shown in Table 4.3.

Standard & Poor Ratings Services

Corporate rating criteria used in the rating process at Standard & Poor Ratings Services are also constructed on both quantitative and qualitative fundamentals, analytical methods and assumptions and can be global, regional or local, be specific to an industry or area. Adapted from 'S&P, criteria', these rating criteria are summarized in Figure 4.3.

The process of rating at S&P begins with the assessment of all the resources available to the issuer for facing its financial commitments regarding the volume and the timing of its debt obligations. This entails taking into account both current and expected future cash flows and their potential level of uncertainty. Reflecting the approach of Moody's, the rating process at S&P has also two aspects, one quantitative and the other qualitative (S&P, 2011b). The first aspect focuses on financial data and may include an assessment of the accounting principles and methods used by the issuer, 'key financial indicators that may include profitability, leverage, cash flow adequacy, liquidity, financial flexibility' (S&P, 2011b), along with temporal trends and comparisons with competitors. The

Table 4.3 Mapping of total factor scores (grid-indicated rating × aggregate weighted = total factor score)

Aaa $x < 1.5$	Aa1 $1.5 \leqslant x < 2.5$	Aa2 $2.5 \leqslant x < 3.5$	Aa3 $3.5 \leqslant x < 4.5$	A1 $4.5 \leqslant x < 5.5$
A2 $5.5 \leqslant x < 6.5$	A3 $6.5 \leqslant x < 7.5$	Baa1 $7.5 \leqslant x < 8.5$	Baa 2 $8.5 \leqslant x < 9.5$	Baa 3 $9.5 \leqslant x < 10.5$
Ba1 $10.5 \leqslant x < 11.5$	Ba2 $11.5 \leqslant x < 12.5$	Ba3 $12.5 \leqslant x < 13.5$	B1 $13.5 \leqslant x < 14.5$	B2 $14.5 \leqslant x < 15.5$
B3 $15.5 \leqslant x < 16.5$	Caa1 $16.5 \leqslant x < 17.5$	Caa2 $17.5 \leqslant x < 18.5$	Caa3 $18.5 \leqslant x < 19.5$	Ca $x \geqslant 19.5$

Source: Moody's Investors' Service (2013), Global Chemical Industry Rating Methodology, at: www.moodys.com/researchdocumentcontentpage.aspx?docid=PBC_160489, retrieved 8 January 2014.

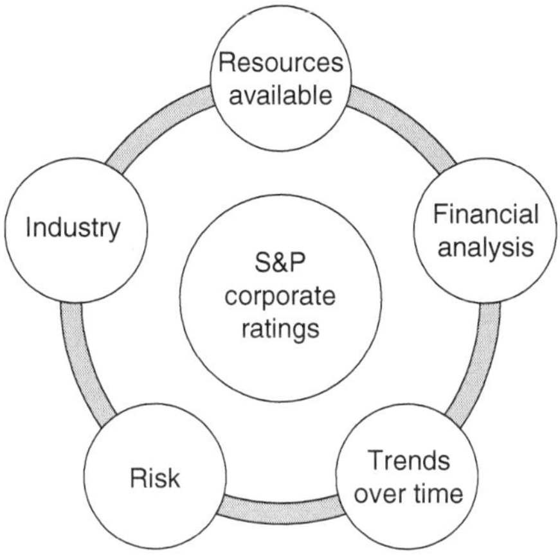

Figure 4.3 Fundamental principles and criteria of corporate ratings (source: 'Fundamental principles of corporate and government ratings and criteria', at: www.standardandpoors.com/prot/ratings/articles/en/us/?articleType=HTML&assetID=1245366284668#ID560).

qualitative aspects of S&P analysis focus on various elements, including country risk, industry characteristics and elements that are specific to the issuer, like industry growth prospects, technological change, and the degree and nature of competition. The approach to credit rating at S&P follows the framework summarized in Figure 4.4.

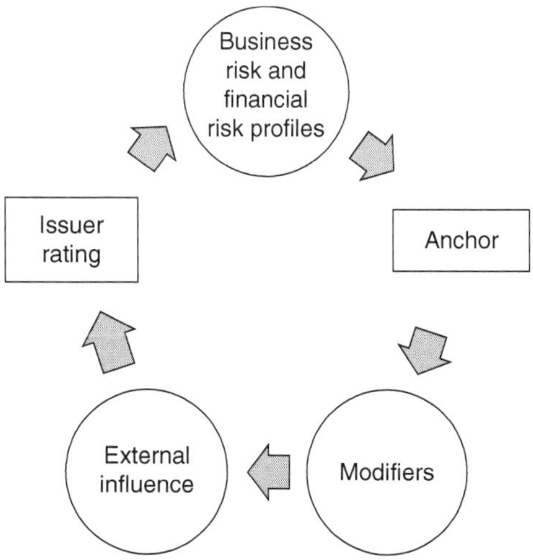

Figure 4.4 S&P corporate criteria framework (source: adapted from Standard and Poor's, at: www.standardandpoors.com/).

Standard & Poor's has a common framework for all its ratings. Its analytical credit rating process is divided in steps, 'in a way that allows answering any questions that may arise during the rating process' (S&P, 2011b). The analytical process always starts with the study of the issuer risk; the issuer business risk profile is analysed, taking into account its industry risk, the country risk and its competitive position. For its part, the financial risk profile of the issuer is assessed through the analysis of its cash flows and debt and according to S&P two situations may be encountered:

i The issuer belongs to the category of investment grade; in this case its business risk profile is then assigned more weight for the assessment of its overall credit rating.
ii The issuer belongs to the speculative grade category; in this case its financial risk profile is assigned more weight.

The two risk profiles (business and financial) are then combined to determine the appropriate anchoring that can be changed by one or more notches, whenever other factors prove to be impacting such as the 'diversification/portfolio effect, capital structure, financial policy, liquidity, and management and governance' (S&P, 2011b). The obtained results will constitute ratings for each factor and determine the number of notches that would apply to the anchorage. The last consideration of the analysis at S&P lies in ensuring comparability to the ratings, based on a global vision of the issuer credit characteristics and taking into account the influence of external factors, and this may lead to a reconsideration of the anchorage (S&P, 2011b).

Fitch Ratings

Credit rating methodology at Fitch Ratings, as represented in Figure 4.5, also reflects qualitative and quantitative factors, covering debt issuers' operational (business) and financial risks. Fitch considers its credit ratings as an assessment of the relative vulnerability of issuers that can cause them to default on their financial obligations under indebtedness (Fitch Ratings criteria). In Fitch's view, ratings are intended to be comparable across sectors and countries.

As shown in Figure 4.5, the key evaluation factors include the industry risk and the issuer financial profile. Industry risk includes the operating environment of the issuer, its management strategy and governance, as well as its organizational structure. The issuer financial profile includes the cash flow generated by the issuer, its profitability, its financial structure and financial flexibilty (Fitch Ratings criteria).

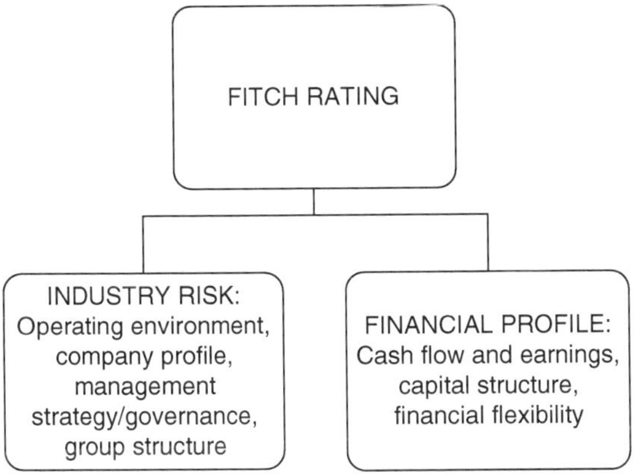

Figure 4.5 Fitch key rating factors.

Agencies' rating default studies

Agencies usually try to validate the accuracy of their methodologies of credit default assessment through their own performance studies, using different but comparable metrics. This section discusses Moody's and S&P default studies.

Moody's default studies

Moody's uses what it calls the accuracy ratio (AR), and S&P the Gini coefficient (GC). Moody's tries to validate the performance of the public Expected Default Frequency (EDF) in a battery of studies entitled 'Validating the public EDF model performance'. Towards this end, Moody's has used the accuracy ratio during the last decade. Moody's accuracy ratio computed as follows:

$$AR = A/(A+B) \tag{4.9}$$

Where:

> A is the area lying between the curve of the CAP and a 45 degree line, and $(A+B)$ is to the total area above the 45 degree line.

A graphic illustration of the Moody's accuracy ratio is provided in the 'Glossary of Moody's Ratings Performance Metrics' (2011b, p. 15). As a rule:

i The closer AR is to 1, the more the rating agency is supposed to discriminate efficiently issuers by assigning high rating to creditworthy issuers and low ratings to issuers at risk of default.

ii A negative AR expresses a particularly inefficient rating.
iii An AR of 0 indicates a random rating process.

Moody's also uses the Average Position (AP) of defaults, which measures the ordinal power of ratings. This is actually an equivalent measure to the accuracy ratio but is supposed to allow a simpler interpretation of the accuracy of credit ratings. According to Moody's, the AP defines the position of any issue in the cohort as the share of issuers rated better than it and assumes that each issue is located in the middle of its rating category. For example, 'the position of every issue rated Aa2 is the share rated Aa1, plus half of the share rated Aa2' (Moody's, 2011b). The AP is simply the average position of non-performing issues. AP is measured between 0 and 1, where 1 indicates perfect discriminating power, 0 indicates a perfectly negative discriminating power and 0.5 indicates no power. Intuitively, a more powerful rating system should have lower rate of defaults and high rated non-defaulting, meaning a higher average position of defaulted issues (Moody's, 2011b).

Moody's validates its process by conducting studies over the period 2001–2010, and covering many sectors areas: North America, European Union, financial companies, etc., and the period under study was divided in two sub-periods: namely 2001 to 2007 and 2008 to 2010. Then the model performance was compared during these two periods. Moody's focused on the ability of the model prospectively to discriminate between defaulting issuers and non-defaulting. For some studies, as in the case of North American companies, Moody's also determines the Altman *Z*-scores, respecting the same conditions as for EDF measures. Table 4.4, adapted from Moody's, shows the accuracy ratios for the EDF credit measures and compares them to *Z*-scores per year/month, for North American companies.

Table 4.4 provides year-end accuracy ratios for North American companies, computed based on cross-sectional data for the period 2000–2009. 'The Expected Default Frequency, EDF outperforms credit ratings on all these cross-sections. This outperformance tends, however, to decrease with the approach of unexpected shocks on the market' (Moody's, 2011b). Table 4.4 also provides the accuracy ratios for the EDF credit measures and *Z*-scores at the end of each year, for the period 2000–2009 for North American companies. EDF credit measure seems to outperform the *Z*-score by large margins, throughout the study period. This allows Moody's to conclude 'that EDF credit measures perform consistently well across different time horizons. Our tests indicate that EDF credit measures provide a very useful measure of credit risk that can be applied throughout North America' (Moody's, 2011b).

Table 4.4 Moody's accuracy ratios for EDF credit measures and Z-Scores by year/month for North American corporate firms (%)

Date (end of)	*Default rates*	*Accuracy ratios EDF*	*Accuracy ratios Z-Score*	*Accuracy ratio differences*
2000	0.4	72.0	66.0%	6.0
2001	3.7	78.7	67.6	11.2
2002	2.6	82.3	64.5	17.8
2003	1.3	86.2	71.1	15.0
2004	1.3	81.5	59.9	21.5
2005	0.6	85.5	70.1	15.4
2006	0.5	93.9	60.7	33.2
2007	1.5	82.9	75.0	7.9
2008	2.4	86.7	63.8	22.9
2009	0.7	87.6	62.1	25.5

Source: Moody's (2011a).

Note
Sales > \$30 million.

S&P default studies

S&P also uses default studies to show the accuracy of its rating defaults. These studies are based on what it called the Gini methodology, used to measure ratings performance/accuracy, by plotting the cumulative proportion of issuers by rating, against the cumulative share of defaulting issuers in a Lorenz curve to take into account the accuracy of their ranking. To construct the Lorenz curve, observations are ordered from the bottom of the rating scale 'CCC'/'C' and moving upward the scale to 'AAA'. The Gini coefficient is located between 0 and 1.

i If the credit rating assesses randomly issuers' default risk, the Lorenz curve will fall along the diagonal line and its Gini coefficient would be 0.
ii If issuers were perfectly ordered by default to ensure that all the defaults have occurred only among low rating entities, the curve would capture the entire area above the diagonal line and its coefficient Gini would be 1.

A graphic presentation of the Lorenz curve is given in S&P document entitled 'How does Standard & Poor's measure performance?' (S&P, 2012b, p. 12).

S&P calculates the Gini coefficient (GC) in the following way:

$$GC = B/(A+B) \tag{4.10}$$

Where:

B is the actual ratings area; and
$A+B$ is the total ratings area.

Table 4.5 S&P global average Gini coefficients and standard deviations (1981–2011)

Time horizon	*1 year*	*3 years*	*5 years*	*7 years*
Average	82.05	75.47	71.58	69.8
Weighted average	84.17	77.35	73.13	70.26
Standard deviation	(5.59)	(5.04)	(5.24)	(5.03)

Source: Standard & Poor's (2011), p. 13.

In other words, the Gini coefficient captures the distance by which actual ratings deviate from random rating scenarios (S&P, 2012b). S&P 2012 'Annual global corporate default study and rating transitions', for instance, indicates that 'All of Standard & Poor's default studies have found a clear correlation between ratings and defaults: The higher the rating, the lower the observed frequency of default, and vice versa' (S&P, 2012a). Table 4.5 provides S&P global average Gini coefficients,[4] for one, three, five and seven year periods (1981–2011). It provides the ratio of actual rank-ordering performance to theoretically perfect rank ordering.

The Gini ratios provided in Table 4.5, allow S&P to demonstrate the accuracy of their credit rating to serve as an effective measure of the relative risk of default, especially during the years of low default rates. In general, 'our default studies have historically shown a strong correlation between ratings and default frequencies: generally the higher the rating, the lower the frequency of default, and vice versa' (S&P, 2011a).[5]

Default studies conducted by agencies suggest high levels of accuracy of their ratings. Moody's accuracy ratio, as well as S&P's Gini coefficient, are both very close to 1, and would indicate a high level of efficiency of agencies' ratings. Agencies' approaches to the determination of the accuracy of credit ratings have, however, their own limitations, since the efficiency of a rating system, according to researchers, cannot be limited to its ability to predict default only, since it is also supposed to rank in an ordering manner issuers in other segments of the rating scale. Rating agencies are, however, convinced of the efficiency of their classification of defaults, despite the fact that agencies' data may contain exceptions, to be presented in the text.

Independent assessment of credit ratings accuracy

Unlike in-house findings, independent research results on rating efficiency are less categorical and still contradictory; they generally lead to unclear conclusions. Researchers have drawn attention to the important degree of subjectivity of the rating processes, especially in the case of sovereign debt and to some extent to the lack of consistency of CRAs' behaviour over time. Indeed recent research show a substantial increase of the 'arbitrary component' of sovereign ratings over recent years and point at the existence of subjective biases in favour or against the rated nations to (partly) explain the differences in sovereign ratings given by two of the major rating agencies (Iyengar, 2010). The author actually concludes, while comparing Moody's and S&P's sovereign ratings of 1995 to those of 2007, that not only have there been a considerable increase in the average difference in agencies' ratings, but also the differences in their ratings are due to the subjective assessments of the countries by agencies. This could be explained by the higher reputational risk attached to rating misspecification in a context of economic crisis and lack of investors' confidence. According to some authors, this may lead CRAs to be 'keener' on lowering sovereign ratings, while they could be keener to attribute higher ratings in boom times, when investors' trust tends to rise. Further, CRAs are accused of not being able to respond to investors' needs in a timely manner. It is underlined that while new information about issuers' performances lead to quick changes in market values, agencies prefer to wait until they can verify their information and their reactions are therefore slower.

Agencies' studies remain particularly silent on the way default is assigned to each market segment, as with regard to the weight of the whole, each default segment is actually representing. Consequently, these in-house findings do not seem to convince researchers, with regard to the rationality of the rating process used by agencies. One straightforward method of judging credit rating quality is by analysing the average rate of default (AD) by category of rating. AD can be determined for each category of rating, by computing the percentage of defaulted issuers during a given period of time (one year, three, five, etc.). Agencies usually calculate them on a cumulative basis. Credit ratings can be considered accurate for a given period of time if default rates associated with rating categories allow their risk classification, with the default rate associated with AAA category assumed to be next to nil and increases by some variable amount of default, by crossing from one category of rating to the next, till reaching the CCC rating category. Appendix 4.1 provides S&P's and Moody's yearly average current defaults by rating symbols for the period 1982–2012 and Table 4.6 provides average yearly default rates and their corresponding standard deviations.

Figure 4.6, depicting actual default variations from one rating symbol to the next, for the period 1983–2012 and based on actual S&P and Moody's data, shows a 'saw tooth' movement in actual default variations from one rating symbol to the next, which may point to a weak accuracy of the whole process.

Table 4.6 S&P's and Moody's yearly average and standard deviation current defaults by rating symbols, 1982–2012

	0	*1*	*2*	*3*	*4*	*5*	*6*	*7*	*8*	*9*	*10*	*11*	*12*	*13*	*14*	*15*	*16*
Year	AAA	AA+	AA	AA–	A+	A	A–	BBB+	BBB	BBB–	BB+	BB	BB–	B+	B	B–	CCC/C
Average	0.00	0.00	0.01	0.14	0.11	0.08	0.11	0.56	0.48	0.63	1.23	3.77	3.00	4.95	11.71	19.60	63.47
Std dev.	0.00	0.00	0.08	0.52	0.31	0.17	0.23	1.93	0.74	0.91	1.62	13.14	2.70	3.88	9.21	14.88	28.95

Source: adapted from Standard & Poors' and Moody's default studies.

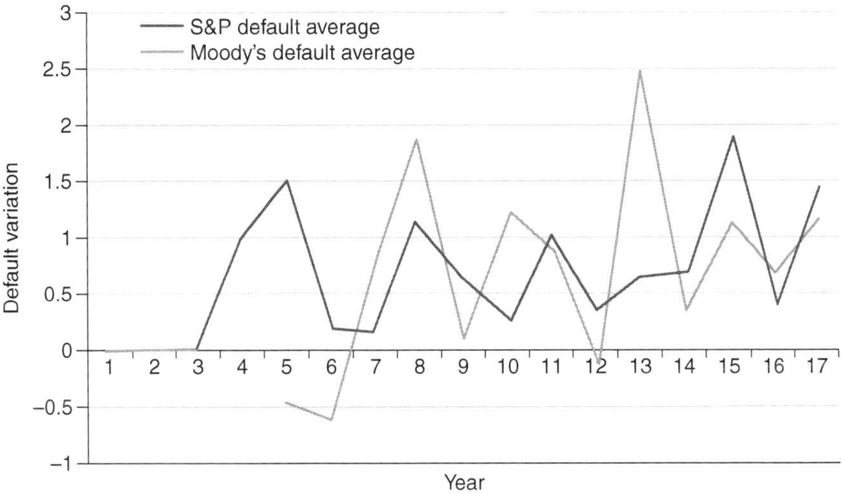

Figure 4.6 S&P default variations by rating symbols.

Figure 4.6 seems to point to the absence of any rationality in the assessment of default by symbol on the part of credit agencies.

- i First, agencies' historical credit rating data, for the period 1983 to 2012, seem to indicate that over 76 per cent of issuers were usually classified at very high risk (CCC and lower) without actually defaulting and would therefore have been unduly denied credit or at least have suffered higher cost of indebtedness.
- ii Second, although default rates associated to the highest rating symbols (AAA and A+) are nil, they don't explain why crossing from the AA category to AA– represents 14 times increase in default.
- iii Third, lags and differences between Moody's and S&P can be unearthed and although both agencies appear to show great inconsistency between rating classes, Moody's seems to suffer even more inconsistencies.
- iv Fourth, impact seems to exist in downgrades, as when a security gets downgraded below the investment grade threshold, managers seem to liquidate their positions in large blocks, thus causing unneeded sudden volatility and possible portfolio losses.
- v Fifth, Moody's and S&P seem to assign divergent ratings much more frequently to sovereign bonds than to corporate bonds.
- vi Finally, as indicated in Table 4.7, is instructive with regard to the confusion in scale classification.

Agencies classified in short-term rating scales as investment grade symbols Aaa to Baa3, and speculative from Ba2 down (equating to a

Table 4.7 Moody's linkage between the global long-term and short-term rating scales

SHORT TERM		LONG TERM		
	Aaa			
	Aa1			
	Aa2	Prime 1		
	Aa3			
Investment				
	A1			
	A2			
	A3		Prime 2	
	Baa1			
	Baa2			Prime 3
	Baa3			
Ba2 to C= Speculative for long term and no prime for short term				

Source: Moody's (2009).

rating of BB as rated by S&P or 'Ba' as rated by Moody's or lower). An investment grade is a rating that indicates that an issue has a relatively low risk of default, while speculative grade issues are considered too risky and therefore unsuitable for investment. Speculative grades are homogeneous, however, Lexicon (*Financial Times*, n.d.), for instance distinguishes

> grade issues [that] can be considered 'less vulnerable in the short run but face major uncertainties and exposures to adverse business, financial and economic conditions' (BB) or 'subject to substantial credit risk' (Ba), to 'a marked shortcoming has materialised' or 'typically in default' (C).

For long term, we can read from Table 4.7, that symbols Aaa to A3 are classified prim-1, and A3 to Baa2 classified prime-2, and Baa2 to Baa3 classified prime-3, with some overlapping: A1, A2 and A3 are, for instance, classified simultaneously as prime-1 and prime-2 and Baa2 classified prime-2 and prime-3. In real life, however, these issuers with the same prime will not accept being charged the same interest rate and any credit rating downgrade from one rating to the next, within any prime class, will usually cause an increase in the interest charged.

Agencies are also silent with regard to the weight assigned to each rating category, among the 17 composing the whole spectrum of rating categories. S&P, for instance, warns that they 'do not ascribe a specific "default probability" to each rating category' and this is where the problem may reside. Agencies' assertions about the probability of default contained in credit ratings should be evaluated *ex post* based on the performance of the rated instruments over time and this may allow market participants to engage in *ex post* monitoring of ratings quality. Indeed, if reputation plays a role in credit rating markets as often asserted, it should be possible to monitor quality (Hunt, 2008).

We believe that the assignment by agencies of default to rating symbols should be based on a better well-defined theoretical model, instead of the simple rank ordering methodology currently in use. It is also feared that this way of doing may have kept agencies from rating effectively fixed-income issuers and may explain why among defaults reported by agencies during the period, 1983–2012, 8 per cent of them have actually emanated from issuers considered to be investment (S&P, 2012a). The demonstration of the accuracy of credit ratings is not made yet, instead, various studies that have compared Moody's and Standard & Poor's ratings, found correspondence once in two only (Kish *et al.*, 1999). Similarities were found for investment grade ratings (Cantor and Parker, 1996) and divergence in speculative-grade issues; however, the impact of ratings seems to exist, but in downgrades only.

Conclusion

Although, CRAs were recently submitted to new rules, by both the SEC and EC, limiting the use of rating for regulatory purposes, and rendering it a voluntary act of capital markets, nevertheless, rating may still be effectively compulsory, despite the fact the methodologies used by agencies in the assessment of debt quality and defaults is questioned; and a suggestion is offered in the next chapter. Agencies are arguing that their methodologies are sound and some users are warning that any alternatives to ratings for use in the regulatory framework must meet the test of delivering the desired diversity of information without compromising the accuracy with which exposures of different credit quality can be distinguished (FSA *et al.*, n.d.). In any case, it should, however, always be possible for investors to tell, even after the fact, whether rating agencies actually performed poorly, or just experienced bad luck (Hunt, 2008). If users can never determine whether goods or services are of high quality or not, there can be no meaningful transparency for high-quality ratings production and this does not seem the case yet.

Appendix 4.1 S&P's and Moody's yearly average current defaults by rating symbols, 1982–2012 (%)

	0	*1*	*2*	*3*	*4*	*5*	*6*	*7*	*8*	*9*	*10*	*11*	*12*	*13*	*14*	*15*	*16*
Year	AAA	AA+	AA	AA–	A+	A	A–	BBB+	BBB	BBB–	BB+	BB	BB–	B+	B	B–	CCC/C
1983	0	0	0	0	0	0	0	0	0	1.33	2.17	0	4.2	1.22	22	25.86	59.97
1984	0	0	0	0	0	0	0	0	1.4	1.06	1.16	3.25	1.49	8.06	14.81	11.77	125
1985	0	0	0	0	0	0	0	0	0	0	1.64	3.12	4.19	7.03	0	19.4	26.78
1986	0	0	0	0	0	0	0.78	0	0.78	3.49	2.71	2.36	4.56	12.47	27.36	31.37	51.68
1987	0	0	0	0	0	0	0	0	0	0	3.79	0.94	3.81	5.55	13.5	17.22	34.48
1988	0	0	0	0	0	0	0	0	0	0	0	0	4.92	6.16	11.28	20.9	70.37
1989	0	0	0	1.418	0	0	0	0.9	1.61	1.02	0.81	1.85	6.79	6.05	16.83	23.48	60.63
1990	0	0	0	0	0	0	0	0.76	0	1.1	6.52	5.93	8.01	12.71	34.86	50.98	106.25
1991	0	0	0	0	0	0	0	10.57	0.74	0	4.84	1.14	10.19	12.24	27.25	59.63	85.77
1992	0	0	0	0	0	0	0	0	0	0	0	0	0.74	1.7	16.4	47.43	61.79
1993	0	0	0	0	0	0	0	0	0	0	0.89	1.94	0.79	3.78	9.16	14.27	37.31
1994	0	0	0	0	0.46	0	0	0	0	0	0	0.86	0.62	3.74	10.17	12.04	23.69
1995	0	0	0	0	0	0	0	0	0	0.63	0	1.55	2.95	7.19	13.88	9.67	52.706
1996	0	0	0	0	0	0	0	0	0	0	0.88	0.65	0.55	3.5	3.74	7.23	17.632
1997	0	0	0	0	0	0	0	0.36	0.35	0	0	0	0.88	0.72	6.44	21.6	30.981
1998	0	0	0	0	0	0	0	0	0.59	1.04	0.68	2.95	1.95	4.71	12.99	17.59	59.327
1999	0	0	0	0.36	0	0.24	0.27	0	3.28	0.65	1.08	1.92	3.36	6.77	15.65	23.58	76.187
2000	0	0	0	0	0	0.24	0.56	0.3	0.26	1.88	0.5	1.45	3.31	8.86	15.61	23.6	75.453
2001	0	0	0	0	0.57	0.69	0	0.53	0.76	0.27	0.52	2.56	8.86	9.13	26.08	41.41	89.87
2002	0	0	0	0	0	0	0.45	1.19	1.39	3.25	3.97	2.4	5.75	5.9	14.37	27.32	98.312
2003	0	0	0	0	0	0	0	0	0.19	0.54	1.14	72.96	1.76	2.07	7.6	13.82	76.007
2004	0	0	0	0	0	0.24	0	0	0	0	0	0.66	1.43	0.46	3.28	5.22	49.716
2005	0	0	0	0	0	0	0	0	0.42	0.33	0.37	0	0.5	0.78	3.2	5.43	26.76
2006	0	0	0	0	0	0	0	0	0	0	0.37	0	0.97	1.33	1.36	3.76	31.405
2007	0	0	0	0	0	0	0	0	0	0	0	0.31	0.23	0.19	0	0.89	51.458
2008	0	0	0.44	2.494	1.52	0.47	0.59	0.46	1.39	1.04	1.2	0.65	3.38	4.83	4.24	15.76	81.834
2009	0	0	0	0	0.3	0.39	0.52	1.54	0.92	1.11	0.7	3.3	1.54	9.67	14.59	26.43	126.35
2010	0	0	0	0	0.36	0	0.25	0	0	0	0.81	0.36	0.54	0.85	0.71	2.64	63.392
2011	0	0	0	0	0	0	0	0	0.244	0.2	0	0	0.541	0.4	1.575	4.01	60.274
2012	0	0	0	0	0	0	0	0.261	0	0	0	0	1.228	0.57	2.297	3.77	92.774
Average	0.00	0.00	0.01	0.14	0.11	0.08	0.11	0.56	0.48	0.63	1.23	3.77	3.00	4.95	11.71	19.60	63.47
Median	0.00	0.00	0.00	0.00	0.00	0.00	0.00	0.00	0.10	0.24	0.76	1.04	1.86	4.77	12.14	17.41	60.45
Std dev.	0.00	0.00	0.08	0.52	0.31	0.17	0.23	1.93	0.74	0.91	1.62	13.14	2.70	3.88	9.21	14.88	28.95
Minimum	0.00	0.00	0.00	0.00	0.00	0.00	0.00	0.00	0.00	0.00	0.00	0.00	0.23	0.19	0.00	0.89	17.63
Maximum	0.00	0.00	0.44	2.49	1.52	0.69	0.78	10.57	3.28	3.49	6.52	72.96	10.19	12.71	34.86	59.63	126.35

Notes

1 The operating cash flow is the cash generated from operations less taxation and interest paid, investment income received and less dividends paid (IAS 7 Cash Flow Statements, January 2007).
2 The capital expenditure is the amount of money spent either to acquire fixed assets or to add to the value of the existing ones.
3 To be long in a security, means the holder of the position owns the security and will profit if the price of the security goes up.
4 As indicated before, the Gini ratios are a measure of the rank-ordering power of ratings over a given time horizon – one through seven years.
5 Acccording to S&P, transition studies have confirmed repeatedly that higher ratings tend to be more stable and speculative grade ratings generally experience more volatility.

Bibliography

Adam, S. and M. Deen (2013), 'France credit rating cut to AA by S&P on growth outlook', Bloomberg, 8 November, at www.bloomberg.com/news/2013-11-08/france-credit-rating-cut-to-aa-by-s-p-on-weak-growth-prospects.html, retrieved 3 March 2014.

Altman, E. (1968), 'Financial ratios, discriminant analysis and the prediction of corporate bankruptcy', *Journal of Finance*, Vol. XXIII(4), pp. 189–209.

Altman, E. (2012), 'Predicting financial distress of companies, revisiting the Z-Score and the Zeta models', at: http://pages.stern.nyu.edu/~ealtman/PredFnclDistr.pdf, retrieved 3 October 2013.

Arezki, Rabah, Bertrand Candelon and Amandou Sy (2011), 'Sovereign rating news and financial markets spillovers: evidence from the European debt crisis', International Monetary Fund (IMF), Working Paper WP/11/68.

Bemmann, M. (2005), 'Improving the comparability of insolvency predictions', Dresden Economics Discussion Paper Series No. 08/2005, at: http://ssrn.com/abstract=731644 or http://dx.doi.org/10.2139/ssrn.731644, retrieved 23 September 2013.

Cantor, R. and F. Packer (1996), 'Determinants and impact of sovereign credit ratings', *Economic Policy Review*, Vol. 2(2), pp. 37–54.

Curzon Price, T. (2012), 'Credit rating agencies: the wrong institutions for public judgement', openEconomy, 12 January.

Economist, The (2012), 'Greece's creditors would all have to take a massive hit to right its finances', at: www.economist.com/node/21543166, retrieved 20 February 2014.

Ederington, L., J. Yawitz and B. Roberts (1987), 'The informational content of bond ratings', *Journal of Financial Research*, Fall, Vol. 10, pp. 211–226.

Financial Times (n.d.), 'Definition of speculative grade', at: http://lexicon.ft.com/Term?term=speculative-grade, retrieved 2 October 2013.

Fitch Ratings (n.d.), 'Understanding credit ratings: limitations and usage', at: www.fitchratings.com/creditdesk/public/ratings_defintions/index.cfm#cm_sp=Criteria-_-intro-_-Ratings%20Definitions, retrieved 22 February 2014.

FSA, HM Treasury and Bank of England (2013), 'The United Kingdom authorities response to the European Commission internal market and services consultation document on Credit Rating Agencies', at: https://circabc.europa.eu/d/d/workspace/

SpacesStore/0d1ea101-b6d0-470b-b8b3-e28e4c1cba30/BoE-FSA-Treasury_EN.pdf, retrieved 1 September 2014.

Hunt, J.P. (2008), 'Credit rating agencies and the "worldwide credit crisis": the limits of reputation, the insufficiency of reform, and a proposal for improvement'. *Columbia Business Law Review*, Vol. 2009(1), at: http://ssrn.com/abstract=1267625 or http://dx.doi.org/10.2139/ssrn.1267625, retrieved 23 September 2013.

Investopedia, at: www.investopedia.com/terms/d/defaultrisk.asp, retrieved 26 September 2013.

Iyengar, S. (2010), 'Are sovereign credit ratings objective and transparent?' *IUP Journal of Financial Economics*, Vol. VIII(3), pp. 7–22.

Kish, R., K. Hogan and G. Olson (1999), 'Does the market perceive a difference in rating agencies?' *Quarterly Review of Economics and Finance*, Vol. 39, pp. 363–377.

Langohr, H. (2006), 'The credit rating agencies and their credit ratings', Presentation to the Bond Market Association's 'Rating Industry Day Conference', 23 February.

Liu, P., F.J. Seyyed and S.D. Smith (1999), 'The independent impact of credit rating changes: the case of Moody's rating refinement on yield premiums', *Journal of Business Finance and Accounting*, April/May, Vol. 26(3), pp. 337–363.

Merton, R. (1974), 'On the pricing of corporate debt: the risk structure of interest rates', *Journal of Finance*, Vol. 29, pp. 449–470.

Moody's (2003), 'Ratings Policy & Approach', at: www.moodys.com/ratings-process/Ratings-Policy-Approach/002003, retrieved 10 February 2013.

Moody's (2006), 'Moody's credit rating prediction model', at: www.moodys.com/sites/products/DefaultResearch/2006200000425644.pdf, retrieved 4 July 2014.

Moody's (2009), 'Rating symbols and definitions', at: www.moody's.com, retrieved 23 September 2013.

Moody's (2011a), 'Validating the public EDF model for North American corporate firms', at: www.moody's.com, retrieved 2 November 2013.

Moody's (2011b) 'Glossary of Moody's ratings performance metrics', at: www.moody's.com, retrieved 2 November 2013.

Moody's Investors' Service (2013), 'Global chemical industry rating methodology', at: www.moodys.com/researchdocumentcontentpage.aspx?docid=PBC_160489, retrieved 8 January 2014.

Ohlson, J.A. (1980), 'Financial ratios and the probabilistic prediction of bankruptcy', *Journal of Accounting Research*, Vol. 18(1), pp. 109–131.

Standard & Poor's (S&P) (2011a), 'Guide to ratings performance', at: http://img.en25.com/Web/StandardandPoors/SP_GuideToRatingsPerformance.pdf, retrieved 2 December 2013.

Standard & Poor's (S&P) (2011b), 'Fundamental principles of corporate and government ratings and criteria', at: www.standardandpoors.com/prot/ratings/articles/en/us/?articleType=HTML&assetID=1245366284668#ID560, retrieved 9 January 2014.

Standard & Poor's (S&P) (2012a) 'Annual global corporate default study and rating transitions', at: www.standardandpoors.com, retrieved 2 December 2013.

Standard & Poor's (S&P) (2012b) 'How does Standard & Poor's measure performance?' at: www.standardandpoors.com, retrieved 2 December 2013.

Standard & Poor's (S&P) (n.d.), 'rating criteria', at: www.standardandpoors.com/

prot/ratings/articles/en/us/?articleType=HTML&assetID=1245319245031, retrieved 8 January 2014.

Stokes, J. (2013), 'Improving on the Altman Z-Score, part 3: Merton's distance to default', at: www.stockopedia.com/content/improving-on-the-altman-z-score-part-3-mertons-distance-to-default-70965/#sthash.oOGyYP3Z.dpuf, retrieved 2 December 2013.

5 Ordinal credit ratings

The threat to rating accuracy

Introduction

The main problem with agencies' methodologies discussed in the previous chapter is the one that relates to agencies' approaches for assessing credit default. Although classifying issuers into 'defaulters' and 'non-defaulters', agencies' ratings do not permit investors to discriminate one level of default from the next or the previous. The level of rating determines, however, how much interest will be charged to issuers and unless there are only two interest rates on the market, one for investment grades and the other for speculative grades issuers, telling investors that 'lower ratings correspond to higher default rates' as agencies do, is just not enough. Given the crucial role played by credit rating agencies in the market, the understanding of the rating incentives that determines rating symbol distribution, is paramount.

This chapter analyses CRAs' mechanism that could lead them to inaccurately assess the credit risk. It raises the possibility that the rating methodology followed by CRAs may suffer a serious limit, residing in their failure to weight default by level of risk, classifying it in ordinal way only. The remainder of the chapter is organized as follows. In the second section, the theoretical background is presented; in the third, the sample and the methodology are discussed; in the fourth section, results and implications are analysed; and, finally, the fifth section concludes.

Theoretical background

Credit ratings are supposed to improve market efficiency, since they aim to give a good assessment of the quality of debts. Ratings are, for instance, used:

i to inform a third party on the possibility that the issuers may default on their debt obligations;
ii to allow achieving easier access to the debt market at a reduced capital costs, given that higher ratings reduce the yield spread to a risk free investment (Gonzales *et al.*, 2004);

iii to signal low investment risk and transparency (Nordberg, 2011) and can therefore be employed to solve principal agent problems (Gonzales *et al.*, 2004);
iv as banking benchmarks for comparisons with banks' own analysis and internal ratings (Erlenmaier, 2006) and even as alternatives for regulatory requirements.

Activities of CRAs are generally considered beneficial, but they are also often perceived as a source of devastating reversals (Theis and Wolgast, 2012); not only are they believed to be at the origin of a major financial crisis, but they are also suspected of doing a bad job and eventually unduly downgrading some issuers, making them pay more than necessary for their funding, consequently mingling with the market efficiency they are supposed to enhance (Kisgen and Strahan, 2010). Credit agencies continuously advocate that their ratings are primarily ordinal. According to Moody's, although a credit rating can give a clear idea about the risk of default of an issuer,

> it is not a statement as to which obligors or obligations will default in the future. Rather, it is expected that lower rated entities and obligations will default, on average, at a higher frequency than more highly rated entities and obligations.
>
> (Moody's Rating System)[1]

In other words, highly rated debt instruments are supposed to default less frequently than lower rated instruments (Hunt, 2008).

Credit ratings are, at the same time, assumed to express 'forward-looking opinions about the creditworthiness of fixed-income securities issuers and obligations and their rank ordering' (Moody's, 2002). The term creditworthiness refers to the question of whether a debt instrument will be paid according to its contractual terms and conditions. CRAs' ratings have had, however, their share of misfortune, the most impacting one is related to the subprime crisis. The likelihood of default is the centrepiece of creditworthiness and seems to be the single most important factor in agencies' assessment of the credit risk of issuers, although, according to S&P, beyond likelihood of default, there are other factors that may be relevant. One such factor is, for example, the payment priority of an obligation following default (Moody's, 2002). Consequently, consistent with the goal of achieving a rank ordering of creditworthiness, higher ratings on issuers (obligations) should reflect the expectation that the rated issuer will default less frequently than issuers and obligations with lower ratings, all other things being equal (Moody's, 2002). Therefore, issuers with higher ratings are judged to be more creditworthy, than issuers with lower credit ratings. Each successively higher rating category should be associated with the ability to withstand successively more stressful economic environments

(Moody's, 2002). Making such an assertion to investors is, however, just not sufficient to explain to them why the crossing from one category of rating to the next is not similar between rating categories, i.e. why such crossing does not initiate the same variation in default risk. This problem can even be exacerbated by the timeliness of ratings (Altman and Rijken, 2005). This can be extremely important, as the cost of indebtedness determination is mainly based on such information. Theoretically, the impact of crossing down in credit rating should be similar to what would happen if an individual credit score is declined: its indebtedness becomes more problematic and its cost of borrowing money is likely to go up.

Linearity in credit rating can be justified in several ways:

i First, by the rating process own characteristic, in fact, ratings rely strongly on publicly reported information (although, when possible, also on private information) not only heavily through audited financial statements, but also through quantitative internal reports, budget forecasts, details of the investment strategy, assessment of the quality of management, strategic vision of the firm's prospects and position within its sector (S&P, 2009). Financial statements and other quantitative reports are therefore heavily used as the basis for the determination of agencies' default categorizations/symbols (Moody's, 2002); thanks to the accounting rules, each transaction contained in financial statements and quantitative reports is supposed to match to, at least, one debit and one credit. Uncertainty is therefore handled using linear rules about any value change, or by reference to quantifiable external real phenomena, such as market value. It is therefore logical to adopt a linear approach to default assessment, whose computation is largely based on financial statement data that are linear in nature. The linear logic of financial numbers should therefore transcend ratings and their classification of default.

ii Second, according to agencies, credit ratings are meant to be forward-looking: credit ratings being at the lower end of the rating scale are the expressions of the vulnerability of issuers, while ratings at the higher end are regarded as having the ability to withstand extreme or severe stress in absolute terms without defaulting. Between the two issuers locating in the middle categories are considered having mild ability to withstand extreme or severe stress (S&P, 2012). This assertion from agencies can in itself be considered as recognition of the linear character of default symbols but does not seem to find application at the level of individual ratings.

iii Third, another argument in favour of linearity resides in the way ratings are used to allow easier access to the debt market, at reduced capital costs. Investors and regulators used ratings in decision-making; investors rely on ratings as key information in determining investment decisions, depending on the degree of risk they are willing to accept (EC, 2013).

iv Fourth, cost of indebtedness charged seems to be linearly related to issuer ratings. The financial market usually distinguishes rating scales and charges interest rates in accordance with their levels of default. There is, indeed, evidence that credit ratings affect issuers' cost of capital specifically due to the regulations based on ratings (Darren *et al.*, 2009). There is, therefore, a need of classifying issuers and obligations in an increasing order of default. Finance theory, especially empirical models motivated by Merton (1973), or the Capital Assets Pricing Model (CAPM) suggests that financial risk, therefore credit default, should evolve progressively and gradually, i.e. in a linear way. Indeed, in almost all aspects of life, the largest risks have the largest payoffs/costs and in competitive financial markets, this holds true almost universally. When using rating, investors usually expect agencies to provide objective information based on sound analytical methods, where linearity plays the key role. Instead, agencies assert that

> obligations carrying the same rating are not claimed to be of absolutely equal credit quality. In a broad sense, they are alike in position, but since there are a limited number of rating classes used in grading thousands of bonds, the symbols cannot reflect the same shadings of risk which actually exist.
>
> (Moody's, 2002)

Without formally recognizing linearity in default assessment, agencies are introducing what they call stress scenarios associated with each rating category. The stress scenario for 'AA',

> should be able to withstand a severe level of stress and still meet its financial obligations. Such a scenario could include GDP declines of up to 15%, unemployment levels of up to 20%, and stock market declines of up to 70%. … [Stress scenarios are used as] benchmarks for enhancing the consistency and comparability of ratings across sectors and over time.
>
> (Moody's, 2002)

The underlying logic of ratings seems therefore to be linear and we expect the change in default risk to affect agencies ranking, in a 'linear' fashion – that is, each change in rating scale adds the same amount of default risk and limits can consequently be drawn between each rating category or symbol and we should, according to financial theory, expect identical increase/decrease in default by moving from one symbol to the next/previous. Failure to do so may explain why the rating does not provide guidance on other aspects essential for investment decisions, and why bonds with the same rating have often very different market prices.

Therefore we can hypothesize that credit ratings are linearly linked to their theoretical level of default.

Sample and methodology

The study is based on agencies' default ratings, during a 30-year period (1983–2012), mainly S&P and Moody's yearly defaults data, reported in their yearly 'Annual global corporate default study and rating transitions' for the years 1983 to 2012. Due to unavailability/insufficiency of data, Fitch is not included. Fitch default studies do not give default information by scale for the whole period covered by the study. The study covers, however, 80 per cent of the world credit market (the portion of the market under the control of Moody's and S&P). This period has witnessed 3,994 default events (54 per cent of the defaults were registered by S&P during the period under study, or 46 per cent were registered by Moody's). Agencies usually divide ratings into two broad classes: investment class (AAA to BBB–) for S&P and (Aaa to Baa3) for Moody's, and the speculative class (BB+ to CCC/C) for S&P and (Ba1 to Caa1/c) for Moody's. We therefore divided the main sample into two sub-samples: the investment sub-sample and the speculative sub-sample.

An issuer is rated default when it 'has either not met a legally scheduled payment or has made it clear that it will miss such a payment in the near future or, in certain cases, that there has been a distressed exchange' (Moody's, 2002). Figure 5.1, depicts all defaults for Moody's and Standard & Poor, for the period 1983–2012.

The study of Figure 5.1 indicates that the covered period has witnessed an unprecedented number of events in global credit markets, particularly sovereign downgrades. Overall credit stability deteriorated three times during this period: first during the period 1990–1991, and drastically later in 1999–2003 and 2008–2009, hitting an all-time high of 265 defaults (total debt outstanding $627.70 billion) in 2009 (SEC, 2013). The count

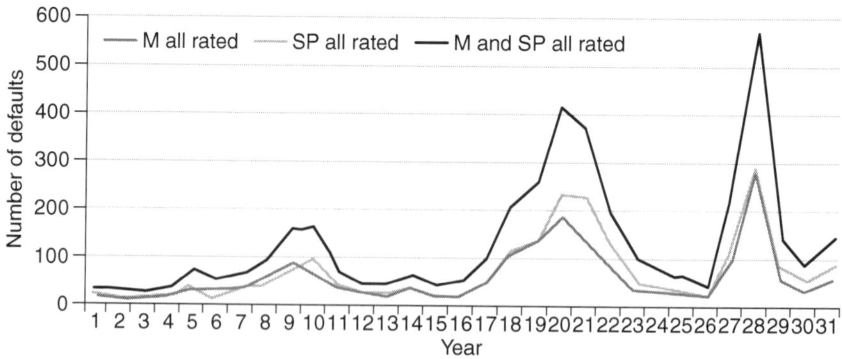

Figure 5.1 S&P and Moody's yearly number of defaults for the period 1983–2012 (source: based on Moody's and S&P data).

of defaulting companies fell off considerably in 2011. This includes publicly and confidentially rated entities as well as entities that were not rated at the time of default. Defaults were, in the 2008–2009 period, related to the fall-out of the financial crisis. Defaults were also generally spread across several sectors: industrial, financial services, government securities and insurance. Defaults over the 2008–2009 period included a relatively high proportion of financial institutions (SEC, 2013), As a rule, synchronization seems to characterize Moody's and S&P ratings: they seem to go hand in hand and such behaviour may be explained by the oligopoly characterizing the rating market. It should, however, be underlined that Moody's seems to take the lead in the rating movement, by always 'opening the ball' followed rapidly by S&P. Their ratings are almost identical, except for the number of notches, which differ marginally: S&P and Moody's use 21 rating symbols, while Fitch uses 24 symbols. For the purpose of the study and in order to respect comparability, the number of notches is reduced to 17 for both Moody's and S&P, with the prime category being classed as 0, see Table 5.1. Note that the Caa1/c classes for Moody's and CCC/C for S&P are presented as summaries for all the subsequent symbols to Caa1/c and CCC/C, for Moody's and S&P respectively. Consequently, S&P's symbols are ranked 0 (for AAA) to 16 (for CCC/C), 0 (for Aaa) to 16 (for Caa1/c) for Moody's. Note that for the rest of the chapter only S&P symbols, composed of 17 main rating categories, are used for both S&P and Moody's. Accordingly, obligations rated 'AAA', 'AA+', 'AA', 'AA–', 'A+', 'A' and 'A–' are considered safe investments. While obligations rated 'BB', 'B', 'CCC' and 'CC' are regarded as having

Table 5.1 Rating symbols and ranking

Rating significance	*Moody's*	*Standard & Poor*	*Ranking*
Prime	Aaa	AAA	0
High grade	Aa1	AA+	1
	Aa2	AA	2
	Aa3	AA–	3
Upper medium grade	A1	A+	4
	A2	A	5
	A3	A–	6
Lower medium grade	Baa1	BBB+	7
	Baa2	BBB	8
	Baa3	BBB–	9
Non-investment grade, speculative	Ba1	BB+	10
	Ba2	BB	11
	Ba3	BB–	12
Highly speculative	B1	B+	13
	B2	B	14
	B3	B–	15
High risk	Caa1/c	CCC/C	16

significant speculative characteristics. 'BB' indicates the least degree of speculation and 'CC' the highest. 'While such obligations will likely have some quality and protective characteristics, these may be outweighed by large uncertainties or major exposures to adverse conditions' (S&P, 2012).

This chapter compares actual average yearly default rates reported by agencies, for the period 1983–2012, to what the finance theory would have assigned to them as level of risk, if they were moving in a linear and progressive way. In order to do so, we first assign a rank, from 0 to 16, to each rating category, in an ascending order in Table 5.1, with 'AAA' ranking 0, 'AA+' ranking 1 and so on, till 'CCC/C ranking 16.

Then, we assume in Table 5.2, that rating symbols used by agencies are arithmetically linear, i.e. the difference in credit quality between any two subsequent symbols is a constant. Therefore the difference in credit quality between an AAA rated firm and an AA+ rated firm is the same as between an A+ and an A rated firm and so on, i.e. it assumes the scale to be uniform and each subsequent symbol sees its default increase by the same decrease in credit quality (increase of risk). In other word, rating defaults follow an arithmetic progression with '*d*' as the common difference of successive members of the progression. An arithmetic progression is a sequence of numbers or quantities, each term of which differs from the succeeding term by a constant amount, called common difference.

$$d = 1/16\ (F_{c16}) \tag{5.1}$$

Where:

F_{c16} is the default frequency registered that year for the CCC/C category (the highest default frequency).

Consequently, we can assign to any rating category for a given year, for the 30 years covered by our study (1983–2012), a default frequency (F_{cn}), as follows:

$$F_{cn} = F_{c1} + d(n-1) \tag{5.2}$$

Table 5.2 Default categories ranking, using arithmetic progression

Standard & Poor	*Assigned rank*	*Theoretical default frequency (F_{cn})*
AAA	0	0
AA+	1	$F_{c1} = F_{c1} + d(1-1)$
AA	2	$F_{c2} = F_{c1} + d(2-1)$
AA–	3	$F_{c3} = F_{c1} + d(3-1)$
...		
CCC/C	16	$F_{c16} = F_{c1} + d(16-1)$

Where:

> F_{cn} is the default frequency for the rating category n, if linearity in default was assumed;
> F_{c1i} is the default frequency for the rating category AA+, i.e. CCC/C/16;
> n is the rank: 0 for 'AAA', 1 for 'AA+' and so on till 16 for CCC/C;.
> d is the common difference of successive members of the progression.

Note that d, is computed by dividing the highest default frequency (for CCC/C = 32) by the number of rating categories with a default different from 0 (16 categories). Note that agencies' average actual default for issuers graded CCC/C for the period 1983–2012 is 34. Take for instance the 'AA' symbol, with a rank of 2, given that d, the common difference of successive members of the arithmetic progression, is 2, i.e. (32/16), its linear default frequency, F_{cn}, will be 4 [$F_{c2} = F_{c1} + d(2-1) = 2 + 2(2-1)$].

The linear progression model allows us to build theoretically agencies' default data (deliverable upon request): the arithmetic linear default frequency ($A_{f)}$ for the period 1983–2012, that will serve for comparing agencies' actual data to their corresponding theoretical data. The classification approach used by agencies is expected to introduce a certain degree of linearity to their default data, although insufficient. Indeed the literature would advance poor predictive ability of credit ratings (Piazolo, 2006; Nakamura and Roszbach, 2010) and remark only few explanatory models of the rating with fair levels prediction, but only when very simplified rating scales are used, and this underlines the problem of rationality in the rating process followed by agencies. The linearity of agencies' default ratings is assessed through an OLS regression analysis. The extent of such linearity, if any, is examined, using two more analyses: (i) the analysis of ratio 'standard deviation to the mean' (the ϕ analysis) and (ii) the marginal default analysis (the Δ_d analysis).

The OLS regression analysis

OLS stands for Ordinary Least Squares, the standard linear regression procedure. One estimates a parameter from data and applyies the linear model:

$$y = Xb + e$$

Where:

> y is the dependent variable or vector;
> X is a matrix of independent variables;
> b is a vector of parameters to be estimated;
> e is a vector of errors with mean zero that make the five equal.

Given that market studies have found some significant correlation between credit rating and market prices only for speculative classes, all agencies' actual defaults are therefore regressed against the corresponding constructed linear data: in a first step (main regression #1: comprising 539 observations) investment defaults and speculative defaults are respectively regressed against their corresponding equal weight data, in a second step. Note that sub-sample investment regression #2 comprises 329 observations and sub-sample speculative, regression #3, 197 observations).

Main sample regression:

$$D_{Ti} = a_i + \beta_i D_{AEWi} + \varepsilon_i \tag{5.3}$$

Sub-sample investment regression:

$$D_{Ii} = a_i + \beta_i D_{AEWi} + \varepsilon_i \tag{5.4}$$

Sub-sample speculative regression:

$$D_{Si} = a_i + \beta_i D_{AEWi} + \varepsilon_i \tag{5.5}$$

Where:

a, β and ε are the intercept, the slope of the regression and the term of error, respectively;
D_{Ti} represents the rate of default i (investment and speculative default rates), during the period 1983–2012;
D_{Ii} represents the rate of default i (investment default rates only), during the period 1983–2012;
D_{Si} represents the rate of default i (speculative default rates only), during the period 1983–2012;
D_{AEWi} represents the arithmetic progressive equal weight rate of default i, during the period 1983–2012.

OLS analysis will be complemented by the study of the ratio of default standard deviation to the mean and the marginal defaults. Indeed, an equilibrated system of rating should have comparable ratios of default standard deviation to the mean and comparable marginal default from one rating to the next. For this reason two more analyses will be performed:

i ϕ, analysis/ratio of the standard deviation to the mean of defaults; and
ii Δ_d, analysis or the marginal defaults analysis.

The φ analysis

In order to gain more insight into the linearity of agencies' data, and as a first step, we compare agencies' actual default standard deviations to their corresponding linear default standard deviations. Standard deviation helps in measuring the variability of a mean. It is used in evaluating values in records set to the mean and measuring of dispersion. If rating symbols were linearly distributed, then they should show the same ratio of standard deviation to the mean *(f)* for each rating symbol.

$$\phi = \sigma / \mu \tag{5.6}$$

Where:

σ is the standard deviation;
μ is the mean.

The Δ_d analysis

As second step, we compare agencies' marginal default increases (variation) by symbols to their corresponding calculated marginal default increases, using theoretical linear values. In general terms, marginal default at each rating symbol includes any additional default required to access the next symbol. Here again if linearity exists within agencies' data, the marginal default increase (Δ_d) from one symbol to the next should be the same.

$$\Delta_d = D_i - D_{i-1} \tag{5.7}$$

Where:

D_i is the default for the *i*-th rating symbol;
D_{i-1} is the default for the previous higher symbol $(i-1)$-th.

Appendix 5.1 presents statistic summary of data used in this study: it gives average default frequency distributions of agencies' ratings, for the period 1983–2012, and the corresponding theoretically constructed default distributions. Linear default means and standard deviations are characterized by their progressive linear behaviour, while actual means and standard deviations tend to follow two different patterns, depending if they belong to issuers (AAA to BB+) or (BB– to CCC/C), with a surprising behaviour of the ratings located between (BB+ to BB–): defaults for rating categories A to BB+ show very low default means and standard deviations and are almost equivalent and tend to vary a little, from one default category to the next. The reverse occurs for categories BB+ to CCC/C that show exponential extraordinary increases in both default means and standard deviations, while moving from one category to the next. The behaviour of defaults for BB+, BB and BB– is difficult to comprehend.

OLS regression analysis results

In order to measure the degree of linearity in agencies' default data, we recourse to the OLS regression analysis. Table 5.3 gives results for regression 1 that investigates the linearity within agencies' default ratings, as measured by the arithmetic progression model.

Regression 1 includes all agencies' defaults registered during the period 1983–2012, with a $p\text{-value} < 0.0001$. The model is statistically significant; however, the R-squared is 0.372, which means that agencies' default data can be described by linearity only approximately 37 per cent of the time. In order to gain even more insight into agencies' defaults methodology, the main defaults sample was divided in two sub-samples, following agencies' dichotomization: (i) the investment sub-sample, for defaulting issuers, graded AAA to BBB– and (ii) the speculative sub-sample, for issuers graded BB+ to CCC/C. Two more regressions are therefore run: regression 2, for investment issuers, and 3, for speculative grades.

Table 5.4 gives results for regression 2, measuring the linearity of agencies' default ratings, emanating from issuers' rated investment, as measured by an arithmetic progression.

The beta of +0.0212 and the R^2 of 0.242 indicate that the linear model cannot describe agencies' investment default ratings and we can only conclude to a very weak linearity in agencies' data.

Results for regression 3, measuring the linearity within agencies' default ratings, emanating from issuers' rated speculative are reproduced in Table 5.5

Although agencies' speculative default ratings can a bit more be described by the linear model, the beta of +0.527 and the R^2 of 0.295 also point to an insufficient linearity.

For all the regressions, p-values are under 0.01,[2] hence indicating the significance of the results. Indeed, the null hypothesis is usually rejected when $0.01 < p\text{-value} < 0.05$. Note, however, that the size of the p-value for a coefficient says nothing about the size of the effect that variable is having on the dependent variable and it is possible to have a highly significant result (very small p-value) for a miniscule effect. Agencies' default ranking seems to completely misclassify linearly investment issuers and only slightly to classify linearly correctly speculative issuers and more analysis of the data can be helpful.

ϕ *analysis results*

A look to actual default standard deviations, by default category, shows lower standard deviations for all actual default categories, and very low for investment categories, compared to the corresponding linear information.

Table 5.3 Main sample, actual defaults regressed against their arithmetic distribution ($Y = -2.27661141858489 + 0.417679011902781 * X$)

	Observations	*A Constant*	*Beta*	*R2*	*F*	*t*	*Pr>F*
Regression 1: main sample	539	–2.277	+0.418	0.372	318.143	17.837	<0.0001

Table 5.4 Investment sub-sample, defaults regressed against their arithmetic distribution ($Y = -0.0514907072638928 + 0.0211804083041991 * X$)

	Observations	*A Constant*	*Beta*	*R2*	*F*	*t*	*Pr>F*
Regression 2: Investment sub-sample	329	–0.051	+0.0212	0.242	104.287	10.212	<0.0001

Table 5.5 Speculative sub-sample, defaults regressed against their linear distributions

	Observations	*A Constant*	*Beta*	*R2*	*F*	*t*	*Pr>F*
Regression 3: Speculative sub-sample	197	–3.625	+0.527	0.295	83.173	91.20	<0.0001

However, leaning only on standard deviation in absolute values can be misleading. Once standard deviations are expressed in their relative value to the mean or ϕ, they may convey another story, as described by Figure 5.2, representing the actual ϕ ratio by rating category, compare to the same ratio based on linear assessment.

A higher ϕ, means higher dispersion around the mean and, except for the CCC/C category, agencies' actual default data show higher dispersion around the mean for each category. Further, actual defaults are not evenly distributed among rating categories, investment categories seem to show higher dispersions around their mean, while speculative categories show lower dispersions around their mean. As general rule, default dispersion around the mean decreases with default category rank, starting with the BB category. This means that speculative defaults are more concentrated around their mean, within each category and investment defaults are highly dispersed around their mean, within each category. Note also the extreme and inexplicable dispersion of defaults for AA, BB+ and BB categories. To better understand the behaviour of the ϕ ratio, we extend analysis to the marginal behaviour of each one of its two components, i.e. the mean and the standard deviation.

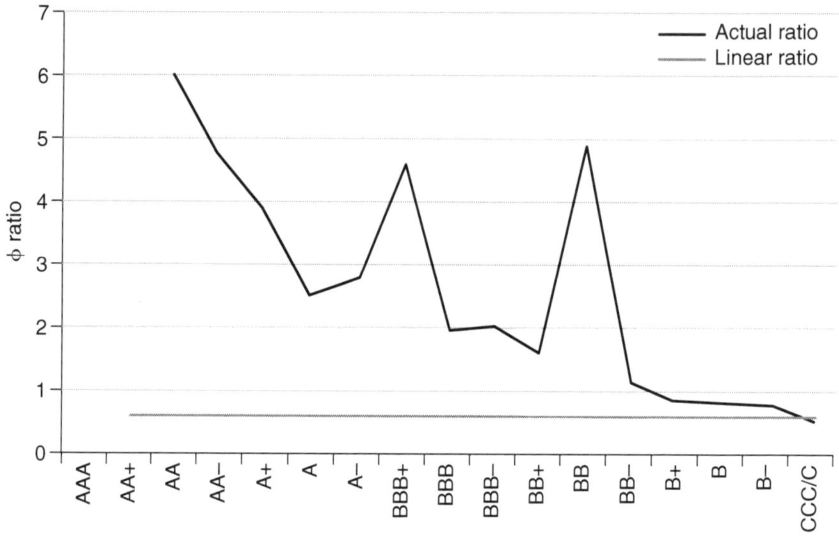

Figure 5.2 φ ratios.

Δ_d *analysis results*

Figure 5.3, allows a better understanding of agencies' actual defaults behaviour. It depicts in panel 1, the variation of actual average defaults, in absolute values, while in panel 2, it depicts the same variations in relative values, i.e. in percentages. In panel 1 it indicates that agencies keep relatively at low and stable levels the changes in default for categories AAA to BBB– and increase it drastically, starting at the BB– default category and lower. Further difference in default, from one category to the next, is far from standardized and does not seem to be based on any rational fact.

Panel 2, in Figure 5.3, depicts marginal variations in relative values (per cent) in default means from one rating category to the next. Inconsistency is here again obvious, while linear defaults indicates steady and stable, they also registered increases in their means, from crossing one default category to the next. Note the extreme increases for BBB+, BB, B and CCC/C categories.

Our analysis of means of defaults can be completed by the study of default standard deviations. Figure 5.4 depicts the changes in standard deviations of default means of both actual and linear data, from one symbol to the next, in absolute (panel 1) and relative (panel 2) values.

Inconsistencies in agencies' default assessment are also obvious. In fact, some crossings of one default category to the next are initiators of larger increases in standard deviations, while others would even experience

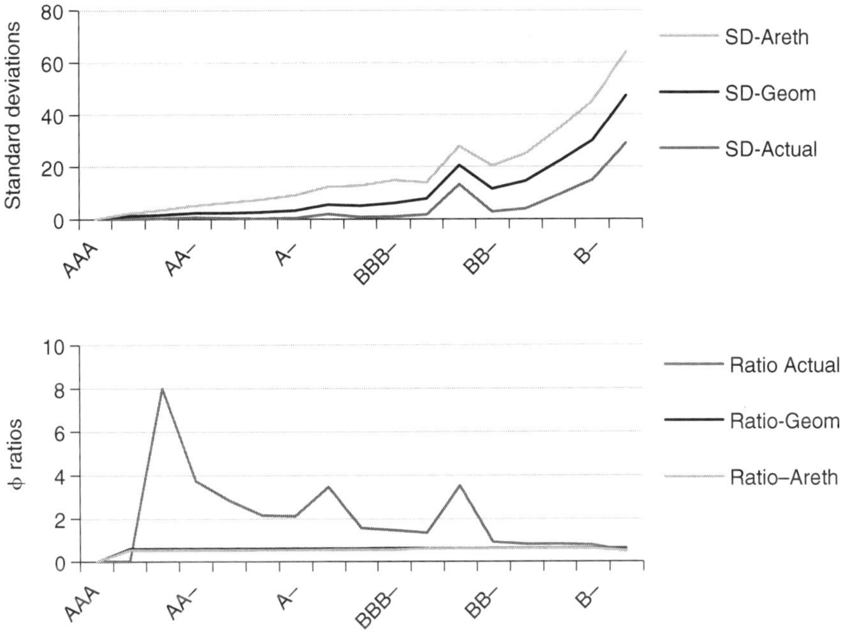

Figure 5.3 Comparing standard deviations and ϕ ratios.

decreases. Panel 1 of Figure 5.4, confirms the segmentation of defaults in three classes: those before BB+, those after BB– and those in between.

The fact that agencies view ratings at the lower end of the spectrum as vulnerable, those at the highest categories as able to withstand extreme or severe stress and those in medium categories to be associated with mild ability to withstand extreme stress, should insure default data with a certain level of linearity. However, this does not seem to be the case and it is possible to think of agencies' systems of categorizing defaults, not only to suffer serious limits in classifying default by symbols, but also to face serious difficulties in distinguishing levels of default within each category. The marginal and the standard deviation analysis point to larger dispersion of defaults within agencies' categories. We can notice, for instance, the highly insignificant variations in default between rating categories AAA to BB+ and the extraordinary variations for categories BB– to CCC/C. It is difficult to explain why it is so. Why, for instance, a single notches change would cause default to double or triple for certain symbols and cause only slight increase for others. It is difficult to think of agencies having in hand rational valuation models that can distinguish, for instance, an 'AAA' rating from an 'AA+'.

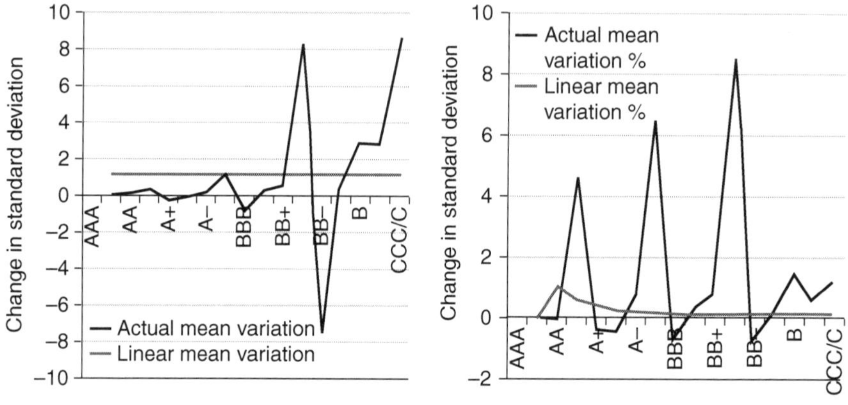

Figure 5.4 Changes in standard deviation of default, from one symbol to the next: actual and linear data (in absolute and relative values).

Discussion and implications

The role of credit rating agencies (CRAs) was recently violently decried all over the world and its quality challenged, especially after their liability was clearly established in the 'subprime' crisis that may have cost the world community a lump sum of US$4.1 trillion, according to the International Monetary Fund. For sure this crisis had and continues to have terrible social consequences: six years after the crisis, families are still suffering. One reason for such failure and frustration with regard to agencies may well be their inability to rationally assess debt issuers' default.

CRAs assert that their ratings are opinions (S&P, 2012), but also acknowledge that they are not mere improbable assertions and describe them as opinions about the likelihood of future events and as forward-looking predictions (S&P, 2012). However, their assertion about the limitations on what their ratings are intended to accomplish might be disregarded by a court or regulator (Moody's, 2007). Agencies assert that history has shown their opinions to be very good predictors of default risk (S&P, 2012) and argue consistently that they are members of the media and publishers (US Senate Turmoil Hearings, 2008) and their ratings as opinions on matters of public concern are protected by the First Amendment of the American Constitution and this bars all manner of efforts to regulate them or hold them liable for the quality of their ratings. Credit rating symbols used by agencies may well be 'mere opinions', but they are opinions that have the power of making a country's borrowing more expensive and a direct impact on the capital levels of financial institutions. Rating symbols do not seem, however, rationally assessed; they are lacking linearity, i.e. the difference in credit quality between an AAA rated firm and an AA+ rated issuer is not the same as between an AA+ and an AA rated issuer. A downgrade from AAA to A– over six notches, for instance, presents a smaller change in default probability than a downgrade from BBB+ to BB+ over two notches. Although, the difference in quality increases with each category, down the scale, agencies' data indicate that over 76 per cent of issuers were usually classified at very high risk, during the period 1983 to 2012, without actually defaulting and would therefore have been unduly denied credit or at least have suffered higher cost of indebtedness. This is may be the reason why Basel II provisions diametrically contradict agencies' weighting and assign to a sovereign debt with a 'AAA' rating 0 per cent risk, 20 per cent risk for another debt with 'A+' and 50 per cent risk to a third with BBB+ (for companies the risk weights are 20, 50 and 100 per cent respectively). This feature is reflected in the measured default frequencies of the individual categories, for example, over a 30-year period, i.e. from 1983 to 2012 there are no one year defaults in the AAA and AA– categories. Yet there are over over notches difference between them.

The linearity of the rating scale could represent an essential characteristic and a key component in understanding empirical observations of ratings and how to apply them, and can be crucial in evaluating credit rating related research (Matthies, 2013), yet it is barely explained or systematically taking care of by agencies. One reason for agencies' apparent failure in assessing risk adequately may be the result of the way they structure risk of default. Our results seem to indicate that agencies' ratings seem unable to classify risk in a progressive and proportional manner. They seem to assign unequal weight to different classes of risk and fail to standardize the passage from one level of default to the next. The rating given to an issuer or security will, however, affect the cost of raising capital. Very often, a deterioration of a debtor's creditworthiness reflected in a rating change may trigger particular contractual obligations (EC, 2013). From Figure 5.5, comparing actual and linear defaults' means and standard deviations, we can see that the agencies' risk assessment model compared to the linear model appears to minimize risk and its progress from one category to the next, for investment issuers, those rated AAA to BB+ and to accelerate the space for ratings from speculative issuers, those rated BB– and lower. As a rule, default risk is underestimated by agencies for all symbols, except CCC/C. The same conclusion can almost be drawn from the analysis of the behaviour of the standard deviations of agencies' actual defaults.

This way of conceiving ratings by agencies and the manner of using them by legislators and investors may have contributed to the flowering of rating bargaining that has been echoed, or that one can easily imagine, most of the time for single notches. Take, for instance, a given bank that is assigned a rating that places it at the upper limit of a given class of risk and making it short of a single notch to advance to the next upper class: what can be expected from a such bank? Indeed, the transition, for

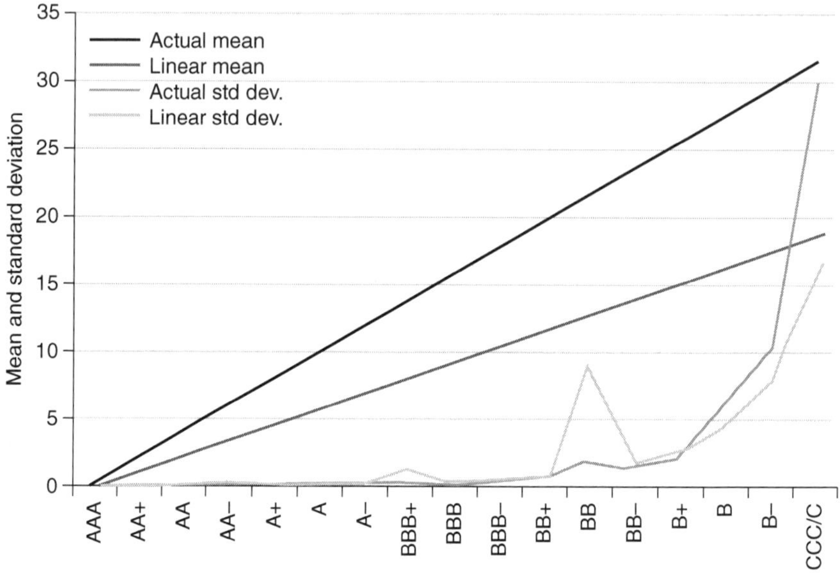

Figure 5.5 Comparison of agencies' default categorization with linear default distributions.

instance, from an 'A+' rating to an 'AAA' would remove virtually any risk for that bank, in the mind of the legislator, allowing saving in cost and expansion in credit. Note that Basel II gives banks the choice to use either their own internal model of assessing credit risk or the Big 3 agencies' ratings and this is probably the reason why some banks will give up the use of their own internal models for assessing risk, whenever Big 3 rating leads to lower requirements in terms of capitalization. Banks would apparently shop for big agencies' ratings, as long as they did not get the desired score. And so these differences shed light on the issue for companies belonging to investment or speculative classes.

Despite the perceived rating weaknesses and setbacks, regulators and investors still, at least till recently, have taken for granted their rationality and let themselves to be guided by them, when it comes time to make regulatory or investment decisions.

Conclusion

Credit ratings can meet an important public need. They seem, however, to lack some rigour; S&P (2012), for instance, warns that agencies do not perform an audit in connection with any issuer credit rating and may, on occasion, rely on unaudited financial information. Our results tend to indicate that beside such limit and many others, the default categorization followed by agencies may push them to make the wrong diagnosis of default, making some issuers pay more than required for their debt, mingling therefore with market efficiency they are supposed to reinforce. Indeed the main reason agencies exist is to assess credit risk accurately and they seem to fail. More performing models of categorizing default should be sought by agencies, otherwise users of ratings may tend to feel that 'a forecaster who is almost always wrong is as good as a forecaster who is almost always right. It is the forecaster who is sometimes right and sometimes wrong … who is dangerous' (Conrad, 2011).

Appendix 5.1 Sample statistic summary for the period 1983–2012

	AAA	*AA+*	*AA*	*AA–*	*A+*	*A*	*A–*	*BBB+*	*BBB*
Actual mean	0.00	0.00	0.01	0.07	0.05	0.04	0.06	0.28	0.24
Std dev.	0.00	0.00	0.06	0.33	0.19	0.10	0.17	1.27	0.48
Actual med.	0.00	0.00	0.00	0.00	0.00	0.00	0.00	0.00	0.00
Actual min.	0.00	0.00	0.00	0.00	0.00	0.00	0.00	0.00	0.00
Actual max.	0.00	0.00	0.44	2.09	1.20	0.45	0.78	9.74	3.00
Linear mean	0.00	1.98	3.97	5.95	7.93	9.92	11.90	13.88	15.87
Linear std dev.	0.00	1.18	2.36	3.54	4.72	5.90	7.08	8.26	9.44
Linear med.	0.00	3.06	6.12	9.18	12.24	15.30	18.35	21.41	24.47
Linear min.	0.00	1.98	3.97	5.95	7.93	9.92	11.90	13.88	15.87
Linear max.	0.00	4.13	8.27	12.40	16.54	20.67	24.81	28.94	33.08

	BBB–	*BB+*	*BB*	*BB–*	*B+*	*B*	*B–*	*CCC/C*
Actual mean	0.30	0.60	1.88	1.49	2.45	5.89	9.67	29.95
Std dev.	0.61	0.98	9.24	1.68	2.14	5.04	7.82	16.40
Actual med.	0.00	0.00	0.63	0.91	2.06	5.18	8.07	26.96
Actual min.	0.00	0.00	0.00	0.00	0.00	0.00	0.00	4.17
Actual max.	3.49	3.79	72.00	9.14	8.72	22.60	32.43	77.41
Linear mean	17.85	19.83	21.82	23.80	25.79	27.77	29.75	31.74
Linear std dev.	10.62	11.80	12.98	14.16	15.35	16.53	17.71	18.89
Linear med.	27.53	30.59	33.65	36.71	39.77	42.83	45.89	48.94
Linear min.	17.85	19.83	21.82	23.80	25.79	27.77	29.75	31.74
Linear max.	37.21	41.35	45.48	49.62	53.75	57.88	62.02	66.15

Notes

1 Moody's Rating System (Moody's, n.d.).
2 The null hypothesis that $\beta = 0$, is to be rejected.

Bibliography

Altman, E. and H.A. Rijken (2005), 'The impact of the rating agencies' through-the-cycle methodology on rating dynamics', *Economic Notes*, Vol. 34, pp. 127–154.

Conrad, V. (2011), 'It is better to be always wrong than sometimes right: the rating agency paradox', 4 November, at: inance.toolbox.com/blogs/credit-eyes-thoughts/

it-is-better-to-be-always-wrong-than-sometimes-right-the-rating-agency-paradox-49180, retrieved 16 November 2013.

Darren, J., P. Kisgen and E. Strahan (2009), 'Do regulations based on credit ratings affect a firm's cost of capital?', National Bureau of Economic Research, Cambridge, MA, Working Paper 14890, March, at: www.nber.org/papers/w14890, retrieved 28 November 2013.

Erlenmaier, U. (2006), 'The shadow rating approach: experience from banking practice', Basel II Risk Parameters, Berlin Heidelberg, pp. 39–77.

European Commission (EC) (2013), 'Transparency report', at: www.esma.europa.eu/page/Credit-Rating-Agencies, retrieved 4 July 2014.

Gonzales, F., F. Haas, R. Johannes, M. Persson, L. Toledo, R. Violi, C. Zins and M. Wieland (2004), 'Market dynamics associated with credit ratings: a literature review', *Banque de France Financial Stability Review*, Vol. 4, pp. 53–76.

Hunt, J.P. (2008), Credit rating agencies and the "worldwide credit crisis": the limits of reputation, the insufficiency of reform, and a proposal for improvement'. *Columbia Business Law Review*, Vol. 2009(1).

Kisgen, D. and P. Strahan (2010), 'Do regulations based on credit ratings affect a firm's cost of capital?' *Review of Financial Studies*, Vol. 23, pp. 4325–4347.

Matthies, B.A. (2013), 'Empirical research on corporate credit-ratings: a literature review', SFB 649, Humboldt-Universität zu Berlin Spandauer Straße 1, D-10178 Berlin, Discussion Paper 2013-003.

Merton, R. (1973), 'An intertemporal capital asset pricing model', *Econometrica*, Vol. 41, pp. 867–887.

Moody's (n.d.), 'Moody's rating system in brief', at: www.moodys.com/sites/products/ProductAttachments/Moody's%20Rating%20System.pdf, retrieved 12 November 2013.

Moody's (2002), 'Ratings definitions', at: www.moodys.com/Pages/amr002002.aspx, retrieved 23 March 2014.

Moody's (2007), 'Structured finance rating performance', at: www.moodys.com/sites/products/DefaultResearch/2007100000520506.pdf, retrieved 3 May 2014.

Nakamura, L.I. and K. Roszbach (2010), 'Credit ratings and bank monitoring ability', European Banking Centre Discussion Paper 2010-10S.

Nordberg, D. (2011), *Corporate governance: principles and issues*, London: Sage.

Piazolo, M. (2006), 'Why have Official rating agencies failed in the past, and will they in the future?' *Ekonomia*, Vol. 9(1), pp. 3–20.

Securities and Exchange Commission (SEC) (2013), 'Annual report to the congress on nationally recognized statistical rating organizations', at: www.sec.gov/divisions/marketreg/ratingagency/nrsroannrep1213.pdf, retrieved 12 October 2013.

Standard & Poor's (S&P) (2009) 'Annual global corporate default study and rating transitions', at: www.standardandpoors.com, retrieved June 25, 2013.

Standard & Poor's (S&P) (2012) 'Annual global corporate default study and rating transitions', at: www.standardandpoors.com, retrieved 25 June 2013.

Testimony of John C. Coffee, Jr, Adolf A. Berle Professor of Law, Columbia University Law School before the Senate Banking Committee on 26 September 2007, 'The role and impact of credit rating agencies on the subprime credit markets', at: www.banking.senate.gov/public/index.cfm?FuseAction=Files.View&FileStore_id=d1c0419e-d84a-4b43-b02d-4e246e2dbec7, retrieved 2 October 2014.

Theis, A. and M. Wolgast (2012), 'Regulation and reform of rating agencies in the European Union: an insurance industry perspective', Geneva Papers 37, pp. 47–76, at: www.palgrave-journals.com/gpp/journal/v37/n1/full/gpp.201133a.html, retrieved 20 June 2012.

World Bank (2009), 'Credit rating agencies', crisis response, at: http://siteresources.worldbank.org/EXTFINANCIALSECTOR/Resources/282884-1303327122200/Note8.pdf, retrieved 10 July 2014.

6 Credit ratings critics

Telling it like it is

Introduction

CRAs have been under intense scrutiny this last decade. An investigation conducted in 2013 by the European Securities and Markets Authority has, for instance, revealed many shortcomings, 'which could pose risks to the quality, independence and integrity of the ratings and of the rating process' (Huw, 2013). According to the World Bank, 'the United States and Europe faulty credit ratings and flawed rating processes are widely perceived as being among the key contributors to the global financial crisis' (2009). Additional to critiques expressed against the credit rating industry and already discussed in Chapters 3, 4 and 5, regarding rating market concentration, methodologies, metrics and rating accuracy, this chapter focuses on independence and integrity of ratings, conflicts of interest and transparency, suggests improvements and warns against pitfalls.

Additional to this introduction, the chapter discusses, in the second section, the independence and integrity of ratings and agencies business models; in the third section, it analyses the conflict of interest in structured finance products; in the fourth section, it deals with the lack of independence as a source of conflict of interest in the rating sector; in the fifth, it suggests the transparency of rating methodologies as an answer to CRA dependence; in the sixth, it discusses credit rating accuracy; and in the final section, it concludes.

Independence and integrity of ratings: agencies' business models

A whole new business domain had been opened for credit rating agencies over the past two decades, much more lucrative than the traditional debt issuer rating activity. This is what came to be known as 'structured finance' or the magic of repackaging existing risky debts, to resell them at much better conditions under a new less risky face. This new activity has placed the rating agencies in a very different moral standing and made them bargain their 'role of judges', to actually become 'judges and parties', by being intimately involved in the issuance process of the structured finance itself. They even became the counsellors that guide issuers on how to obtain the necessary favourable ratings for their issuers of structured finance transactions and they received very generous fees for their appreciable services. Agencies' revenue from structure finance operations, has actually over-shaded all other sources of agencies' income, unfortunately it also confronted them with a serious problem of conflict of interest and moral hazard.

Credit rating agencies generally do not make their rating accessible to debt issuers for free. Ratings users have to pay a subscription fee for access to ratings, and currently, and although agencies also provide other types of services than just ratings, this accounts for a large share of their revenue. Up until the 1970s, agencies' remuneration model was simple and straightforward: investors bought a subscription to receive ratings. Since then things have changed and as indicated in Figure 6.1 agencies use different remuneration models for their services: the subscriber pay business model, the issuer pays business model and the pay-if-rating-is-good model.

The three remuneration models presented in Figure 6.1 are defined as follows:

i The subscription model was the prevailing business model until the early 1970s and it refers to the situation where investors pay the rating agency a subscription fee to access the ratings (Alessi *et al.*, 2013).
ii The issuer pays business model is a model where an agency receives compensation from issuers/investors for rating, but credit rating agencies are allowed to make the ratings freely available to the broader market, especially via the Internet (Alessi *et al.*, 2013).
iii The pay-if-rating-is-good model allows a client to decide not to seek the rating if it learns that it would be less favourable than expected. Indeed,

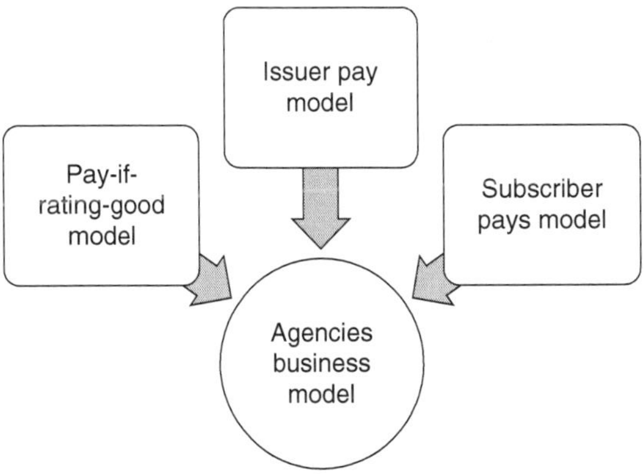

Figure 6.1 Agencies business models.

> today, the rating agency receives one fee to consult with a client, explain its model, and indicate the likely outcome of the rating process; then, it receives a second fee to actually deliver the rating (if the client wishes to go forward once it has learned the likely outcome).
>
> (Coffee, 2008)

The issuer pays model is, today, by far the dominant compensation model of credit rating agencies, and also their favourite. Our discussion will therefore be limited to the understanding of this model. One reason that seems particularly to have significantly contributed to the exclusion and expansion of the issuer pays model and may explain its generalization, is the so-called 'free-ride investors'. These are investors who use rating reports without having paid for them (Partnoy, 2006). On average, the revenue generated by the issuer pays model represents more than two-thirds of total CRA revenues. Despite its bias, CRAs defend the issuer pays model, on the basis that its generalization did not affect credit rating accuracy. CRAs have, however, difficulties explaining how they can maximize their utilities, and both issuers and investors' utilities simultaneously; they usually argue 'they have nothing to benefit from adjusting their ratings to their client's needs because they have a reputation to uphold' (Partnoy, 2006). Reputation seems to work, however, only when a large proportion of agencies' revenues come from other sources than the rating of complex products (McAndrews and Rochet, 2009). Within the issuer pays model, whether issuers want the rating or not, agencies can make them public, since 'If the issuer does not request a rating, then the rating agency will simply do the rating on the basis of [only] the publicly available information' (White, 2011). Agencies may, of course, argue that after all this is a good way of forcing issuers to supply them with all the necessary information required for the making of well-balanced rating decisions. In all cases, many suspect that the issuer pays model has allowed agencies to bill clients with excessive fees and are wondering 'why should S&P and Moody's earn such vast sums?' and their answer is 'Certainly not for their oracular genius – the agencies have as much foresight as Mr Magoo' (Chakrabortty, 2012).

Although, the other agencies remuneration models are not free from potential conflicts of interest either, overall, the issuer pays model may reflect the following inherent conflicts of interest as reported by the SEC (2011):

i Conflicts of interest may occur when in order to gain favour with an issuer and secure its business, an agency may issue a credit rating that is more favourable than the quality of the issuer would justify. 'This conflict could be even more acute when an agency determines higher credit ratings for a whole class of issuers in order to retain or attract business across all issuers in that class' (SEC, 2011).

ii Conflicts of interest may occur whenever a debt issuer is able to shop from different rating agencies for a more favourable rating; this may render agencies more inclined to issue a rating that is higher than objectivity would justify in order to retain a client.
iii Conflicts of interest may occur when higher fees are offered to rating agencies in exchange for improving credit ratings of issuers.
iv Conflicts of interest may occur when issuers may seek to hire rating agencies that provide the more favourable ratings (rating shopping). Consequently, 'agencies whose rating methodologies required lower levels of credit enhancement to reach a given rating level than competitors tended to increase their market share' (Cantor and Packer, 1996) and the presence of a new entrant could result in an increase in 'issuer-friendly' ratings (Becker and Milbourn, 2008).
v Conflicts of interest may occur when agencies assign sovereign credit ratings under political considerations.
vi Conflicts of interest may occur when agencies may issue unsolicited ratings as a means of increasing their market shares. By assigning issuers low and unsolicited ratings, agencies may try to force reluctant issuers that refuse to pay for unsolicited ratings they did not require, to become clients. Unsolicited ratings are usually of weaker quality, since they are primarily based on accessible public information only, as agencies have rather limited access to recalcitrant issuers' private information. Despite the controversy surrounding the practice, unsolicited ratings is commonly in use in all major agencies.

With regard to unsolicited ratings, agencies believe it to be their right to engage in such activity. Moody's, for instance, underlines that, as a publisher of opinions about credit, it reserves the right at any time to issue unsolicited credit ratings, conditional however to the respect of the following conditions:

i a meaningful credit market exists and an investor's interest is served by the publication of such a rating; and
ii agency has sufficient information to support adequate analysis and, if applicable, ongoing monitoring.

Moody's reports an additional restriction; this agency will not seek or accept remuneration for its analytical services from the issuer for at least one year after the publication of unsolicited credit rating (Moody's, 2013a). In the absence of convincing disciplinary rules the issuer pays model can lead to unduly inflated ratings, often mentioned in the literature, as in 1975, for instance, of the city of New York that had been literally running out of money not even paying for its operating expenses, yet CRAs were grading it favourably. Other instances of potential conflicts of interest can be mentioned: the next section will focus on the biggest conflict of interest ever, the one related to structured finance products.

The conflicts of interest between CRAs and debt issuers, from whom they receive fees, can drive the entire agency business model and can undermine the CRA's ability to give an unbiased assessment of credit default. In most cases, CRAs run the risk of the issuers recoursing to ratings shopping which 'not only does enhance ratings distortion, but it also corrupts the entire rating process by giving issuers an incentive to trick their clients into buying overrated securities' (UKEssays, 2010). According to Bolton *et al.* (2009) the former president and CEO of Moody's Investor's Service (Brian Clarkson) acknowledged that 'there is a lot of rating shopping that goes on. What the market doesn't know is who's seen certain transactions but wasn't hired to rate those deals' (Bolton *et al.* 2009). Credit rating agencies are playing both coach and referee in the debt game. Further, the results of a poll conducted by the CFA Institute shows that some 211 of the 1,956 respondents said they have indeed witnessed a CRA 'change ratings in response to external pressures' (2008).

Conflict of interest in structured finance products

Potential conflicts of interest involving rating agencies can be exceptionally serious in structured finance products, specifically the transformation process in subprime residential mortgage-backed security (RMBS), asset-backed securities (ABS) and collateralized debt obligation (CDO). A structured finance product is a particular class of debt issue initiated through a process known as securitization. 'Securitization involves pooling individual financial assets, such as mortgage or auto loans, and creating, or structuring, separate debt securities that are sold to investors to fund the purchase of these assets' (S&P, 2011a). These transactions are launched and operated by a relatively small group of players, enjoying tremendous power: sponsors, underwriters and managers, and where costs are particularly high (SEC, 2013b). These transactions have actually fuelled the mortgage securitization pipeline (FCIC, 2011). The subprime term is used to define the mortgages that were granted to individuals who would not normally be financially qualified for them, i.e. people generally considered insolvent. As summarized in Figure 6.2, a typical structured finance instrument involves four parties (S&P, 2011a); an originator, an arranger, a special purpose entity (SPE) that issues the securities and an investor to buy it. A special purpose entity (also named special purpose vehicle (SPV)) is created to fulfil the specific objective of isolating business risk from financial risk.

The process of structured finance instruments is traditionally initiated with a bank, or another financial institution, called an 'originator' which either has made loans to individuals or has purchased them from other originators. Then comes the 'arranger', an investment bank or other specialized financial institution, which may also be the transaction originator, using the

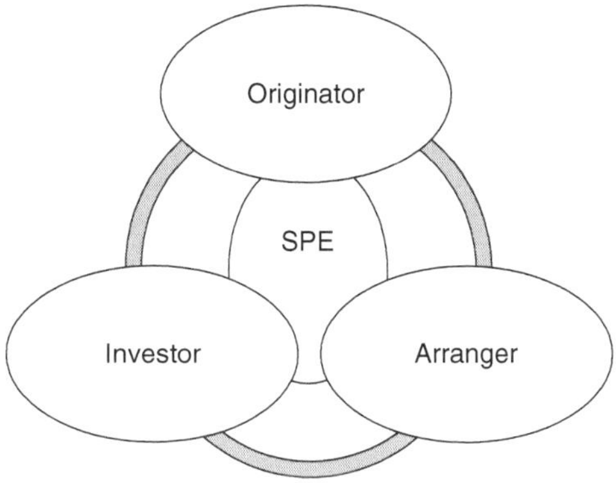

Figure 6.2 Structured finance instruments (source: adapted from S&P, 2011a).

mortgage for the purpose of guaranteeing more complex structured financial instruments, such as RMBS, CDO and ABS. One or more of these sophisticated financial instruments is issued when the arranger puts important numbers of individual mortgages into a pool and transfers them to a special purpose entity (S&P, 2011a). Then comes the crucial step of the process of structured finance instruments: the stratification step of the pool, consisting of dividing undifferentiated risk into multiple classes of debt securities with varying degrees of seniority, called tranching: (i) senior tranches, (ii) junior tranches and (iii) equity tranches.[1]

According to the SEC (2008) there are three ways of security stratification or tranching that are commonly used by SPEs: subordination, over-collateralization and excess spread:

i Subordination comes first and consists of establishing a loss absorption hierarchy between the tranches of debt securities, and later any loss of interest and principal suffered by the SPE 'is first allocated to the lower tranche until all its principal amount is consumed, then the attention is shifted to the next upper tranche on the ladder and so on to climb the entire capital structure' (SEC, 2008).
ii Over-collateralization consists of establishing a loss reserve or provision, out of the amounts by which the principal balance of the mortgage pool exceeds the principal balance of the tranche of securities issued by the SPE, and used to create an 'additional' equity 'tranche below the Lowest tranche security to absorb Losses' (SEC, 2008). And meant to protect it from the early losses created by the defaulting loans.
iii Excess spread finally describes the amount by which the monthly interest income of the SPE exceeds its monthly financial commitments. This surplus can be used to accumulate loss reserves or to adjust the overdue interest of a particular tranche security.

Based on one of the three methods of credit stratification presented, the SPE issues securities of its own to investors who evaluate them based on their new credit risk classification, and three situations can be encountered:

i First, the situation of investors who opt for the senior tranche: this is a tranche presenting the profile of the highest quality debt and also paying the lowest interest rate from a credit perspective. These investors are the first to be repaid from the cash flow generated by the underlying assets.
ii Second, the situation of investors who opt for the next-lower tranche, which pays a somewhat higher rate of interest than the previous tranche, but also bearing higher risk than the previous tranche, and so forth.
iii Third, finally, the situation of investors who purchase the lowest tranche generally hoping for the potential of earning the highest interest rate, but also expected to bear the highest risk.

Investors buy mortgage-backed securities and their senior tranches end up being acquired by many financial institutions, including banks. Many of these financial institutions have also established their own 'structured investment vehicles' (SIV), which also borrow funds through the issuance of short-term 'asset-backed' commercial paper. These funds are then used to finance the purchase of tranches of the CDOs backed by subprime mortgages (White, 2010). What is even more interesting is that when mortgage-backed securities are given high credit ratings, the asset-backed commercial papers will also receive a high credit rating and this will make borrowing cheaper. 'In addition for regulated financial institutions structured prime mortgages rated AA qualify for the same reduced capital requirements[2] as asset-backed securities issued by reputable financial institutions' (White, 2010).

Contrary to what logically should have happened, to see agencies reluctant to mingle with these structured finance transactions, they were actually becoming actively implicated in their design and they were not only requiring compensation for rating structured securities transactions, but were also requiring to be paid for being consulted on how to structure their tranches to achieve issuers' desired if abnormally high ratings. They were, for instance, consulted extensively by issuers of these securities on matters like what kinds of mortgages would earn what levels of ratings, for what sizes of tranches of these securities, etc. (Mason and Rosner, 2007). Unlike the market for rating corporate or government debt, the market for rating mortgage-related securities involved only a relatively small number of investment banks as securitizes with high volumes (SEC, 2008) and this may have had many moral hazard consequences for:

i It gives, for instance, the securitizes the dreamed opportunity to pressure rating agencies for delivering unjustified favourable ratings and render rating process almost on demand. Consequently, abnormally high profit margins were unregistered on these mortgage-related securities.

> Not coincidentally, the commissions and fees involved in the subprime lending business were the highest of all, as the end borrower was being charged interest rates well above the base or wholesale rate in recognition of his or her poor credit standing.
>
> (Hunt, 2008)

ii It makes also any displeased securitize, with an agency's rating on any specific security, to be inclined to exercise its decisive bargaining power, by just threatening to move all of its securitization business to a different rating agency. This is may be the reason behind agencies providing more favourable ratings for the structured products issued by clients that provide them with more overall bilateral rating business (Swiss Finance Institute, 2013).

iii CRAs that were intimately implicated in the design of the securitization business, may have also found themselves under considerable financial pressure to deliver the rating that issuers wanted to see. Indeed,

> because credit rating agencies issue ratings to issuers and investment banks who bring them business, they are subject to an inherent conflict of interest that can create pressure on the credit rating agencies to issue favourable ratings to attract business.
>
> (FCIC, 2011)

iv Securitizes, for their part, being aware that for any given packaging of underlying mortgages to be securitized, their profit will be intimately linked the highest ratings on a largest percentage of the tranches of securities issued against mortgages, will fight for the highest ratings on a largest percentage of the tranches of securities possible.

v Further, given the complexity of mortgage-backed securities, rating errors are less likely to be quickly discovered by agencies. 'It is therefore not surprising to see CRAs becoming complacent and less worried about the problems of protecting their long-run reputations' (Mathis *et al.*, 2009).

One main factor seems to have particularly contributed to the explosion of the subprime mortgages securities business, namely the favourable ratings conferred by agencies on the more senior tranches. 'From 2000 to 2007, Moody's rated nearly 45,000 mortgage-related securities as triple-A. This compares with six private-sector companies in the United States that carried this coveted rating in early 2010' (FCIC, 2011). Many bond investors were inclined to enter this market only because of the trust they had in agencies, due to the favourable reputations they had established. At the beginning agencies were maybe too optimistic for the securities backed by subprime mortgages, however, unable to adjust and change past practices on time, they proved to be slow to downgrade those securities as their negative fates became obvious (Hunt, 2008). For instance, the CDO tranches that were originally rated AAA by Standard & Poor's had been downgraded 80 per cent below investment grade (Arezki *et al.*, 2011). Moody's and S&P were found guilty of triggering the worst financial crisis in decades (FCIC, 2011).

Table 6.1, adapted from NRSRO, provides mid-year and full-year CRA ratings activity of structured finance. Among CRAs, the Big 3 have increased the number of their deals in the past few years especially in the commercial mortgage-backed securities market. Their share has, however, decreased in the number of deals by 23 per cent, from 84 per cent in 2010, to 61.04 per cent in 2012, while their volume in dollars has remained almost unchanged, registering a slight decrease of less than 1 per cent from its level of 2010.

Moody's had registered the largest rated commercial mortgage-backed security (CMBS) market share in the first half of 2012. It rated 50 per cent of rated CMBS transactions during this period. In terms of the number of transactions, Fitch rated 19 transactions, placing it second largest in numbers.

Lack of independence as a source of conflict of interest

Big 3 rating has been criticized for maintaining too familiar ties with client managements, possibly opening them to undo influence and to the risk of being misled. It seems that Big 3 managers used to meet frequently

Table 6.1 Rating agencies for CMBS issued in the first half of 2012

Agency	*1H-2012 issuance ($ million)*	*No. of deals*	*1H-2011 issuance ($ million)*	*No. of deals*	*1H-2010 issuance ($ million)*	*No. of deals*
Moody's	17,831.4	23	13,190.9	13	9,761.1	17
Fitch	11,787.5	19	13,847.2	13	8,260.4	11
S&P	2,546.4	5	6,544.2	8	9,285.6	14
Total Big 3	29,618.9	47	33,582.3	34	18,021.5	42
Total all agencies	38,516.3	77	38,098.4	50	23,152.8	50
Big 3/Total	76.90%	61.04%	88.15%	68.00%	77.84%	84.00%

Source: adapted from SEC (2012).

personally with the management of many clients, and advise them on actions that should be taken for reaching/maintaining a certain rating (Partnoy, 2006). The Big 3 were perceived to be hesitating in downgrading companies with whom they were in consulting business. For example, issuers' ratings were kept at investment grade only a few days before these issuers went bankrupt, despite awareness of their problem a while before: this the case of Enron, Freddie Mac and many others. The Big 3 seem to have actually become victims of their own system, 'When you get into a situation like with AIG, the rating agencies are basically trapped into maintaining high ratings because they know if they downgrade, they don't only have this regulatory effect but they have all these effects' (Partnoy, 2006) and 'in a crisis a downgrade can be like firing a bullet in company's heart' (Fons and Partnoy, 2009). Therefore, when the AIG bailout was debated in 2009, US officials made sure that agencies would not downgrade the company. It is, of course, argued that theses were unfortunate aberrations and that agencies' ability to rate debts bonds remained unaffected (Fons and Partnoy, 2009). The SEC, points out also to circumstances where the independence of agencies can seriously be challenged:

i In the case, for instance, where an agency feels the need to revise its rating of a particular debt security to allow one of its major clients to acquire it, knowing that its current low level of rating will not permit the client to go ahead with the investment without overriding own internal guidelines or contractual provisions.
ii In the case where an agency, for the sake of gaining an influential client's favours, makes him benefit from updated ratings that may lead to an increase of market value of securities in hand. This would also be the case when influential issuers investing in new bond issues aspire achieving higher yields in the case of a low rating.
iii In the case where a credit analyst, participating in an issuer rating, is also seeking a job with an issuer.
iv When an issue is of large size. It is often argued that, during the financial crisis, for instance, large size issuers were better rated than those of smaller size issues of comparable quality (He *et al.*, 2011).
v In the case where an agency rates its own controlling shareholders, such ownership structure could indeed be problematic. This will be also the case when controlling shareholders invest in products rated by their controlled agency.
vi In the case where an investor holds substantial interests in several large CRAs, allowing him to 'steer the odds' for its own sake.
vii In the case where an issuer linked to a credit rating agency provides advisory services to an entity, which later, rated it.
viii Whenever an agency rates structured products, where issuers are separate legal entities established and operated by a select group of sponsors, underwriters, managers (NRSRO).

It is argued that, in this last case, the complexity of the structured financial products adduced to the inability of issuers to control the flow of information on the underlying assets, may create an information asymmetry problem, where the arranger is better informed on the transaction in hand than investors. This information imbalance, combined with the ratings oligopoly, increases the risk of conflict of interest and undermines the integrity of the market as a whole.

Transparency of rating methodologies can be the answer to CRA dependence

Concerns about transparency in the rating process are not new; it was an important issue even before the global financial crisis run-up and it is still today. The rating agencies had always failed documenting significant steps in the ratings process, like they had failed documenting significant participants in the ratings process (SEC, 2009). Further, 'generally, when the issuer-paid model is employed, much of the information relied on by the hired NRSROs to rate structured finance products is non-public' (SEC, 2011). Finally, issuers themselves may use tactics that prevent some agencies from obtaining information needed to assign ratings. All these actions contribute significantly to the weakening of rating transparency.

The damaging effect of the lack of transparency is widely recognized, even by agencies themselves that are beginning to revaluate their rating processes. It is, however, felt that transparency cannot be increased industry wide on a voluntary basis only and best practices that are endorsed by the regulator may prove to be necessary (FIDC, 2007), Consequently attempts to address the issue of methodological transparency were made by both the SEC and EC, requiring agencies to render public their registration material, including their rating procedures, although, this might represent the least bad approach to the fundamental problem of transparency. As of January 2011 the SEC adopted the set of rules applicable to NRSROs, listed in Table 6.2.

Usually agencies' Annual Certification of Form NRSRO, Exhibits 1 through 9, contain information about each agency with NRSRO status, including (SEC, 2011):

- i performance statistics;
- ii procedures and methodologies for determining credit ratings;
- iii procedures to prevent the misuse of material non-public information;
- iv organizational structure;
- v code of ethics (or explanation of why it does not have a code of ethics);
- vi conflicts of interest and procedures to manage conflicts of interest;
- vii credit analysts; and
- viii designated compliance officers.

Table 6.2 Exchange act rules applicable to NRSROs, regarding independence and transparency

Rule 17g-1	Requires a credit rating agency to apply for NRSRO status and issue credit ratings for various classes of securities by filing a Form NRSRO with the Commission, and prescribes how an NRSRO must keep its registration up-to-date and file an annual certification. Additionally, an NRSRO must make its current Form NRSRO and information and documents submitted in Exhibits 1 through 9 to Form NRSRO publicly available.
Rule 17g-2	Requires an NRSRO to make and retain certain types of business records and publicly disclose certain ratings history data.
Rule 17g-3	Requires an NRSRO to file certain audited and unaudited annual financial reports and reports of the number of credit rating actions with the Commission.
Rule 17g-4	Requires an NRSRO to establish and enforce written policies and procedures designed to address specific areas in which material, non-public information could be inappropriately disclosed or used.
Rule 17g-5	Identifies a series of conflicts of interest arising from the business of determining credit ratings. Some of these conflicts must be disclosed and managed, while others are expressly prohibited.
Rule 17g-6	Prohibits NRSROs from engaging in certain unfair, abusive or coercive practices.
Rule 17g-7	Requires NRSROs to include information regarding the representations, warranties and enforcement mechanisms available to investors in an asset-backed securities offering in any report accompanying a credit rating issued in connection with such offering, including a preliminary credit rating, as well as how those representations, warranties and enforcement mechanisms differ from those in similar offerings.

Major agencies are therefore already issuing regular performance reports, but there is no required standardized format for their reporting; they are simply required to attach their already public performance reports to the annual certification. However, 'If investors cannot determine how an agency's ratings have performed, they cannot develop informed views about the quality of those ratings' (Hunt, 2008). Unfortunately, no increase in pertinent information about agency methodologies seems to have resulted yet: 'current rules on methodologies only require disclosure of underlying assumptions for structured finance products, creating varying degrees of transparency for different asset classes' (Hunt, 2008). And it is further argued that

> the fact that agencies are willing to give away their models suggests that something is wrong with the reputational capital model. It suggests that the rating agencies credit-assessment techniques are not valuable, so that ratings derive their value from something other than high quality.
>
> (Hunt, 2009)

The lack of transparency of rating methodologies is suspected of contributing to the increase of uncertainty in the market and hence its instability. Further, in the case of revised methodologies, when they are misunderstood or investors are not aware of the reasons for changes, a risk of disruption may result. Of the large agencies, only Moody's is a separate, publicly held corporation that discloses its financial results without dilution by non-ratings businesses.

Accuracy of credit ratings

Agencies respond to the lack of transparency and rating inaccuracy critiques by warning that rating 'is not investment advice, or buy, hold or sell recommendations' (S&P, 2012) and is not intended to be used as 'prognosis' (forecast) and is 'not guarantee of credit quality or of future credit risk' (S&P, 2012) (but what are they?); they are 'global benchmarks' that are comparable 'over time asset classes and economic sectors'. Agencies also react to critiques by a number of in-house studies, as discussed in Chapter 4 that defend the accuracy of their ratings.

Figure 6.3, based on the sample presented in Chapter 4, depicts S&P and Moody's number of defaults for each year, for the period 1982–2012 and due to unviability/insufficiency of data Fitch is not included.[3] Figure 6.3 covers, however, 80 per cent of the global credit market (i.e. the portion of the market under the control of Moody's and S&P). This period has witnessed 3,994 default events (1,820 default events registered by S&P during the period under study or 46 per cent and 2,174 registered by Moody's or 54 per cent). The vertical axis represents the yearly number of defaults and the horizontal axis the years from 1 to 31, with 1 corresponding to the year 1982 and 31 to the year 2012.

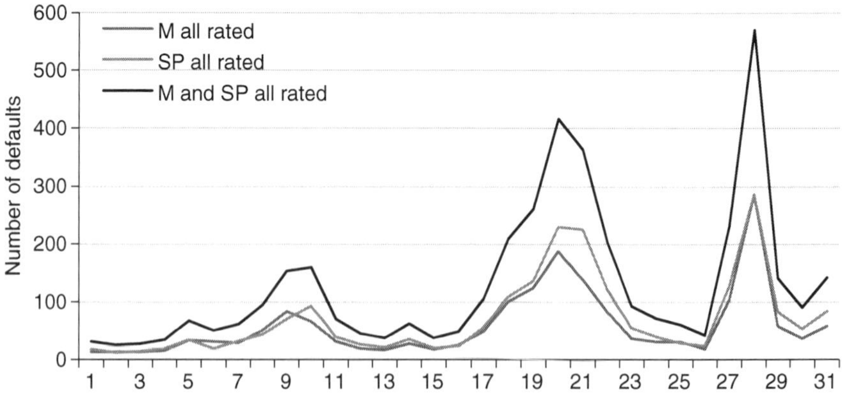

Figure 6.3 S&P and Moody's yearly number of defaults for the period 1982–2012 (source: adapted from S&P and Moody's data, for the period 1982–2012).

As expressed by Figure 6.3 the period 1982–2012 has witnessed an unprecedented number of events in global credit markets particularly sovereign downgrades. As mentioned in Chapter 4, overall credit stability deteriorated three times during the period covered by the study and defaults were generally spread across several sectors: industrial, financial services, government securities and insurance. In general, agencies' default ratings seem to covariate perfectly with some lag for S&P. S&P and Moody's default variations by rating symbols, for the period 1983–2012, are depicted in Figure 6.4. Results seem to point to the absence of any rationality in the assessment of default by symbol and unearth time lags and differences between agencies. Although both agencies appear to show great inconsistency between rating classes, Moody's seems to suffer even more inconsistencies.

It seems that default assignment to rating symbols should be based on a well-defined theoretical model instead of the simple rank ordering methodology currently used by agencies. It is possible that this situation may have kept agencies from rating effectively fixed-income investment issuers and may explain why among defaults reported by agencies during the period 1983–2012, 8 per cent emanated from issuers considered to be investment (S&P, 2012). This may also explain why credit rating upgrades

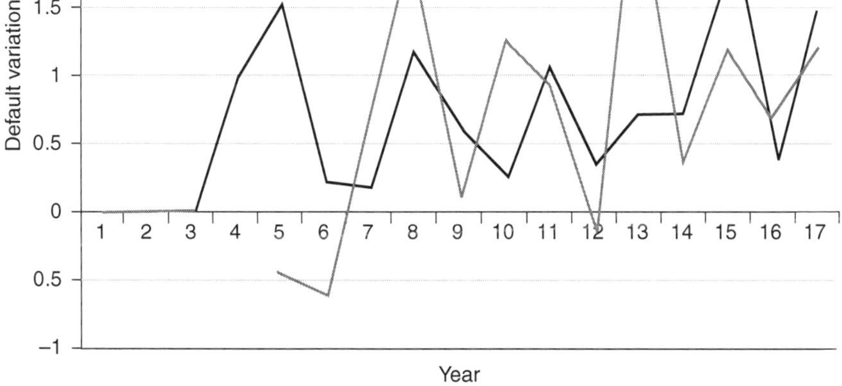

Figure 6.4 S&P and Moody's default variations by rating symbols for the period 1983–2012.

Note
The number 1 in Figure 6.4 corresponds to AAA symbol and 17 to CCC symbol.

seem to have little effect on bond prices and why an impact seems to exist in downgrades. It is believed also that when a security gets downgraded below the investment grade threshold managers have to liquidate their positions in large blocks thus causing unwarranted sudden volatility and possible portfolio losses hence the need to create quantitative ratings instead of using letters.

A number of empirical studies analysed the effectiveness of ratings accuracy (Božovic *et al.*, 2011). Some have suggested that behaviour of sovereign credit ratings have practically no predictive power vis-à-vis crises (Reinhart and Rogoff, 2011). Their explanation on why this may be the case is related to the fundamentals used by CRAs, which are dominated by financial ratios that are generally poor predictors of distress of sovereign debt. Others find that the anticipative power of corporate ratings varies with time or noticed that the moral hazard induces conflict between borrowers and lenders, leading to lending rates that are lower than optimal (Mishkin, 2009) and also pointed to the crucial relationship between credit ratings and capital adequacy requirements. To such inaccuracy of the ratings, agencies usually respond that their views are opinions and acknowledge that the opinions they offer are not mere improbable assertions. Instead agencies describe their ratings as opinions about the likelihood of future events and as forward-looking predictions (S&P, 2011a).

Inaccurate credit ratings can have, at least, two distinct negative setbacks. On the one hand, they can downgrade unduly a certain issue, and, on the other hand, they can destabilize the financial markets at a systemic level. Various studies which have compared Moody's and Standard & Poor's ratings, have found a great similarity for investment grade ratings (Cantor and Packer, 1996; Ammer and Packer, 2000): in the case of speculative-grade issues, however, Moody's and Standard & Poor's assign divergent ratings much more frequently to sovereign bonds than to corporate bonds. Individual issuers and institutional investors still find it useful to be guided by a rating when making their investment decisions that can destabilize the financial market if ratings prove to be inaccurately assessed. Especially, in case of a rating downgrade movement resulting in a mass selling. It is difficult, however, to see CRAs 'monitor continuously the unpredictable behaviour of myriads of individual debt issues' (Goodhart, 2008).

Conclusion

This chapter has discussed numerous cases where agencies may have lacked transparency and/or demonstrated conflicts of interest mostly inherent to the issuer pays model. A deep look at rating history and activity may show numerous instances where agencies have erred. Indeed, past activities of agencies carry much suspicion as expressed by their many failures to 'flag up' problems. They had often downgraded companies, too late to be helpful to investors, just days before their bankruptcy. Agencies' ratings gave positive, investment-grade ratings to AIG and Lehman Brothers up until their collapse. It was, however, in the area of structured finance, where their built-in conflict of interest has had far more prejudicial consequences and grievous repercussions. The Financial Crisis Inquiry Commission of the US underlines, for instance, the following breakdowns at Moody's:

i the flawed computer models;
ii the pressure from financial firms that paid for the ratings;
iii the relentless drive for market share;
iv the lack of resources to do the job despite record profits; and
v the absence of meaningful public oversight.

The FCIC also concluded 'indeed, without the active participation of the rating agencies, the market for mortgage-related securities could not have been what it became' (FCIC, 2011). CRAs are constantly asserting that independence is crucial to their role and it seems difficult to perceive any immediate solution to this problem, but the transparency of the rating methodology constitutes the best bet. A key lesson to be learned from the last financial crisis is that it is vital for ratings agencies to be able to provide a reliable indication of a debtor's creditworthiness even in times of crisis. Obviously, the self-disciplining role played by reputation cannot always be relied on and may only function over the long term. Hence, an international and several national, regulatory regimes for CRAs are suggested and will be discussed in the next chapter.

Notes

1 Some SPE stratify pools in ten tranches.
2 Currently such capital requirement is 1.6 per cent of asset value.
3 Fitch studies do not give default information by scale for the whole period covered by the study.

Bibliography

Alessi, C., R. Wolverson and M.A. Sergie (2013), 'The credit rating controversy', Council on Foreign Relations, at: www.cfr.org/financial-crises/credit-rating-controversy/p22328, retrieved 12 February 2013.

Ammer, J. and F. Packer (2000), 'How consistent are credit ratings? A geographic and sectoral analysis of default risk', Board of Governors of the Federal Reserve System, International Finance Discussion Papers, No. 668, June.

Arzeki, Rabah, Bertrand Candelon and Amandou N.R. Sy (2011), 'Sovereign rating news and financial markets spillovers: evidence from the European debt crisis', International Monetary Fund (IMF) Working Paper WP/11/68, March.

Becker, B. and T. Milbourn (2009), 'How did increased competition affect credit ratings?' Harvard Business School Working Paper, No. 09-051.

Bolton, P., X. Freixas and J. Shapiro (2009), 'The credit ratings game', NBER Working Paper No. 14712, February.

Božović, M., B. Urošević and B. Živković (2011), 'Credit rating agencies and moral hazard', *Panoeconomicus*, Vol. 2, pp. 219–227.

Cantor, R. and F. Packer (1996), 'Determinants and impact of sovereign credit ratings', *Economic Policy Review*, Vol. 2(2), pp. 37–54.

CFA Institute (2008), 'CFA Institute Member Opinion Poll Confirms Support for CRA Reform', 7 July, at: www.cfainstitute.org/aboutus/press/release/08releases/20080707_01.html, retrieved 12 July 2013.

Chakrabortty, C. (2012), 'Time to take control of the credit rating agencies', at: www.theguardian.com/commentisfree/2012/jan/16/time-control-credit-ratings-agencies, retrieved 5 April 2014.

Coffee, J.C. (2008), 'Testimony before the U.S. Senate Committee on banking, housing and urban affairs', at: www.gpo.gov/fdsys/pkg/CHRG-110shrg50399/pdf/CHRG-110shrg50399.pdf, retrieved 4 June 2014

European Securities and Markets Authority (ESMA) (2013), 'ESMA identifies deficiencies in CRAs sovereign ratings processes', at: www.esma.europa.eu/news/Press-Release-ESMA-identifies-deficiencies-CRAs-sovereign-ratings-processes, retrieved 9 July 2014.

Federal Deposit Insurance Corporation (FIDC) (2007), 'Supervisory insights, enhancing transparency in the structured finance market', at: www.fdic.gov/regulations/examinations/supervisory/insights/sisum08/article01_transparency.html, retrieved 23 July 2014.

Financial Crisis Inquiry Commission (FCIC) (2011), 'Financial crisis inquiry commission report: final report of the national commission on the causes of the financial and economic crisis in the United States', ISBN 978-0-16-087727-8.

Fons, F. and F. Partnoy (2009), 'Rated F for failure', *New York Times*, 16 March.

Goodhart, C.A.E. (2008), 'How, if at all, should credit ratings agencies (CRAs) be regulated?' Special Paper LES Finance Market Group Paper Series, June.

He, Jie, Jun 'QJ' Qian and Philip E. Strahan (2011), 'Are all ratings created equal? The impact of issuer size on the pricing of mortgage-backed securities', at: www2.bc.edu/~strahan/Ratings-July2011.pdf, retrieved 5 May 2014.

Hunt, J.P. (2008), 'Credit rating agencies and the "worldwide credit crisis": the limits of reputation, the insufficiency of reform, and a proposal for improvement', *Columbia Business Law Review*, Vol. 2009(1).

Huw, J. (2013), 'EU watchdog slams "big three" rating agencies, sees failings in sovereign debt process', at: www.theglobeandmail.com/, retrieved 23 June 2014.

McAndrews, M. and J.-C. Rochet (2009), 'Rating the raters: are reputation concerns powerful enough to discipline rating agencies?' *Journal of Monetary Economics*, Vol. 56(5), pp. 657–674.

Mason, J.R. and J. Rosner (2007), 'Where did the risk go? How misapplied bond ratings cause mortgage backed securities and collateralized debt obligation market disruptions', at: http://ssrn.com/abstract=1027475 or http://dx.doi.org/10.2139/ssrn.1027475, retrieved 15 July 2014.

Mathis, J., J. McAndrews and, J.-C. Rochet (2009), 'Rating the raters: are reputation concerns powerful enough to discipline rating agencies?' Toulouse School of Economics Working Paper

Mishkin, F. (2009), 'The financial crisis and the Federal Reserve', National Bureau of Economic Research.

Partnoy, F. (2006), 'How and why credit rating agencies are not like other gatekeepers'. In R.E. Litan and Y. Fuchita, *Financial gatekeepers: can they protect investors?* Washington, DC: Brookings Institution.

Reinhart, C. and K.S. Rogoff, (2011), 'From financial crash to debt crisis', *American Economic Review*, August, Vol. 101(5), pp. 1676–1706.

Securities and Exchange Commission (SEC) (2008), 'Summary report of commission staff's examinations of each NRSRO', at: www.sec.gov/, retrieved 5 October 2014.

Securities and Exchange Commission (SEC) (2011), 'Annual report on nationally recognized statistical rating organization', December, at: www.sec.gov/divisions/marketreg/ratingagency/nrsroannrep1212.pdf, retrieved 10 July 2014.

Securities and Exchange Commission (SEC) (2012), 'Annual report on nationally recognized statistical rating organization', at: www.sec.gov/ retrieved 29 March 2014.

Securities and Exchange Commission (SEC) (2013a), 'Annual report on nationally recognized statistical rating organization', at: www.sec.gov/ retrieved 29 March, 2014.

Securities and Exchange Commission (SEC) (2013b), 'Summary report of commission staff's examinations of each NRSRO', at: www.sec.gov/news/studies/2013/nrsro-summary-report-2013.pdf, retrieved 26 September 2014.

Standard & Poor's (S&P) (2011), 'Default study', at: www.standardandpoors.com/, retrieved 12 November 2013.

Standard & Poor's (S&P) (2011), 'Guide to credit rating essentials', at: www.standardandpoors.com/, retrieved 12 November 2013.

Standard & Poor's (S&P) (2012), 'Default study'. at: www.standardandpoors.com/ retrieved November 12, 2013.

Standard & Poor's (S&P) (2013), 'Default study', at: www.standardandpoors.com/, retrieved 12 November 2013.

Swiss Finance Institute (2013), 'Study of structured debt ratings from Standard & Poor's, Moody's Investors Service, and Fitch Ratings', at: www.swissfinanceinstitute.ch/, retrieved 19 May 2014.

Thoughtsworththinking.net (2010), 'Will financial reform negatively bias U.S. sovereign credit ratings?' at: www.thoughtsworththinking.net/?p=487, retrieved 10 May 2014.

UKessays (2010), 'Problems of the credit rating agencies', at: www.ukessays.com/dissertations/economics/problems-of-the-credit-rating-agencies.php, retrieved 3 March 2014.

White, L.J. (2010), 'The credit rating agencies', *Journal of Economic Perspectives*), Spring, Vol. 24(2), pp. 211–226.

White, L.J. (2011), 'Market: the credit rating agencies', *Journal of Economic Perspectives*, Spring, Vol. 24(2), pp. 211–226.

World Bank (2009), 'Credit rating agencies', crisisresponse, at: http://siteresources.worldbank.org/EXTFINANCIALSECTOR/Resources/282884–1303327122200/Note8.pdf, retrieved 10 July 2014.

7 Credit rating agencies

External monitoring

Introduction

Before the 2007 financial crisis, credit rating agencies (CRAs) were hardly submitted to any regulatory framework to ensure their transparency and were constantly advocating the free speech defence to escape any liability. Following the financial crisis, however, a strong consensus emerged, especially among long time allies, that were suddenly convinced of the usefulness of stricter regulatory intervention to curb CRAs' perceived excesses. The new rules are mainly aiming to reduce reliance on CRA ratings for regulatory purposes and are looking for ways to increase their transparency and independence. Agencies must now (if registered with a national security exchange commission) provide additional information in a way that investors can make better decisions. They must also publicly disclose how their ratings are made and how well they performed over time. Further, CRAs are considered to be commercial in character and therefore are subject to liability and oversight.

This chapter will focus on CRAs' recent regulatory and supervision frameworks. Additional to the introduction, the second section discusses CRAs' monitoring and registration with supervisory authorities; the third section deals with the Financial Stability Board action; the fourth section introduces the IOSCO Initiative; the fifth section introduces the Basel Committee for Banking Supervision reaction; the sixth views national jurisdictions (US, EC and others); and the final section concludes the chapter.

CRAs' monitoring and registration

Agencies were unanimously blamed for being one of and the biggest aggravating factor of the 2007 crisis, mainly because of their failure, where they were supposed to succeed, i.e. predicting the crisis happening, for reacting nervously in the period following the crisis and becoming excessively conservative in their ratings to the point of 'daring' downgrading loyal supporters like the United States and major European countries. Such affront may have finally cost them dearly and, for sure, has earned them the wrath of their long-time supporters: the United States, the European Commission and international agencies. The United States, for instance, has recently filled a $5 billion US fraud case against Standard & Poor's (Barrett, 2014). Denounced by S&P, this lawsuit is considered retaliation, intended to punish the agency for 'exercising its First Amendment rights'. According to Wikipedia, the First Amendment (Amendment I) to the United States Constitution, adopted on 15 December 1791, 'prohibits the making of any law … impeding the free exercise of religion, abridging the freedom of speech, infringing on the freedom of the press'. The time of regulation has definitely sounded and the wind of change keeps increasing stronger for agencies. The international community acts in concert and rarely was such homogeneity recorded in any international regulatory initiative. The G20, the International Organization of Securities Commissions (IOSCO), the US and the EC, and other countries and jurisdictions all have recently launched their own regulatory initiatives for monitoring rating agencies. We should 'never spit on the hand that feeds us', like they say. Further, the applicability of the First Amendment protection to credit ratings, often advocated by agencies was recently seriously challenge, the 'Court has ruled that there is no blanket First Amendment protection for published credit ratings' (Baklanova, 2009). Described in Figure 7.1, are CRAs' recent regulatory frameworks.

The Group of Twenty (G20) is the premier forum for international economic cooperation and decision-making, not to be confused with the G7, another forum of the world's seven most industrialized economies, formed in 1975 and initially composed of six nations: France, Germany, Italy, Japan, UK and US, and later joined by Canada in 1976. Russia's inclusion

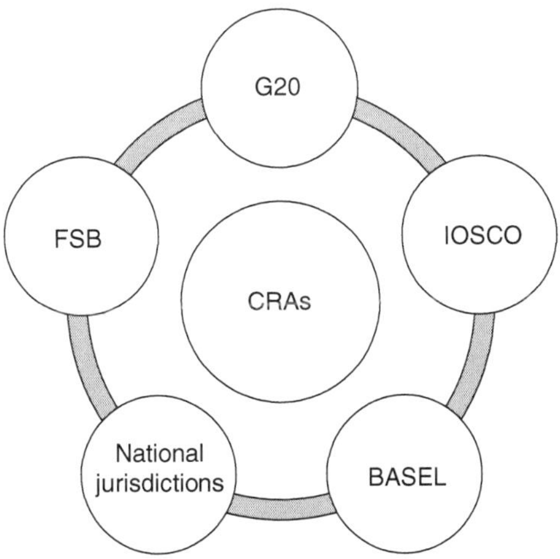

Figure 7.1 An overview of the international dynamic in favour of regulating CRAs' activities.

in 1999 led to the establishment of the G8. Members of the G7 and the G8 meet on a semi-annual basis for discussing economic policy issues as well as political and security matters. In addition to the annual meeting of heads of state and governments, annual meetings of foreign ministers and other ad hoc ministerial meetings take place.

The G20, the last born of the 'G' groups, was finally created in the aftermath of the Asian financial crisis, to allow the representation of emerging markets countries. The 20 nation members were actually selected by the original G7 and are in addition to the European Union: Argentina, Australia, Brazil, Canada, China, France, Germany, India, Indonesia, Italy, Japan, Republic of Korea, Mexico, Russia, Saudi Arabia, South Africa, Turkey, UK and US (G20). As can be seen, G20 members are well scattered around the globe and represent around 85 per cent of its gross domestic product, over 75 per cent of its global trade and two-thirds of its population (G20, members).[1] The main objective of the G20 members is try to exercise a continuous monitoring of the world economy. Finance ministers and central bank governors meet regularly to (DFATA, 2009):

i discuss ways to strengthen the global economy;
ii reform international financial institutions; and
iii improve financial regulation.

The G20 members also attribute the fundamental causes of the global deep financial disturbance to major failures in financial regulation and supervision of financial intermediaries and the financial sector. They are concerned and convinced that confidence in the financial system will be restored only if trust is rebuilt. A consensus among the G20 members has emerged and was embodied in the G20's 2009 declaration, known also as the London Declaration, concerning the strengthening of the financial system (the 'G20–2009 Declaration'), which firmly stated that all CRAs whose ratings are used for regulatory purposes should be subjected to a stricter regulatory oversight regime, that includes their registration with national monitoring authorities. The stated objective is to ensure that rating agencies 'meet the international code of good practice, particularly to prevent unacceptable conflicts of interest' (G20, 2009). More precisely, G20 members agreed that:

i All credit rating agencies whose ratings are used for regulatory purposes must register with a national/regional regulatory oversight authority and be submitted to its monitoring and control. Such a regulatory oversight system should be in line with the principles of the IOSCO Code of Conduct.
ii The IOSCO should coordinate member jurisdictions' regulatory regimes.
iii Monitoring frameworks in different environments should be consistent

across jurisdictions with appropriate sharing of information through IOSCO and between national authorities.

iv National authorities should be invited to enforce compliance and ask for changes in rating agencies' practices and procedures for guaranteeing transparency and quality of rating systems and managing conflicts of interest.

v Credit rating agencies should be required to provide full disclosure of their ratings track record and the information and assumptions that underpin the ratings process.

vi The Basel Committee is invited to continue its review of the use of CRAs' ratings in prudential regulation purpose and identify any adverse effect.

Three key international organizations were therefore entrusted with the implementation of the London Declaration provisions of the G20 that can be considered as the world policy towards agencies and has set up the foundations of a 'global regulatory reform agenda'. They are:

i the Financial Stability Board (FSB) for the follow up;

ii the International Organization of Securities Commissions (IOSCO) for the sharing of information and coordinating full compliance between the IOSCO CRA Code and member jurisdictions' regulatory regimes; and

iii the Basel Committee for the review on the role of external ratings in prudential regulation.

The following section will discuss the role of each one of these pillar international organizations in the build up to the recent process of CRAs' international regulatory oversight regime.

The Financial Stability Board

One of the international organizations entrusted with the implementation of the London Declaration provisions of the G20 is the FSB. The predecessor of the Financial Stability Board was the Financial Stability Forum (FSF), founded in 1999 by central bank governors and finance ministers from the G7 countries. It was then intended to bring together:

i national authorities responsible for financial stability;

ii sector-specific international groupings of regulators; and

iii supervisors and international financial institutions in charge of surveillance of domestic and international financial systems.

In 2009 the FSB was created by finance ministers and central bank governors from the G7 countries, in replacement of the FSF, and is hosted by the Bank for International Settlements. The FSB has its Secretariat located in Basel with a membership that includes, along with international organizations, Argentina, Australia, Brazil, Canada, China, France, Germany, Hong Kong, India, Indonesia, Italy, Japan, Mexico, Netherlands, Republic of Korea, Russia, Saudi Arabia, Singapore, South Africa, Spain, Switzerland, Turkey, United Kingdom and United States. Its main objective is coordinating, at the international level, the work of national financial authorities and international standard setting bodies and developing and promoting the implementation of effective regulatory, supervisory and other financial sector policies in the interest of financial stability. Within its mandate with the G20, the FSB took decisive actions towards more supervision of CRAs. It has, for instance:

- i endorsed the 2010 principles, approved by the G20 to reducing overreliance of authorities and financial institutions on CRA ratings;
- ii made in 2012 its Principles for Reducing Reliance on CRA Ratings endorsed by the G20 (G20, Gyeongju, Korea, 23 October 2012); and
- iii adopted in 2012 a roadmap to accelerate their implementation (Seoul Summit, 11–12 November 2010).

Typically the FSB invites large financial institutions not to rely anymore on CRA ratings mechanically and to develop their own capability to conduct their own credit assessment. It is believed that 'the wide and free availability of external ratings as a measure of risk has in all likelihood reduced financial institutions' private incentives to research and develop potential alternatives' (FSA *et al.*, 2013). Instead, they should master the risk of all assets that they hold and be able to prove that they have carried out the requisite level of due diligence (FSA *et al.*, 2013). One important thing that might render the FSB action towards CRAs more impacting is its membership that includes such international agencies (FSB website) as the Bank for International Settlements (BIS), European Central Bank (ECB), European Commission (EC), International Monetary Fund (IMF), Organisation for Economic Co-operation and Development (OECD) and the World Bank, international standard-setting bodies and other groupings, such as the Basel Committee on Banking Supervision (BCBS), Committee on the Global Financial System (CGFS), Committee on Payment and Settlement Systems (CPSS), International Association of Insurance Supervisors (IAIS), International Accounting Standards Board (IASB) and the International Organization of Securities Commissions (IOSCO).

IOSCO initiative

The other key international organization, entrusted with the implementation of the London Declaration provisions of the G20, is the International Organization of Securities Commissions (IOSCO), established in 1983 and considered as the international body that brings together the world's securities regulators. It imposed itself as the leading global standard setter for the world securities exchanges. Its membership includes over 120 securities regulators and 80 other securities markets participants (i.e. stock exchanges, financial regional and international organizations etc.) (IOSCO website). It currently regulates over 95 per cent of the world's securities markets and develops, implements 'and promotes adherence to internationally recognized standards for securities regulation, and is collaborating intensively with the G20 and the Financial Stability Board (FSB) on the global regulatory reform agenda' (IOSCO website). IOSCO derives its power from the G20's 2009 Declaration, assigning it the responsibility of coordinating member jurisdictions' regulatory regimes.

IOSCO was the first international organization to deal with the credit rating issue and has published its Code Fundamentals since 2003 that gained the G20 recognition (G20 2009 Declaration). The IOSCO Code for CRAs seems to be the product of intense discussions among many interested parties and is mainly intended to offer a set of 'robust, practical measures as a guide to and framework for CRAs with respect' (IOSCO, 2004a):

i protecting the integrity of the rating process;
ii ensuring that issuers and users of credit ratings, including investors, are treated fairly; and
iii safeguarding confidential material information provided them by issuers.

The main objective of the Code is therefore to promote informed, independent analyses and opinion by CRAs, as indicated in Figure 7.2 (IOSCO, 2014).

Figure 7.2 underlines the specific mechanisms CRAs can use 'to protect their analytical independence, eliminate or manage conflicts of interest, and help ensure the confidentiality of certain types of information shared with them by issuers' (IOSCO, 2004b). Structurally the fundamentals of the IOSCO Code are broken into three sections:

i The quality and integrity of the rating process: the IOSCO Code Fundamentals require credit agencies to incorporate in their code of conduct provisions showing how they deal with the quality, the integrity of their rating process, and the monitoring and updating of such rating process.
ii CRA independence and the avoidance of conflicts of interest: the IOSCO Code requires credit agencies to include in their code of conduct provisions 'that insure that the determination of a credit rating is influenced only by factors relevant to the credit assessment, to make sure of the quality of procedures and policies, and to insure analyst and employee independence' (IOSCO, 2004b).

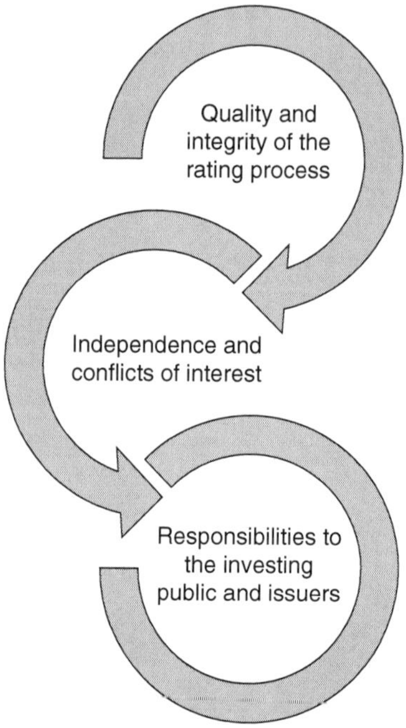

Figure 7.2 IOSCO's Code fundamentals.

iii CRA responsibilities to the investing public and issuers: the IOSCO Code requires credit agencies to include in their code of conduct provisions assuring transparency and timeliness of the rating process, and the confidential treatment of information.

According to IOSCO, CRAs should endeavour to issue ratings that aim at reducing the information asymmetry among market participants. Asymmetry of information usually occurs when one of the two parties involved in a transaction has access to more or superior information compared to the other. CRA ratings decisions should also be taken in all independence, i.e. away from any pressures or conflict of interest that may arise from ownership structure, business activities or employees' own interests. The term conflict of interest occurs when a fiduciary fails his trust obligation and acts for personal benefit. The IOSCO Code requires CRAs not only to incorporate into their own codes of conduct the IOSCO Code's provisions, but also to indicate how each provision is addressed. In case of non-incorporation of a specific provision, the reason should be disclosed and how otherwise its objective is addressed.

It seems that the IOSCO Code Fundamentals have gained much recognition, since their publication and 'CRAs of all sizes and methodologies are more aware of the concerns surrounding the credit rating industry and are taking steps to address those concerns' (IOSCO, 2009).

The Basel Committee for Banking Supervision

With members from Argentina, Australia, Belgium, Brazil, Canada, China, France, Germany, Hong Kong SAR, India, Indonesia, Italy, Japan, Korea, Luxembourg, Mexico, Netherlands, Russia, Saudi Arabia, Singapore, South Africa, Spain, Sweden, Switzerland, Turkey, United Kingdom and United States, the third key international organization entrusted with the implementation of the London Declaration provisions of the G20, is the Basel Committee for Banking Supervision (BCBS). It is also the primary global standard-setter for the prudential regulation of banks; it provides a forum for cooperation on banking supervisory matters. Its mandate is to strengthen the regulation, supervision and practices of banks worldwide with the purpose of enhancing financial stability. The BCBS reports to the Group of Governors and Heads of Supervision (GHOS) and advises supervisory authorities in all countries. The BCBS's secretariat is located at the Bank for International Settlements in Basel, Switzerland, and is staffed mainly by temporary transferred professional supervisors from member institutions. In addition it undertakes the secretarial work for the committee and its many expert sub-committees (BIS website).

The BCBS is the main user of CRAs' ratings in prudential supervisory activity within its standardized approach for capital requirements. Following, however, the G20–2009 Declaration, it engaged itself to reduce its reliance on CRAs' ratings in its securitization framework by 2014. The BCBS has indeed set up a Task Force on Standardized Approaches, with the objective of reducing or removing, where possible, the reliance on external ratings. The Task Force is studying whether appropriate alternatives to CRAs' ratings exist and 'is developing policy recommendations to reduce mechanistic reliance on ratings' (FSB, 2013). The BCBS is expected to come up with a consultative proposal, in line with the FSB roadmap timetable, on the review of standardized approaches. In considering potential alternatives to the use of CRAs' ratings for banking regulatory requirements, the BCBS is, however, facing the important challenge of identifying credible alternative standards of creditworthiness and is also aware of the difficulties related to reliance on banks' internal models. Any changes, warns the Bank of England, 'must be carefully assessed' (FSA *et al.*, 2013).

National jurisdictions

In line with the policy developed by the international community within the Financial Stability Board (FSB), IOSCO and the Basel Committee, other jurisdictions, such as the United States, the EU and also Australia, Canada and other countries are taking impacting actions to remove or replace references to CRA ratings for regulatory purposes, in their laws and regulations, always with the aim in mind of ensuring an international consistency to the global financial system. Many national jurisdictions have, indeed, adopted their own framework and rules for monitoring CRAs in their environment of control. This section will present the Securities and Exchange Commission (SEC) and the European Commission (EC) initiatives, and other countries' regulatory efforts.

CRAs' statutory framework and rules in the US

The Credit Rating Agency Reform Act of 2006 (SEC, 2006) and Dodd–Frank Wall Street Reform and Consumer Protection Act (Dodd–Frank Act) of 2010 are the main foundations of the US statutory framework for credit rating agencies. The Credit Rating Agency Reform Act gives authority to the SEC to implement a transparency rule to CRAs that register with the Commission as nationally recognized statistical rating organizations (NRSROs). US regulators first used credit ratings in the 1930s to limit the riskiness of assets held by regulated entities, though the practice has expanded significantly since the 1970s (Levich *et al.*, 2002) The Commission implemented the NRSRO registration and oversight programme created by the Rating Agency Act in 2007. It also amended several of its rules in February and December 2009, in accordance with the G20 Global Plan, with the goals of (SEC, 2013):

i further increasing the transparency of NRSRO rating methodologies;
ii strengthening the disclosures of rating performance; and
iii enhancing NRSRO record keeping.

In July 2010 the Dodd–Frank Act was enacted and amended Section 15E of the Securities Exchange Act of 1934 of the United States (the 'Exchange Act') to enhance the regulation, accountability and transparency of NRSROs. By adding Section 15E and amending Section 17 of the Exchange Act, the Rating Agency Act provided the Commission with rule-making authority in a variety of areas. The Commission adopted the six rules provided in appendix 1, in June 2007 (SEC, 2007). As required by the Dodd–Frank Act and in support of its mission of protecting investors, facilitating capital formation and maintaining fair, orderly and efficient markets, the SEC created the Office of Credit Ratings (OCR),[2] charged with administering the rules enacted by the Commission for NRSROs' supervision, with respect to:

i the practices of NRSROs in determining credit ratings, for the protection of users of credit ratings and in the public interest;
ii the promotion of accuracy in credit ratings issued by NRSROs;
iii ensuring that credit ratings are not unduly influenced by conflicts of interest; and
iv helping to ensure that firms provide greater disclosure to investors.

Table 7.1 Agencies with NRSRO registration, as of December 2013

Agency	*Country*
A.M. Best Company, Inc. (AMB)	US
DBRS, Inc. (DBRS)	Canada
Egan-Jones Ratings Company (EJR)	US
Fitch Ratings, Inc. (Fitch)	US
HR Ratings de México, SA de CV (HR)	Mexico
Japan Credit Rating Agency, Ltd (JCR)	Japan
Kroll Bond Rating Agency, Inc. (KBRA)	US
Moody's Investors Service, Inc. (Moody's)	US
Morningstar Credit Ratings, LLC (Morningstar)	US
Standard & Poor's Ratings Services (S&P)	US

Source: SEC, 2013.

In order to assess and promote compliance with statutory and Commission requirements and in support of this mission, OCR monitors the activities and conducts examinations of registered NRSROs. The list of agencies with NRSRO certification appearing in the SEC Annual Certifications report for the year ended 31 December 2013, Item 7A is provided by Table 7.1.

All agencies with NRSRO registration are from the United States or from a country member of the North American Free Trade Agreement (NAFTA), except for the Japanese JCR. The two other NRSRO agencies that are non-US, are DBRS from Canada and HR Ratings from Mexico. It appears that each group wants to have an axe to grind and defends its own interests first. The NRSRO status is granted only to agencies with appropriate experience. The SEC recognizes the difficulty of reconciling its willingness to encourage new entrants with their limited experience.

The SEC at the beginning of 2014 amended its rules in order to remove where appropriate, references to external credit ratings.

CRAs' statutory framework in the European Commission

The EC rules are broadly in line with the policy developed by the international community within the FSB and the Basel Committee. Consequently, in accordance with G20 recommendations, the European Commission published in 2009 a proposal of regulating credit rating agencies (Regulation (EC), No. 1060/2009), which was amended in 2011 by Regulation (EC) No. 513/2011. Accordingly the European Securities and Markets Authority (ESMA), was also put in charge for carrying out policy work to prepare future legislation, such as regulatory technical standards, and guidelines. This work is undertaken through the CRA technical committee, which has representatives from all the national competent authorities. ESMA was declared to be exclusively responsible for the registration and supervision of credit rating agencies in the European Union and was required to:

i establish a central repository (CEREP)

> where credit rating agencies shall make available information on their historical performance data including the ratings transition frequency and information about credit ratings issued in the past and on their changes. The CEREP allows users to search, filter, download and print statistics for individual CRAs for time periods of varying length and different rating types.
>
> (ESMA)

ii define the standardized form in which the credit rating agencies shall provide information to that repository;
iii ensuring accessibility of information to the public;
iv publish summary information on the main developments observed on an annual basis;
v submit draft regulatory technical standards for endorsement by the Commission on the presentation of the information, 'including structure, format, method and period of reporting, that credit rating agencies shall to the central repository' (ESMA).

Table 7.2 gives the list of registered and certified CRAs as 3 June 2013 in accordance with Regulation (EC) No. 1060/2009 of the European Parliament and of the Council of 16 September 2009 on credit rating agencies (the Credit Rating Agencies Regulation).

Of the 37 agencies listed with ESMA on January 2014, 12 agencies are affiliated to one of the Big 3, Moody's, Standard & Poor's or Fitch. Nine agencies are German, seven from UK, three Italian, two French and two Spanish.

The European CRA-3 Regulations focused on registration, conduct of business and supervision (European Commission, Memo of 18 June 2013). ESMA has been entrusted since July 2011 with responsibility for registering and directly supervising credit agencies in the EU. In order for credit rating agencies to be registered with ESMA, they must fulfil a number of obligations relative to the conduct of their business, that are all intended to ensure the independence and integrity of their rating processes and to enhance the quality of the ratings they issue. The previous Regulation (CRA-I) required also credit rating agencies to avoid conflicts of interest, for instance: any rating analyst employed by a credit rating agency should not rate an entity in which he/she has an ownership interest; to ensure the quality of ratings, requiring, for example, the ongoing monitoring of credit ratings; rating methodologies should be rigorous and systematic; and a high level of transparency, meaning

Table 7.2 Agencies with EC registration, as of June 2013

Name of CRA	*Country of residence*	*Name of CRA*	*Country of residence*
Euler Hermes Rating GmbH	Germany	Moody's Investors Service Cyprus Ltd	Cyprus
Japan Credit Rating Agency Ltd	Japan	Moody's France SAS	France
Feri EuroRating Services AG	Germany	Moody's Deutschland GmbH	Germany
BCRA-Credit Rating Agency AD	Bulgaria	Moody's Italia Srl	Italy
Creditreform Rating AG	Germany	Moody's Investors Service España SA	Spain
Scope Ratings GmbH	Germany	Moody's Investors Service Ltd	UK
ICAP Group SA	Greece	Standard & Poor's Credit Market Services France SAS	France
GBB-Rating Gesellschaft für Bonitätsbeurteilung mbH	Germany	Standard & Poor's Credit Market Services Italy Srl	Italy
ASSEKURATA Assekuranz Rating-Agentur GmbH	Germany	Standard & Poor's Credit Market Services Europe Limited	UK
ARC Ratings, SA (previously Companhia Portuguesa de Rating, SA)	Portugal	CRIF SpA	Italy
AM Best Europe-Rating Services Ltd (AMBERS)	UK	Capital Intelligence (Cyprus) Ltd	Cyprus
DBRS Ratings Limited	UK	European Rating Agency, AS	Slovakia
Fitch France SAS	France	Axesor SA	Spain
Fitch Deutschland GmbH	Germany	CERVED Group SpA	Italy
Fitch Italia SpA	Italy	Kroll Bond Rating Agency	USA
Fitch Polska SA	Poland	The Economist Intelligence Unit Ltd	UK
Fitch Ratings España SAU	Spain	Dagong Europe Credit Rating Srl	Italy
Fitch Ratings Limited	UK	Spread Research	France
Fitch Ratings CIS Limited	UK		

Source: ESMA, at: www.esma.europa.eu/.

periodically reporting. ESMA has also been given comprehensive investigatory powers, allowing it:

i to require from registered agencies any document or data considered significant;
ii to summon and hear persons, to conduct on-site inspections; and
iii to impose administrative sanctions, fines and periodic penalty payments.

CRA-1 and CRA-2 European regulations have already strengthened disclosure requirements and enabled effective enforcement of those requirements by ESMA. ESMA made new proposals in 2011, aiming the to reinforce the existing regulatory framework and remedying their outstanding weaknesses. They enter into application in 2013 and, as of that date, credit rating agencies have to follow stricter rules, which make them more accountable for their ratings. The new rules also aim to reducing over-reliance on credit ratings while at the same time improving the quality of the rating process. Agencies registered with ESMA are submitted to annual transparency reports, similar to NRSROs' transparency requirements

At the beginning of 2014 and in accordance with the European Credit Rating Agencies Regulation (CRA-3), ESMA has reviewed all its existing guidelines and recommendations in order to identify, and where appropriate remove, references to external credit ratings that could trigger sole or mechanistic reliance on such ratings.

Although the EU and US approaches to CRAs' monitoring share certain common principles like better governance, greater transparency and strict requirements concerning conflicts of interest, their philosophies are not the same. US authorities, for instance, believe that, by eliminating a regulatory requirement for ratings and transparency, they can re-establish a competitive, reputation-driven market for ratings. By contrast, because EU authorities are more preoccupied by ratings shopping, it doesn't suggest any market-driven regulation and aim to promote CRAs' accountability through supervision (UKEssays, 2010).

Other jurisdictions' CRA statutory frameworks

According to the Financial Stability Board 'robust transparency requirements are a fundamental component of the CRA registration and oversight programs administered by IOSCO members' (FSB, 2013). Indeed, in accordance with international regulations, many other IOSCO members besides the US and the EC have initiated their own regulatory frameworks for rating agencies. Australia, for instance, required since 1 January 2010, all CRAs operating in the country to hold an Australian financial services (AFS) licence. A CRA may choose to apply for an AFS licence that either authorizes it to issue credit ratings to retail and wholesale clients (retail authorization), or to wholesale clients only (wholesale authorization) (Australian Securities and Investments Commission website). For their part, Canadian securities regulators adopted in 2012 a new regulatory regime for credit rating agencies that want to have their credit ratings eligible for use in securities legislation (Shecter, 2012). CRAs are required to apply to become a 'designated rating organization' and adhere to rules concerning conflicts of interest, governance, conduct, a compliance function and required filings.[3] The Monetary Authority of Singapore (MAS) has also implemented a regulatory framework for CRAs with effect from 17 January 2012. CRAs become subject to licensing obligations. CRAs will be required to comply with existing Regulations, Guidelines and Notices under the Securities and Futures Act that apply to all capital markets services licensees. In addition, CRAs will also have to comply with a new Code of Conduct for CRAs that MAS will introduce in conjunction with establishing of a regulatory regime for CRAs (Asiatrading). Most developed economies have indeed implemented laws and regulations that require CRAs to disclose information 'about rating methodologies, rating performance, conflicts of interest, and other operational matters' (FSB, 2013).

Although, the US has moved the furthest in removing references to ratings in statutory frameworks, the EU has also made significant progress in this direction (FSB, 2013). The challenge is to identify credible alternative standards of creditworthiness. Competition among CRAs is, however, considered to be the best enhancing factor of reducing the mechanistic reliance on ratings, enforcing transparency and disclosure that enables the comparability of different CRAs, and removing unnecessary barriers to entry. Transparency and disclosure are also key reforms particularly with regard to securitizations and covered bonds, where the complexity of the products and lack of transparency around underlying asset pools renders them difficult to deal with.

Conclusion

Thanks to a well-orchestrated international regulatory initiative, backed up by the US and the EU, and reinforced by international standard setters,[4] there are now rules in many jurisdictions providing their members with guidance on steps to further discourage reliance on CRA ratings, and will facilitate sharing of ideas and best practices amongst their membership (FSB, 2013), CRAs seem to have started strengthening their disclosure and sanitize their governance. Although jurisdictions have faced different starting positions, the US has made the most progress in weaning itself off credit ratings agencies, followed by the EU. There are, however, dissident voices, the United Kingdom authorities (FSA *et al.*, 2013) believe that 'an effective reform package should be more narrowly focused on the key priorities that address the remaining causes of instability associated with credit ratings'. It is, however, important to underline that regulation will only work in the absence of sound principles. CRAs must therefore be encouraged to learn how to behave themselves ethically and efficiently and the two next chapters will tell if this is possible.

Notes

1 See www.g20.org/about_g20/g20_members, retrieved 26 September 2014.
2 The OCR is located in New York and Washington, DC, and is staffed with examiners, attorneys and accountants with expertise in structured finance, corporate finance, municipal finance, financial institutions, insurance companies and credit rating agencies.
3 New standards are consistent with international regimes, www.investmentexecutive.com/-/csa-adopts-regulatory-regime-for-credit-rating-agencies, retrieved 26 October 2013.
4 IOSCO on disclosure and accounting, market intermediaries and investment management, International Association of Insurance Supervisors on insurers, and Organisation for Economic Co-operation and Development on pension funds.

Bibliography

Asiaetrading, at: http://asiaetrading.com/mas-introduces-regulatory-framework-for-credit-rating-agencies/, retrieved 27 October 2013.

Australian Securities and Investments Commission (ASIC) website at: www.asic.gov.au/asic/asic.nsf/byheadline/Disclosure-of-credit-ratings-in Australia?OpenDocument/, retrieved 26 October 2013.

Baklanova, V. (2009), 'Regulatory use of credit ratings: how it impacts the behaviour or market constituents', *International Finance Review*, Vol. 10, pp. 65–104, at: http://ssrn.com/abstract=1378627/, retrieved 12 December 2013.

Bank for International Settlements (BIS) website at: www.bis.org/, retrieved 20 March 2014.

Barrett, Paul M. (2014), 'A $5 billion U.S. fraud case against Standard & Poor's enters critical phase', Bloomberg, 16 January, at: www.businessweek.com/articles/2014-01-16/5-billion-u-dot-s-dot-fraud-case-against-standard-and-poors-enters-critical-phase, retrieved 28 January 2014.

Basel Committee on Banking Supervision (BCBS) website, at: www.bis.org/bcbs/, retrieved 20 March 2014.

Department of Foreign Affairs and Trade, Government of Australia (DFATA), website at: www.dfat.gov.au/trade/g20/, retrieved 23 June 2014.

European Commission (EC) (2013), 'Memo on new rules on credit rating agencies (CRAs) enter into force: frequently asked questions', at: http://europa.eu/rapid/press-release_MEMO-13–571_en.htm, retrieved 4 May 2014.

Financial Stability Board (FSB) website at: www.financialstabilityboard.org/about/overview.htm, retrieved 11 October 2013.

Financial Stability Board (FSB) (2013), 'Credit rating agencies reducing reliance and strengthening oversight, progress report to the St Petersburg G20 Summit', 29 August, at: www.financialstabilityboard.org/press/pr_130905.htm, retrieved 20 March 2014.

FSA, HM Treasury and Bank of England (2013), 'The United Kingdom authorities response to the European Commission internal market and services consultation document on credit rating agencies', at: https://circabc.europa.eu/d/d/workspace/SpacesStore/0d1ea101-b6d0-470b-b8b3-e28e4c1cba30/BoE-FSA-Treasury_EN.pdf, retrieved 2 July 2014.

G20 website at: https://www.g20.org/about_g20/g20_members, retrieved 20 March 2014.

G20 (2009), 'Global plan annex: declaration on strengthening the financial system', at: www.g20.utoronto.ca/2009/2009ifi.pdf, retrieved 20 March 2014.

G20 (2012), 'The meeting of finance ministers and central bank governors', Gyeongju, Korea, 23 October 2012.

International Organization of Securities Commissions (IOSCO) website at: www.iosco.org/about/, retrieved 20 March 2014.

International Organization of Securities Commissions (IOSCO) (2004a), 'Code of conduct fundamental for credit rating agencies', December.

International Organization of Securities Commissions (IOSCO) (2004b), 'IOSCO release code of conduct fundamentals for credit rating agencies', Media release, at: www.fsa.go.jp/inter/ios/f-20041224-3/02.pdf, retrieved 24 March 2014.

International Organization of Securities Commissions (IOSCO) (2009), 'A review of implementation of the IOSCO code of conduct fundamentals for credit rating agencies', Technical Committee of the International Organization of Securities Commissions, at: www.iosco.org/library/pubdocs/pdf/IOSCOPD271.pdf, retrieved 27 March 2014.

International Organization of Securities Commissions (IOSCO) (2014), 'Consultation report titled Code of Conduct Fundamentals for Credit Rating Agencies'.

Levich, R.M., G. Majnoni and C. Reinhart (eds) (2002), *Ratings, rating agencies and the global financial system*. New York: Kluwer Academic Publishers.

Securities and Exchange Commission (SEC) (2006), 'The Credit Rating Agency Reform Act', at: www.sec.gov/divisions/marketreg/ratingagency/cra-reform-act-2006.pdf/, retrieved 2 June 2013.

Securities and Exchange Commission (SEC) (2007), 'Annual report on nationally recognized statistical rating organizations', at: www.sec.gov/ retrieved 29 March, 2014.

Securities and Exchange Commission (SEC) (2013), 'Annual report on nationally recognized statistical rating organizations', at: www.sec.gov/ retrieved 29 March, 2014.

Securities and Exchange Commission (SEC) 'Dodd–Frank Wall Street Reform and Consumer Protection Act' 'Dodd–Frank Act', at: www.sec.gov/about/offices/ocr/ocr-about.shtml/, retrieved 29 October 2013.

Shecter, B. (2012), 'Canada imposes oversight on credit rating agencies', at: http://business.financialpost.com/author/bshecter/, retrieved 6 May 2013.

UKessays (2010), 'Problems of the credit rating agencies', at: www.ukessays.com/dissertations/economics/problems-of-the-credit-rating-agencies.php, retrieved 3 March 2014.

Wikipedia website, at: http://en.wikipedia.org/wiki/First_Amendment_to_the_United_States_Constitution, retrieved July 4, 2014.

8 Credit rating agencies

Internal monitoring

Introduction

The previous chapter shows how strong is the determination of the international community to monitor credit agencies in order to correct their perceived behavioural gaps. One main reason that may have motivated such public intervention in credit ratings affairs is the weakness of their internal oversight mechanisms. CRAs can therefore ease much of the regulatory pressure they are submitted to, by having efficiently operated internal structures. The structure of ownership and the functioning of the board regarding rating oversight may affect the accuracy of the ratings and the independence of agencies. This chapter is intended to have a close look into rating agencies' ownership, and board of directors and management team efficiency in ensuring rating quality. It suggests implementing Rating Committees of the Board as a mean of improving rating accuracy.

Additional to the introduction, the second section discusses the dynamic of CRAs' organizational structure; the third section underlines the impact of the separation of power and credit ratings accuracy; the fourth section emphasizes the effect of ownership on credit rating accuracy; the fifth section analyses internal credit rating monitoring in agencies; the sixth discusses the result of the SORT analysis; and the final section concludes the chapter.

The dynamic of CRAs' organizational structure

The board derives its legitimacy and power from the shareholders of the organization who elect its members. As members of the board owes a duty of care and duty of loyalty to the organization, they owe the same duties and care to shareholders, as they are considered their fiduciaries during the performance of their function. The board, through its members, establishes strategies and policies relating to the management of the organization, makes decisions on major issues of concern to the organization and ensures their implementation by overseeing the management. Further, section 15E(t)(3) of the SEC entrusts the board within credit agencies with additional responsibilities and the following are underlined:

i 'The Board must oversee: the establishment, maintenance, and enforcement of policies and procedures for determining credit ratings and to address, manage, and disclose any conflicts of interest' (SEC, 2013b).
ii 'The effectiveness of internal controls for determining ratings; and compensation and promotion policies and practices' (SEC, 2013b).

The efficiency with which the board is operated in credit agencies, can have an impacting effect on the whole efficiency of the agency and so on the quality of its governance, but also on the accuracy of its ratings. Rating agencies' governance presents own specification, as it can be seen as a system by which agencies are governed, but also a system by which ratings are developed and communicated, in addition to being sincere, proactive and spontaneous in communicating with internal and external issuers and rating users. As indicated in Figure 8.1, such communication should be largely based on a sound relationship between the five main stakeholders of agencies, namely: owners, the board of directors, the management team, ratings users and regulators.

As for any organization, a credit agency's board should play the strategic role of constituting the interface platform, linking all organizational stakeholders to each other. The board should set the strategy of the rating agency, and by doing so it will give the agency the appropriate strategic direction that impacts virtually everything it does. The identification of right strategy is the starting point for agency independence, transparency and success. The board has also a vital role to play by overseeing the implementation of agency strategy and codes of conduct and making sure

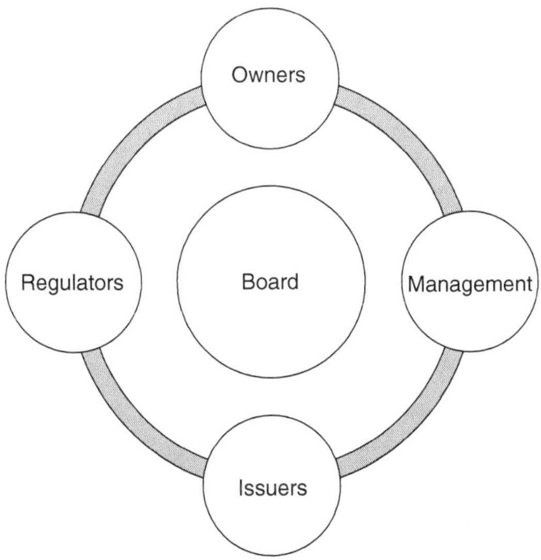

Figure 8.1 The credit rating governance structure.

they are translated into daily practice by the management. This can, however, be challenging area, as it may require directors to thoroughly understand their rating organization and its industry, including its emerging trends and risks. Only if equipped with the right information and disposing of the necessary time, can the directors fulfil their roles efficiently and 'engage in robust discussion that allows them to contribute to the enhancement of agency governance. Ideally directors' involvement should help the agency adopt a strategy that is most likely to enhance issuers' satisfaction and ultimately shareholder value' (PWC, 2014).

Board members are nominated (elected) by agencies' owners and the main role of the board of directors in credit rating agencies, like in any other organization, should be the hiring of the most capable management team (CEO) for the job, as the management team should be held responsible for the quality of the ratings. Such responsibility can, however, only be fulfilled when two conditions are met:

i when the appropriate and competent analytical staff is selected and hired;
ii when the effective supervision of rating operations is ensured, without interference with rating processes.

Usually governance problems arise when these guidelines are not respected, resulting in conflicts triggering, especially whenever supervisors interfere with the day-to-day rating operations. A challenge for an agency's board is to appear either too active or too passive, in both cases reproaches may be harvested. Passive ownership can lead to the full control of the agency by its management and managed parameters may not always be in the interest of all stakeholders. While active ownership may allow some agencies' boards to intervene for their own benefit, in the rating process, this may put the independence of the ratings to the test. By contrast, agency management should not be responsible for the agency's strategic orientation; the power separation between the board and the management is a major governance requirement for credit rating agencies, as the independence and effectiveness of ratings depend on it.

The structure of a board and the planning of its work can be key elements to effective governance and establishment of committees can be one way of enhancing the work of the board, thereby strengthening its governance role. Generally, board committees focus on specific board activity areas, allowing the board to concentrate on broader and strategic issues and orientation. Board committees can be of two types: standing and ad hoc. The first deals with ongoing issues, internal control for instance, while the latter deals with specific issues that are ad hoc in nature. One standing committee can specifically be of very high importance for a CRA's board, although such a committee does not currently appear to exist within rating agencies' structure, namely 'the Standing Rating Committee' of the Board

(SRCB) whose primary purpose should be the overseeing of the rating activities by the board and should have the same power as the Audit Committee. CRAs do have technical rating committees whose role is the technical study of ratings, not to be confounded with the suggested SRCBs. In the absence of an SRCB, agencies should have the activities of audit committees extended to cover rating activities. One way of ensuring SRCBs within CRAs is by upgrading existing credit policy groups (CPGs). Indeed, the main agencies do have CPGs, which are supposed to be a key part of the control and analytical support framework. Although, they seem to be independent of and separate from the ratings teams, they also seem to have limited access to the board, except for Moody's, as will be discussed in the next chapter.

Further, if the credit rating governance system is to be efficient and the ratings to be produced accurate, it is necessary that a sound relationship exists between the board and the management team, and their respective responsibilities must be clarified and clearly separated. The board of directors should elect the CEO, and lay down the strategic direction to be followed, and management should put into practice such strategic orientations and periodically provide the board with all the necessary operating and financial information, as well as progress reports. Specific to CRAs, the management should allow some kind of rating quality control to operate an independent rating quality control. The power sharing within credit agencies should therefore be threefold:

i between shareholders and the board (S-B);
ii between the board and the management (B-M);
iii between the management and the rating quality control, that can be embodied by a Standing Rating Committee of the Board (SRCB) with the necessary power and direct access to the board (M-RC).

Following the recent financial crisis persistent need has arisen for a more balanced relationship based on confidence between agencies and their main stakeholders. Such confidence can only be guaranteed through transparency. This need has put rating agencies under growing pressure to publish more information about their processes of rating, methodologies, metrics and so on (see Chapter 7). Further, for a rating governance programme to be successful, agencies should increase the participation of rating users in rating processes. Rating issuers and users are agencies' partners, as such they should be allowed to participate and stay informed of the strategic decisions taken by the rating agencies and those responsible for them. For this to happen, agencies are invited to bring the issuer/investor relations area within the board's scope, thus communicating information like board members' profiles and compensation, policies on sustainability, management of conflicts and risks, internal controls, as well as corporate culture and ethics (PWC, 2014). Regulators have taken the necessary steps for making agencies communicate some information regarding their independence, transparency and methodologies of rating, but they do not deal specifically with internal considerations. Consequently, as represented in Figure 8.1, in order to assess the efficiency of credit rating agencies' organizational structure for the sake of rating accuracy, four elements are to be considered crucial, namely:

i the separation of power;
ii the ownership structure;
iii the rating monitoring; and
iv the transparency.

These SORT elements will be used in this chapter to test the effect the Big 3's organizational structures may have on rating accuracy.

The Big 3's organizational structures

Agencies have different organizational structures; their description will help assessing the accuracy of the ratings performed by them, based on SORT elements. Figure 8.2, derived from NRSRO Forms of Fitch Inc., Moody's Corporation and McGraw Hill Financial Inc., dated 27 March 2013, illustrates their respective structure.

Panel 1 (Figure 8.2) represents the Fitch Group organizational structure, previously known as Fitch Ratings and currently has three subsidiaries:

i Fitch Ratings provides 'core' products and services including public and private ratings, credit assessments, the issuance of preliminary or indicative ratings and rating assessments (Fitch Ratings, 2010).
ii Fitch Solutions, is an affiliate of Fitch Ratings and subsidiary of the Fitch Group, Inc., the parent entity of Fitch Ratings. It provides market-implied ratings, which include credit default swap (CDS) implied ratings and equity implied ratings.
iii Fitch Training, an affiliate of Fitch Ratings, is a training firm focused on the provision of credit and corporate finance training.

Panel 2 (Figure 8.2), on the other hand, derived from NRSRO Forms of Moody's Corporation and dated 27 March 2013, illustrates Moody's organizational structure. Moody's Corporation (NYSE: MCO) is the parent company of Moody's Investors Service, and Moody's Analytics. Moody's Investors Service provides credit ratings and research covering debt instruments and securities, while Moody's Analytics, offers leading-edge software, advisory services and research for credit and economic analysis and financial risk management (Moody's).

Finally, panel 3 (Figure 8.2) presents McGraw Hill Financial, Inc. organizational structure, which has two subsidiaries:

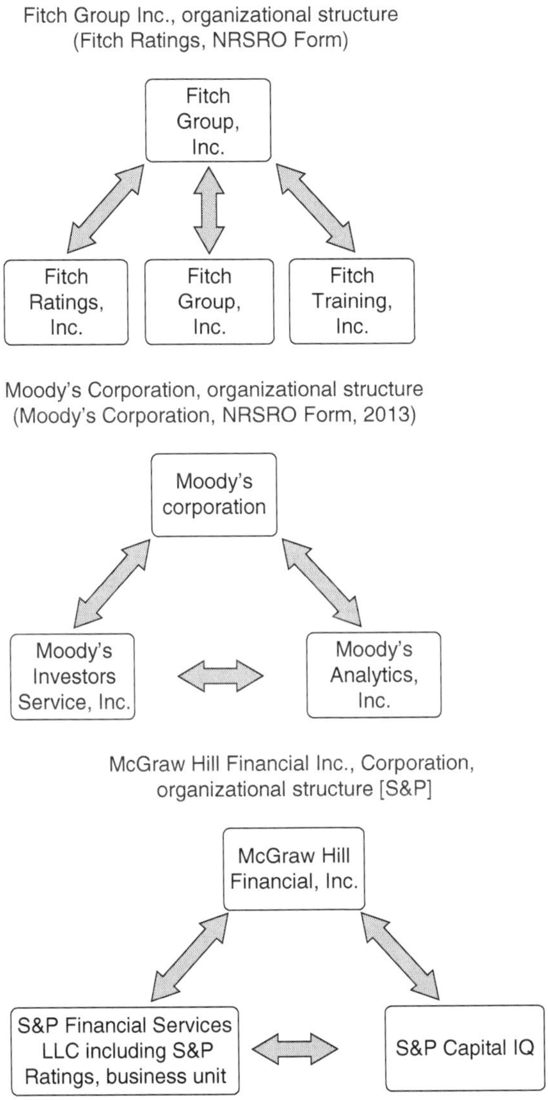

Figure 8.2 The Big 3's organizational structures (sources: adapted from Fitch Ratings, NRSRO Form, 27 March 2013, Exhibit 4; Moody's Corporation, NRSRO Form, 27 March 2013, Exhibit 4; and McGraw Hill Financial Inc., NRSRO Form, 27 March 2013, Exhibit 4).

i S&P Financial services LLC, which includes the S&P Ratings Business Unit; and
ii S&P Capital, IQ, S&P financial services providing credit ratings to investors as well as financial information on stocks, mutual funds, corporate bonds and municipal bonds.

S&P Capital IQ is not part of the registered NRSRO, and is described as a separate segment of the McGraw Hill Companies (S&P NSRO Form).[1] It provides a variety of financial and analytical products to a variety of clients (S&P's NRSRO Form, 2013).

Among the Big 3, Moody's is the only agency that operates its rating activity as an independent corporation.

Separation of power and credit rating accuracy

The separation of power between shareholders/owners and the board (S-B), between the board and the management (B-M) and between the management teams and rating quality control teams (M-RC), is a major enhancing factor of CRAs' efficiency and ratings accuracy. Shareholders/owners, as supreme organization controllers, actually delegate their authority to the board, via the election of directors. The main role of the board of directors in a credit rating agency, as underlined, should be the hiring of the most knowledgeable management team for the rating job and setting agency overall orientation and strategies; while the role of the management team is the operationalization of these rating directions and strategies. Finally, the role rating quality control is to ensure the accuracy of credit ratings and reporting to the board. Evaluating the quality of the separation of power, between owners, board, management and quality control teams, in the Big 3 seems to be more difficult than in other organizations. Of the three major global credit agencies, only Moody's (a spin off of the Dun & Bradstreet Corporation in 1999) has become a publicly traded corporation. The two other major credit ratings agencies, Standard & Poor's and Fitch, are managed by their controlling companies. Standard & Poor's is a subsidiary of McGraw Hill, a major publishing company with a strong business information focus, while Fitch Ratings is a jointly owned subsidiary of two private companies, Hearst Corporation and Fimlac.

The relation between management teams and rating quality control teams in the Big 3 is not clear, although most agencies assert the existence of such independence but there are no real rules guaranteeing it. We cannot therefore assume, beyond any doubt, that the separation of power between the board and the management, and the management and rating quality control teams within credit rating agencies, is always fully encountered, like there is no sufficient proof that management of each Big 3 enjoys all the independence it needs to fulfil the ratings independently, or rating quality control teams to ensure their accuracy.

Big 3 ownership and credit rating accuracy

Among the Big 3 only Moody's exercises its rating activities as a separate corporation. This section gives an overview of major shareholders of Moody's Corporation, but also those of McGraw Hill as controlling

Table 8.1 Big 3 shareholding and ownership breakdown, as of February 2014

Shareholders	*Moody's*	*McGraw Hill*	*Fitch Ratings*
% of shares held by all insider and 5% owners	0	3	–
% of shares held by institutional and mutual fund owners	96	87	–
Number of institutions holding shares	468	552	–
Others	–	–	100%

Source: adapted from diverse SEC NRSRO Forms.

company of Standard & Poor's and Hearst Corporation and Fimlac as controlling interests of Fitch Ratings. Table 8.1 gives the breakdown of the Big 3 shareholding and ownership, as at beginning of 2014, as collected from agencies' diverse NRSRO Forms, submitted to the SEC.

In their majority, Moody's shareholders are institutional and mutual fund owners. As indicated in Table 8.1, as of February 2014, 468 institutions hold 96 per cent of Moody's outstanding shares and the percentage of shares held by all insider and '5% owners' is insignificant. Major direct holders are: Berkshire Hathaway Inc. (number of shares unknown), McDaniel Raymond W. with 185,491 shares, Almeida Mark with 113,782, McKinnell Henry A with 112,153 and Cantor Richard with 55,678. McGraw Hill shareholders, as Standard & Poor's controlling company, are also, in the majority, institutional and mutual fund owners. As indicated in Table 8.1, 552 institutions hold McGraw Hill shares, as of February 2014, representing 87 per cent of all McGraw Hill outstanding shares. The percentage of shares held by all insider and '5% owners' is only 3 per cent. As of February 2014, major direct holders (Yahoo Finance) of McGraw Hill shares are: Graw Harold III, with 2,175,796 shares, Vittor Keneth M., with 127,296 shares, Peterson Douglas, with 122,289 shares, Teschner Charles L. JR, with 76,783 shares and Smyth D. Edward I, with 61,928 shares. Fitch Rating shareholding does not include any institutional or mutual fund owners. Fitch is rather owned by two family groups. Fimalac and Hearst Corporation are, indeed, the controlling entities of Fitch rating, with 50 per cent of ownership each; they are two groups, where the family plays a decisive role. In fact, Fimalac does not seem to have any board at all and Hearst has a board of five members with committees. Fimalac is in the ownership of one individual, the French businessman Marc Eugène Charles Ladreit de Lacharrière and was created by him in 1991. He serves as the CEO, and holds 100 per cent of the shares of the FIMALAC Group, which holds 80 per cent of Fimalac. Hearst Corporation, the other 50 per cent owner of Fitch Ratings, is a multinational mass media family group, founded by William Randolph Hearst as an owner of newspapers. The company's holdings have subsequently expanded to include a highly diversified portfolio of media interests. The Hearst family is involved in the ownership and management of the corporation.

Given the ownership structure described, the voluntary policy of opacity followed by the Big 3 may have increased the incentive to acquire information privately, for those users in a position of exploiting it profitably, like institutional investors (Bushman *et al.*, 2004). The opacity of firms' financial reporting is likely to be an important factor in determining the extent of the benefit an informed rating user can withdraw. Overall, there are compelling reasons to believe that the extent of institutional investors' informed trading could be increasing in the opacity of agencies' financial reporting (Maffett, 2011). The Big 3's shareholding and ownership breakdown presented in Table 8.1 seems to point to the existence of strong ties to financial institutions and/or family groups. This kind of ownership structure may present a serious risk of conflict of interest and eventually allow sophisticated investors to take advantage of agencies' opacity (the unavailability of specific information). The SEC relates two situations where an agency may succumb to a conflict of interest (SEC, 2012), as discussed in Chapter 6, when, for instance, an agency acts according to the desire of an influential client and when it is aware that such client wishes to acquire a particular security. According to the SEC, however, 'these potential conflicts are mitigated to the extent that subscribers [may] have different interests with respect to an upgrade or downgrade of a particular security' (SEC, 2012).

Internal credit rating monitoring

In this section we will assess the Big 3's boards' efficiency in exercising their effective monitoring on credit rating activities. To effectively oversee rating activity, CRAs' boards need well-defined and complete credit rating policies. The mere existence of such policies will not, however, be enough to ensure board efficiency. Indeed, if the Big 3's boards depend solely on reports supplied by the CEOs, asserting there is compliance with policies, they may fall short in their monitoring responsibilities. A good practice is to undertake periodically policy compliance audits that each time should focus on different selected policies. While board members could undertake such a direct audit themselves, they barely have the time, or the capacity to do so. Therefore, such work, as we suggested in the previous section, should be entrusted with a special standing committee of the board, which can recourse to external resources, the Standing Rating Committee of the Board (SRCB). In the case of absence of an SRCB its monitoring activity should be specifically entrusted to the audit committee of the board (AC). As indicated, the SRCBs should be distinguished from the technical rating committees, operating at the analytical level in most agencies. The main objective of SRCBs should be the coordination of rating oversight and

Table 8.2 Board oversight of credit rating activity within the Big 3

Agency	*Board*	*Standing Rating Committee of the Board (SRCB), or equivalent*	*Compliance audit*
Moody's	Yes	Yes	No
Standard and Poor's	No	No	No
Fitch	Fitch Rating Ltd	Yes	Fitch Credit Policy Group

direct reporting to the board. Table 8.2 gives an overview of board oversight of credit rating activity within the Big 3.

As we know, of the Big 3, only Moody's has its own board of directors and of the five members composing Moody's board, two directors only come from Moody's Corporation. The role of the board at Moody's is setting 'high standards for the Company's employees, officers and directors. Implicit in this philosophy is the importance of sound corporate governance' (Moody's, 'Corporate governance'). 'To fulfil its responsibilities and to discharge its duty, the Board relies on three committees' (Moody's website). Moody's Investors Service (MIS)[2] committee, is of special interest to this chapter, for its monitoring role of rating activity. Moody's MIS Committee is composed of at least three directors, including a chairman, as appointed by the board upon the recommendation of the Governance and Compensation Committee. At least half of the members of the MIS Committee including the chairman must meet independence requirements of section 15E(t)(2)(B) of the Exchange Act. Its duties and responsibilities are summarized in the following, as reported by Moody's Investors Service Committee Chart:

i the overseeing, the establishment, the maintenance, and the enforcement of MIS's policies and procedures for determining credit ratings and for addressing, managing, and disclosing any conflicts of interest;
ii the overseeing of the effectiveness of MIS's internal control system with respect to policies and procedures for determining credit ratings; and
iii the overseeing of the compensation and promotion policies and practices of MIS and of MIS's compliance and governance processes, including the performance of the credit policy function.

Standard & Poor's, as an affiliate of McGraw Hill, is submitted to the oversight of the McGraw Hill board of directors, composed of 13 members. According to McGraw Hill its board oversees the company's business and affairs pursuant to the Corporation Law and Incorporation and By-Laws, under the Company's Certificate of Incorporation. McGraw Hill underlines that its board 'is strongly committed to the highest standards of corporate governance'. Of the five Committees of the Board of McGraw Hill there is no Rating Committee of the Board, and there is no other Committee that can fill its function. According to the McGraw Hill Audit Committee Chart, the Audit Committee at McGraw Hill is appointed by the board to assist its oversight of the following:

i the integrity of the financial statements of the company;
ii the compliance by the company with legal and regulatory requirements;
iii the independent auditor's qualifications and independence; and
iv the performance of the company's internal and external auditors.

As can be seen, there is no mention of credit rating monitoring, within the mandate of the McGraw Hill Audit Committee.

Fitch Ratings Limited[3] has a board of directors composed of 13 members: three insiders from Fitch Ratings Ltd, two from Fimalac, one from Swiss Life Holding AG, one from SAES Getters SpA, one from R2 Financial Technologies Inc. and five university representatives (from Columbia University, Massachusetts Institute of Technology, Universität Bonn, Universität Ulm and Harvard University) (*BusinessWeek* website). Fitch Ratings Ltd has only one advisory committee composed of ten members. Fitch Ratings Inc., through Fitch Ratings Limited, each operates according to governance and supporting board procedures and the objective is to ensure an efficient oversight of all Fitch policies and procedures in relation to them (Fitch Ratings, 2012):

i to the creation, maintenance and enforcement of policies and procedures for determining credit ratings;
ii to the management and the disclosure of conflicts of interest;
iii to the effectiveness of the internal control system with respect to policies and procedures for determining credit ratings; and
iv to the compensation and promotion policies and practices of Fitch.

Although, the implementation by Fitch of a Rating Advisory Committee is an interesting example and a step in the right direction, such an advisory organ does not seem to have strong ties to the board.

All the Big 3 have Credit Policy Groups (CPGs) responsible 'for ensuring that rating criteria are appropriate and that rating committees take the necessary actions when a sustained shift in a risk profile is identified' (SEC, 2013b). Except for Moody's, none of the agencies seems to have the board exercising efficiently its monitoring of rating activities, nor do they have a formal compliance audit for the rating. Beside their weak oversights of ratings a number of additional weaknesses regarding credit rating agencies' boards' supervision, were identified by the SEC (2013b):

i It is not always sufficient evidence that the Board is discharging its obligations under Section 15E(t).
ii Board composition or oversight was in need of improvement at larger and smaller agencies.
iii Many boards did not meet certain requirements with respect to composition or needed improvement in the execution of their duties.
iv Boards of some smaller agencies demonstrated insufficient engagement in executing their duties.
v Many agencies' boards' lack of preparedness to discharge duties at board meetings and a lack of command of the details of key compliance issues facing the agency.
vi Boards of smaller agencies were not required by their governing bodies to oversee compensation and promotion practices as required.

Boards usually struggle with their oversight role: at one end of the spectrum are boards that depend almost exclusively on management reports to know what is going on in their organization, and, at the other end of the spectrum, boards that manage details because that is what they believe their oversight function should be. In the Big 3 the result is mitigated and probably leaning towards the situation where the board is not efficiently performing its job for rating monitoring. Indeed, only Moody's has a board that can exercise direct monitoring over the credit rating activity of the company through its Moody's Investors Services committee. The Big 3, however, operate ratings through technical credit rating committees. If conducted efficiently these committees may prove to be very helpful for ensuring rating accuracy. The technical credit rating committees will be discussed in the next chapter.

Result of the SORT analysis

In order to assess the efficiency of credit rating agencies' organizational structure and transparency for the sake of rating accuracy, this chapter tested the SORT elements presented and considered crucial to the quality of ratings, namely separation of power, ownership, rating monitoring and transparency. Table 8.3 summarizes its findings with regard to these elements and their impact on the accuracy of ratings.

Table 8.3 SORT analysis result summary

Element	*Test result*
Separation of power and board efficiency	Weak
Ownership	Mostly financial
Rating monitoring	Unclear
Transparency	Improving, but not enough to allow replication of rating computations

It is obvious that the board of directors in the case of large agencies does not perform its role efficiently; of the Big 3 only Moody's exercises its rating activities as a separate entity, where the board is totally devoted to rating activities. S&P's and Fitch's boards have also other activities, besides ratings, to deal with. With regard to the independence of ratings, Moody's like Standard & Poor's (McGraw Hill shareholders) are, in their majority, institutional and mutual fund owners and Fitch is under the control of two family groups. These kinds of ownership structure, may not present a real guarantee of independence of rating. Despite real improvement in the volume and the quality of information, regarding the description of methodologies to determine rating, the enforcement rating written policies and procedures, etc., made public to users by agencies since 2007, it is still impossible for an issuer to be reasonably sure of the accuracy of the rating assigned. Technical rating committees exist in agencies, but their work seems generally not to be continually audited and monitored.

Given the weaknesses identified in agencies' internal oversight, the legal monitoring of credit rating activities finds its full significance and relevance and becomes the main means of improving agencies' activities.

Conclusion

This chapter considered whether the Big 3 have the appropriate organizational structures that allow them to exercise an effective monitoring of their rating activities, in order to ensure the accuracy of credit ratings, and concludes that, although the Big 3 have substantially improved the integrity of the credit rating process and the procedures to increase the accuracy of ratings, much remains to be done and this may have justified the regulatory frameworks they are increasingly submitted to. The wave of regulatory initiatives aiming to curb credit agencies' behavioural gaps can be seen as the direct consequence of the weaknesses in their internal organizational structures; therefore, 'the priority should be to establish a capital framework that ensures robust internal risk assessment, better oversight of such risk assessment, and improved access to credit-relevant information' (FSA *et al.*, 2013).

Notes

1 See Exhibit 4 of S&P's NRSRO Form, describing S&P as a business unit within Standard & Poor's Financial Services LLC, a company wholly owned by the McGraw Hill Companies, Inc. ('McGraw Hill').

2 Other Moody's committees are: (i) the Audit Committee and (ii) the Governance and Compensation Committee.

3 By simplifying we can say that Fitch Ratings Limited is 100 per cent owned by Fitch Ratings, Inc., which in turn is 100 per cent owned by Fitch Group, Inc., a holding company, which in turn is 50 per cent indirectly owned by Fimalac SA, France, and 50 per cent indirectly owned by the Hearst Corporation, US: both Fimalac and Hearst are family group holdings (Fitch Ratings, 2013).

Bibliography

Bushman, R., J. Piotriski and A. Smith (2004), 'What determines corporate transparency?' *Journal of Accounting Research*, Vol. 42, pp. 207–252.

Businessweek website, at: http://investing.businessweek.com/research/stocks/private/snapshot.asp?privcapId=705307, retrieved 2 April 2014.

Fitch Ratings (2010), 'Statement on definition of ancillary business', at: https://www.fitchratings.com/, retrieved 23 January 2014.

Fitch Ratings (2012), 'Fitch Ratings: European Union transparency report', March, at: www.fitchratings.com/web_content/compliance/eu_transparency_report_fiscal_year_2012.pdf, retrieved 21 November 2013.

FSA, HM Treasury and Bank of England (2013), 'The United Kingdom authorities response to the European Commission internal market and services consultation document on credit rating agencies', at: https://circabc.europa.eu/d/d/workspace/SpacesStore/0d1ea101-b6d0-470b-b8b3-e28e4c1cba30/BoE-FSA-Treasury_EN.pdf, retrieved 2 July 2014.

Maffett, M. (2011), 'Who benefits from corporate opacity? International evidence from informed trading by institutional investors', University of North Carolina at Chapel Hill.

Moody's, 'Moody's Investors Service committee charter', at: http://files.shareholder.com/downloads/MOOD/3007345420x0x429937/286f7283-200c-48e3-babc-a25bcdcfc16f/MCO_WebDoc_8060.pdf.

Moody's, 'Corporate governance', at: http://ir.moodys.com/committeechart.aspx?iid=108462, retrieved 4 October 2013.

Moody's website at: www.moodys.com/Pages/atc.aspx.

PriceWaterHouse (PWC) (2014), 'Board effectiveness', at: www.pwc.com/us/en/corporate-governance/publications/board-effectiveness.jhtml, retrieved 20 January 2014.

Securities and Exchange Commission (SEC) (2012), 'Annual report on nationally recognized statistical rating organizations', at: www.sec.gov/ retrieved 29 March 2014.

Securities and Exchange Commission (SEC) (2013a), 'Annual report on nationally recognized statistical rating organizations', at: www.sec.gov/ retrieved 29 March 2014.

Securities and Exchange Commission (SEC) (2013b) 'Summary report of commission staff's examination of each NRSRO section 15E examinations', at: www.sec.gov/ retrieved 30 March 2014.

Securities and Exchange Commission (SEC) 'Section 15E(t)(2)(B) of the Exchange Act' at: www.sec.gov/, retrieved 30 May 2014.

Securities and Exchange Commission (SEC) 'Section 15E(t)(3) of the SEC', at: www.sec.gov/, retrieved 30 May 2014.

Standard & Poor's (S&P) (2013), 'Form NRSRO', at: www.standardandpoors.com/ratings/form-nrsro/en/us, retrieved 23 June 2014.

Yahoo Finance (n.d.), 'Moody's major holders', at: http://finance.yahoo.com/q/mh?s=MCO+Major+Holders, retrieved 12 March 2014.

9 Agencies' rating quality control systems

Just as much an efficient board is necessary for the accuracy of ratings as underlined in Chapter 8, the practice of a sound internal audit/control is also required to enhance the quality of the ratings and to meet debt issuers'/investors' expectations and needs (SEC, Section 15E(c)(3)(A)); it also contibutes to dissipating their suspicions and fears with regard to agencies' suspected governance breaches. In accordance with current international (IIA) standards (IIA standard 1300), rating agencies must, for their efficient functioning, establish, maintain, enforce and document an effective internal control structure governing the implementation of and adherence to policies, procedures and methodologies for determining credit ratings (SEC, 2013b). Internal quality assessments include a combination of ongoing monitoring of performance criteria and periodic reviews against standards and external quality assessments.

This chapter will assess the quality of rating agencies' internal control systems. Additional to the introduction, the second section shows how the quality of ratings can be enhanced through a sound internal quality control system; the third section presents the sample and the methodology; the fourth analayses the results; the fifth discusses the results; the sixth wonders if transparency can be the answer; and the final section concludes the chapter.

Enhancing the quality of ratings through a sound internal audit system

Internal audit (IA) functions in credit rating agencies are faced with additional challenges that are regarded as a key element of agencies' corporate governance frameworks and rating accuracy. According to the Institute of Internal Auditors (IIA), internal audit can be defined as: 'an independent, objective assurance and consulting activity'. Its main objective is twofold: (i) adding shareholders' value and (ii) improving organizations' operations. An effective IA is supposed to help organizations to attain efficient operations mainly by introducing a systematic and disciplined approach to the evaluation and the continuous improvement of the effectiveness of risk management, control and governance processes (IIA website). It also forces organizations to periodically examine and evaluate their activities as services providers (IIA Handbook). Practically, internal auditing assists members of the organization in the effective discharge of their daily responsibilities, by supplying them with analyses, appraisals, recommendations, counsel and information concerning the activities reviewed (Aksoy and Sezer, 2013). Credit agencies' stakeholders and especially debt issuers should, therefore, be able to rely on an agencies' internal audit for assurance on agencies' corporate governance, risk management and internal surveillance processes. Hence, agencies must have a great tendency to establish relatively more sophisticated and dynamic IA functions than other business sectors, which can provide much needed assurance on the effectiveness of ratings. In this respect, IA should serve as an essential pillar of the agencies' corporate governance frameworks. Internal auditors need to be dynamic, keep pace with change and not leave major risks unattended. It is a fact that IA cannot act directly on the rating process; however, it should play a significant role by maintaining a flexible and risk based audit rating approach and dynamic audit plan to address emerging and potential rating problems.

Ideally, the IA charter (or the charter of the Standing Rating Committee of the Board (SRCB), suggested in the previous chapter) should express the formal agency policy, subject to periodical review and approval by the Audit Committee/SRCB. In this way, it will be guaranteed that the IA/SRCB charter accurately reflects the authority, responsibility and accountability assigned to the IA/SRCB function and clearly articulates functional and administrative reporting relationships. Further, Section 15E(c)(3)(A) of the SEC requires that each credit rating agency establishes, maintains, enforces and documents an effective internal control structure governing the implementation of and adherence to policies, procedures and methodologies for determining credit ratings. SEC Section 15E(g)(1) requires an agency to establish, maintain and enforce written policies and procedures reasonably designed to prevent the misuse of material, non-public information by the agency or by any person associated with the agency. Further, Rule 17g-4(a)(3) provides that these written policies and procedures must include policies and procedures reasonably designed to prevent the inappropriate dissemination of pending credit rating actions within and outside the agency before issuing the rating on the Internet or through another readily accessible means (SEC, 2013a). It can therefore be assumed that agencies are subjected to the following requirements with regards to internal control:

1 establishing an effective internal control structure;
2 maintaining an effective internal control structure;
3 enforcing an effective internal control structure;
4 documenting an effective internal control structure;

5 establishing, maintaining and enforcing written policies and procedures designed to prevent the misuse of material, non-public information;
6 establishing, maintaining and enforcing written policies and procedures designed to prevent the inappropriate dissemination of pending credit rating actions;
7 assessing internal quality.

Methodology

A questionnaire was prepared and first sent to a sample of 106 rating agencies scattered all over the world, seeking information on how internal audit functions and/or rating committees of the board conform to international standards on quality and monetary authorities requirements. This sample included:

i the ten agencies registered as CRAs for the year ended 31 December 2012;
ii the 37 ESMA registered CRAs in accordance with Article 18(3) of the Credit Rating Agencies Regulation as of December 2013; and
iii all credit rating agencies listed by Defaultrsik.[1]

Unfortunately very few rating agencies felt the need to answer our questionnaire, even after a second sending. We therefore recoursed to agencies' publications to assess the quality of their rating quality internal control systems and even then only few agencies allow this option. For that reason our study on the quality of agencies' internal control was limited to rating agencies that are expected and supposed to publish information regarding their control system, mainly due to their NRSRO or ESMA registration requirements. They are:

A.M. Best Company, Inc. (A.M. Best)
DBRS Ltd (DBRS)
Egan-Jones Rating Company (EJR)
Fitch, Inc. (Fitch),
Japan Credit Rating Agency, Ltd (JCR)
Kroll Bond Rating Agency, Inc. (KBRA)
Moody's Investor Services, Inc. (Moody's)
Morningstar and
Standard & Poor's Rating Services (S&P) (through McGraw Hill).

Answers regarding rating quality internal control requirements were sought from the published information by agencies and their different filing with the SEC and ESMA. The sources of information used included:

i agencies' codes of conduct;
ii agencies' audit committees chart;

iii agencies' more recent Form and associated Exhibits;
iv agencies' EU transparency reports; and
v 2013 Section 15E Examinations Summary Report of SEC staff's examination of each NRSRO.

Results of our data collection and analysis are presented in the next section

Analysis of results

Table 9.1 presents several demographic-related data that were first collected, and presented in order to assist in comprehending how factors such as size may impact agencies' practices related to rating quality assurance and process improvement.

Agencies usually indicate that they operate under a single professional code of conduct based on the IOSCO code. Agencies' codes usually set out the principles under which agencies, their managers and staffs are expected to operate and offer a set of robust, practical measures that serve as a guide to and a framework for implementing the principles' objectives (IOSCO, 2004). Structurally, the IOSCO code fundamentals, supposed to be binding to agencies, are broken into three sections and draw upon the organization and substance of the principles themselves: (i) the quality and integrity of the rating process, (ii) CRA independence and the avoidance of conflicts of interest and (iii) CRA responsibilities to the investing public and issuers (IOSCO, 2004).

Agencies indicate reviewing regularly their codes of conducts to take account of changes in legislation on a global basis. The nine agencies composing the sample assert in their publications to being managed under a governing board with an audit committee, but exceptions are encountered. DBRS, for instance, although, having a board of directors, its founder Walter Schroeder maintains voting control. Walter Schroeder currently holds the role of Chairman of DBRS and his son holds the role of Deputy Chairman (DBRS, 2013). Similarly, although, Fitch Ratings, Inc. indicates

> having a board that operates according to a governance charter and supporting board procedures to ensure they have oversight of all Fitch policies and procedures related to the effectiveness of the internal control system with respect to policies and procedures for determining credit ratings,
>
> (Fitch, 2013)

it gives a little indication of how this board is actually operating. For its part, S&P Ratings Services indicated having 'established a governance hierarchy and committee framework that implements policies, procedures and methodologies for determining Credit Ratings as well as an independent

Table 9.1 Demographic data of the agencies in the sample

Agency	*A.M. Best Company, Inc.*	*DBRS Ltd (DBRS)*	*Egan-Jones Rating Company (EJR)*	*Fitch, Inc.*	*Japan Credit Rating Agency, Ltd. (JCR)*	*Kroll Bond Rating Agency, Inc. (KBRA)*	*Moody's Investor Services, Inc.*	*Morningstar*	*Standard & Poor's Rating Services*
Leadership structure[1]	Independent	Independent DBRS Holdings Limited, a private company incorporated in Ontario, Canada	Independent	French Fimalac (50%) US Hearst Corporation (50%)	Financial institutions	Marsh & McLennan Companies[2]	Board	Joe Mansueto and Japanese Softbank	McGraw Hill
Existence of a technical rating committee	Yes	Yes	Yes	Yes	Yes	Yes	Yes	Yes	Yes
Existence of a rating committee of the board	–	DBRS' internal review function	–	Fitch's Credit Policy Group	–	–	–	Yes	S&P Ratings Services' Global Risk Management
Existence of an audit committee of the board	Yes	Yes	Yes	Yes	Yes	Yes	Yes	Yes	Yes
2012 number of ratings[3]	6,452	46,112	1,161	350,370	714	18,993	923,323	13,935	1,143,300
2012 total number of credit analysts (4)	126	93	5	1,092	59	37	1,123	22	1,436
Ratings to analysts ratio	51	496	232	321	12	513	822	633	796
Designated compliance officer	Yes	Yes	Yes	Yes	Yes	Yes	Yes	Yes	Yes

Notes
1 Yahoo Finance.
2 Marsh & Mclennan Companies is a global professional services firm offering clients advice and solutions in the areas of risk, strategy and human capital.
3 NRSRO Annual Certifications for the year ended 31 December 2012, Item 7A; 2013 NRSRO Forms, Exhibit 8.

governance and control structure aimed at fully adhering to policies, procedures, and methodologies for determining Credit Ratings' (S&P, 2013).

Agencies' practices with regard to board functionning are often subject to critiques, according to the SEC (2013a):

i instances were identified where some agencies' board members were required to certify the code of conduct every six months, but where certifications had not been made as required;
ii documentation of the board meetings at three smaller agencies does not sufficiently evidence that the board is discharging its obligations; and
iii board composition[2] and oversight were found in need of improvement at some large and small agencies.

All agencies seem to have a Designated Compliance Officer and operate under a credit rating committee system, where ratings are determined by a rating committee (see next section) in accordance with the policies and procedures governing the rating committee process and not by any individual rating analyst. All agencies published rating methodologies and practices and procedures, but some agencies, at times, did not follow certain aspects of their rating procedures (SEC, 2013a). The number of analytical staff assigned to the rating activity varies between agencies and allows for comparison based on the size of the rating functions. Of the nine agencies in the sample most have 20 or more analyst staff, with the Big 3 having between 1,092 and 1,436. The ratio of the number of ratings to the number of analysts unveils interesting information: the bigger the agency the higher the ratio. Except for two small agencies, A.M. Best and JCR, all agencies process hundreds of ratings per analyst, per year. Of the Big 3, Fitch devotes more analytical staff to rating activities, an analyst per 321 ratings per year, compared to an analyst per 822 and 796 ratings for Moody's and S&P respectively.

Technical credit rating committees

One way of improving accuracy and consistency of the ratings is by setting efficient technical credit rating committees (TCRCs) that can represent 'a critical mechanism in promoting the quality, consistency and integrity of credit rating process' (Fitch Ratings, 2013). This committee should have no permanent members; it should be formed anew for each case from senior members of the agency. It is important that the issuer does not know its members, to avoid improper encouragement to fraud. These are individuals who collectively have the required knowledge and experience of rating development and monitoring for a specific type of rated entities. The composition of TCRCs may vary depending on the nature and complexity of the credit rating at issue, but generally should include the following:

i a chairperson, serving as head of the committee;
ii an assigned analyst, responsible for the issuance of the rating recommendation;
iii other analysts who support the assigned analyst; and
iv others that may include specialists, etc.

The chairman of any TCRC should have some specific responsibilities in order for the TCRC to operate efficiently. According to Fitch Rating:

i The chair should be required to encourage broad-based participation from all members, regardless of their expression of dissenting views or position in the hierarchy in the agency or seniority and credit ratings are decided by vote of all members.
ii The chair should make sure all rating committee members are eligible and vote, and each voting member is entitled to one vote, with all votes carrying equal weight.
iii The chair must also be required to make sure and determine 'if committee members possess sufficient depth and breadth of expertise to allow the rating committee to be properly constituted' (Fitch Ratings, 2013).
iv He must be required to make sure of the proper constitution of the committee, the appropriate application of ratings criteria, the review of all relevant information and materials, the compliance with policies, guidelines and procedures, and the reaching of a ratings decision (Fitch Ratings, 2013).
v The chair should be required to make sure that any rating recommendation is made by the assigned analyst following the technical rating committee discussion.
vi The chair should be required to make sure that the vote begins with the assigned analyst, and continues with other members voting, with the chair voting last.
vii Rating analysts should be allowed to have different views on financial strength and rating factors and although the lead analyst should prepare a rating proposal for the committee, the rating decision should come from the committee.
viii The actual rating decision should be made by a ratings committee, not an individual analyst.

The chair should specially be given the necessary power to suspend the rating proceedings if he considers that the rating committee needed more time for discussion, additional information or a wider participation, before reaching a conclusion (Moody's, 2013a).

A meeting of ratings analysts with the issuer's senior managers should usually be called and the topics to be discussed should focus on qualitative information not available from public data: corporate form capital structure information flow between executives and line personnel; strategic objectives, financial goals, recent acquisitions and divestitures, competitive strategies for underwriting, pricing, etc. For an initial meeting, rating agencies should ask issuers to provide extensive background material and should provide checklists, to ensure complete information. Rating analysts should question the insurer's views, but avoid specifying the data they want (Feldblum, 2011). Although TCRCs in agencies can play a determinant role in ensuring rating accuracy, to our view their role is dependent of the existence within agencies of a specialized rating audit organ, independent from the management and reporting directly to the board, a Standing Rating Committee of the Board (SRCB), as discussed in a previous chapter.

Each Big 3 seems to have its own code of conduct, relating to the quality and integrity of the rating process and avoidance of conflicts of interest. None of the codes specifically addresses the issue of the structure and the functioning of the technical rating committees.

Do agencies establish an effective internal control structure?

In addition to understanding the demographics of the agencies, we tried to identify what actions were taken in agencies' efforts to meet quality of ratings and whether or how they differed based on some of the demographic information collected, knowing that the IOSCO code requires that

> the CRA should adopt, implement and enforce written procedures to ensure that the opinions it disseminates are based on a thorough analysis of all information known to the CRA that is relevant to its analysis according to the CRA's published rating methodology.
>
> (IOSCO, 2013)

As a first step, we tried to know whether agencies establish an effective internal control structure. Agencies seem to maintain internal audit programmes 'that were designed to provide verification that the firm and its employees were complying with the firms' internal policies and procedures' (SEC, 2008a). The nine agencies composing the sample, also indicate having an auditing committee. The largest agencies do, however, have well-operating audit committees. Moody's, for instance, asserts that its Audit Committee's primary purpose 'is to represent and assist the Board of Directors in fulfilling its oversight responsibilities' (Moody's, Audit Committee Charter).

There seems usually to be no specific mandate given to audit committees in rating agencies, with regard to rating integrity. At Moody's, for instance, the audit committee's primary purpose is to represent and assist Moody's board of directors in fulfilling its oversight responsibilities relating to (Moody's 2013):

i the integrity of Moody's financial statements and the financial information provided to Moody's stockholders and others;
ii Moody's compliance with legal and regulatory requirements;
iii Moody's internal controls;
iv the audit process, including the qualifications and independence of the auditors, and the performance of the internal audit function and of the independent auditors;
v Moody's policies and practices with respect to financial risk assessment and risk management; and
vi the review of contingent liabilities and risks that might be material to Moody's.

The review of the information based on the size shows that some smaller agencies, were not even adhering to recordkeeping procedures (SEC, 2013a).

Do agencies maintain an effective internal control structure?

Most agencies declare maintaining a control function as well as a compliance function, as required by law and regulations that are supposed to be independent from the practice areas responsible for credit rating activities, ancillary services, and other services (S&P, 2014). Most agencies also indicate they have taken appropriate steps 'to avoid issuing any credit analysis, Credit Ratings or reports that contain misrepresentations or are otherwise misleading as to the general creditworthiness of an Issuer or obligation' (Moody's, 2013a). They are also underlining maintaining internal records to support their ratings and rating outlooks (Fitch Ratings, n.d.). According to the SEC the following breaches can be found in some agencies (SEC, 2013a):

1 Some small agencies did not consistently conduct surveillance within the time frames set forth in their procedures, while some of the required documentation was not maintained in a manner specified in the procedures, and some meetings of the criteria committee were not held with the frequency required by the procedures.
2 Some of the procedures and supervisory controls governing the rating process at two larger agencies were tainted with significant weaknesses.
3 Weaknesses were identified in criteria development and disclosure at two larger and four smaller agencies.
4 Weaknesses were identified in one larger NRSRO and four smaller NRSROs, in certain rating procedures or in certain public disclosures of those policies and procedures.
5 Certain improvements were needed in the internal audit or testing programmes at one larger and five smaller agencies.

6 Four smaller agencies require improvements to their programmes for training employees on compliance policies and procedures.

The European Securities and Markets Authority (ESMA) has also found some weaknesses in agencies' internal audits. ESMA has even 'issued a public notice against Standard & Poor's Credit Market Services on June 2014, for breaches of Regulation 1060/2009 CRA Regulation, as results from its investigation into the erroneous publication on 10 November 2011:'

> ESMA found that this incident was the result of a failure by S&P to meet certain organisational requirements set out in the CRA Regulation, relating to sound internal control mechanisms, effective control and safeguard arrangements for information processing systems and decision-making procedures and organisational structures.
>
> (ESMA, 2013)

Do agencies enforce an effective internal control structure?

Agencies indicate they usually proceed to rigorous and formal review of the rating methodologies and models and significant changes to the rating methodologies and models used. Weaknesses with respect to the testing programme for rating criteria and models, were also discovered in this area (SEC 2013a):

i Some agencies' audit departments and compliance departments were not adequately monitoring criteria function to ensure independence from business and market considerations.
ii In some larger agencies, the model quality review processes were tainted with weaknesses, 'including lack of communication between criteria and model quality review functions and inadequate follow-up on model quality review recommendations and insufficient procedures for rating model validation and testing' (SEC, 2013a).
iii There was a lack of coordination at one agency, between the compliance function and the internal audit function in way that the compliance department was not constantly provided with copies of internal audit reports with direct impact on the compliance programme (SEC, 2013a).

The European market authority, ESMA, also unearthed a number of weaknesses and required improvement in the following areas (ESMA, 2013):

i the validation of rating methodologies, to ensure that a credit rating assessment is a comprehensive risk assessment leading to high quality ratings;

ii the enhancement of internal governance, ensuring the full independence of the internal review function and thereby reducing the risk of potential conflict of interest; and
iii the increase in the robustness of IT systems to support the rating process, including information security controls and protection of confidential rating information.

Do agencies document effective internal audit structures?

Agencies declare maintaining internal records related to credit ratings and internal audit for a reasonable period of time, in accordance with the applicable laws. Most agencies also assert having policies of classifying documents according to different criteria, based on:

i whether the documents are central to the procedures and determinations of rating decisions;
ii refer to the commercial relationships with clients and customers; or
iii are documents that agencies keep to satisfy their legal and regulatory obligations.

Over all, 'records are maintained in such a manner as to protect the integrity, confidentiality and security of the records and to enable the records to be made available, as necessary' (DBRS, 2013). It seems usually ensured that there are procedures in place which adequately detail record retention practices and requirements applicable to the records under their control. These procedures usually identify relevant record types and focus on (DBRS, 2013):

i establishing and maintaining a records management system in their department to ensure availability, retention and appropriate destruction of the records;
ii ensuring that multiple versions of the same record are not maintained within their departmental records; and
iii ensuring that records are retained for the applicable retention period.

S&P, for instance, has specific retention guidelines and records in relation to credit ratings that are subject to a number of requirements (S&P, 2013):

i For each rating decision, the identity of the analysts participating in the determination of the credit rating and of the identity of the persons who have approved the credit rating, information as to whether the credit rating was solicited or unsolicited, and the date on which the credit rating action was taken.
ii An account record for each rated entity, related third party or other user that has paid for the issuance or maintenance of a credit rating. In

accordance with applicable policies, analysts do not have access to such account records.

iii The records documenting the established procedures and methodologies used by the entity to determine its credit ratings.

iv The final version of internal records, including non-public information and work papers, used to form the basis of the rating decision taken.

v Records of the procedures and measures implemented to comply with the regulation.

vi Copies of internal and external communications, including electronic communications, received and sent by the entity and its employees that relate to credit rating activities.

Further, designated records are retained for at least five years after the records are made or received in relation to credit rating activities, ancillary services and other services. The heads of each practice area, as well as the heads of certain departments and functions, are responsible for their respective group's compliance with record-keeping policy and guidelines (S&P, 2013).

Do agencies establish, maintain and enforce written policies and procedures designed to prevent the misuse of material, non-public information?

All agencies of the sample indicate having written policies and procedures providing detailed interpretations of rules governing the ways in which agencies operate and designed to prevent the misuse of material, non-public information, unless otherwise permitted by a specific confidentiality agreement. Standard & Poor's, for instance, asserts that 'S&P and its Employees will protect Confidential Information entrusted to it and its Employees by Issuers in connection with the performance of Credit Rating Activities' (S&P, 2014). Agencies' employees are usually required to maintain the confidentiality of all non-public information. They are usually forbiden from disclosing confidential information in press releases, through research conferences, to future employers or in conversations with investors, other issuers, other persons or otherwise (A.M. Best, 2014). According to the SEC (2013b), however:

i Three smaller agencies did not have procedures to manage other conflicts of interest of the agency and its employees.

ii Two smaller agencies did not disclose certain conflicts of interest on their NRSRO Forms; the staff further found that a smaller agency's procedures did not address all prohibited acts and practices set forth in Rule 17g-6 (SEC, 2013).

iii Four smaller agencies did not have sufficient procedures and controls for separating business and analytical functions or for preventing rating analysts from being involved in fee discussions and from having access to rating fee information.

iv One larger agencies and four smaller agencies had weaknesses in certain rating procedures or in certain public disclosures of those policies and procedures.

v One larger agency and five smaller agencies had weaknesses in procedures and controls governing certain prohibited acts and conflicts of interest, including employee securities ownership.

vi One larger agency and five smaller agencies needed to improve management of the conflict of interest associated with employee securities ownership.

Do agencies establish, maintain and enforce written policies and procedures designed to prevent the inappropriate dissemination of pending credit rating actions?

According to the IOSCO Code each CRA 'should adopt procedures and mechanisms to protect the confidential nature of information shared with them by issuers under the terms of a confidentiality agreement'. Agencies usually indicate maintaining and enforcing written policies and procedures designed to prevent the inappropriate dissemination of pending credit rating actions. Agencies do have policies and procedures reasonably designed to prevent the inappropriate dissemination of pending credit rating actions within and outside agencies before issuing the rating on the Internet or through another readily accessible means. It seems that there are weaknesses in some agencies' internal controls over the handling of material, non-public information, including pending rating actions (SEC, 2013a).

Do agencies assess internal quality?

The assessments of internal quality include a combination of ongoing monitoring of performance criteria and periodic reviews against the standards and external quality assessments. Agencies do not seem to have formal quality control functions; the largest agencies, especially the Big 3, and also DBRS, do, however, have specific functions responsible for monitoring, testing and reporting on the quality of credit ratings. These are:

i Fitch's Credit Policy Group;
ii Moody's Credit Policy Group;
iii S&P Ratings Services' Global Risk Management ; and
iv DBRS' Internal Review function.

S&P Ratings Services, for instance, is intended to evaluate the effectiveness of its internal control structure and make changes to its organizational structure and processes as and when it deems appropriate (S&P, 2013). Moody's Credit Policy Group, in the other hand, is supposed to be independent of and separate from thc ratings teams.

> Its responsibilities fall into three broad areas: promotion of the consistency and quality of MIS's credit ratings; review and approval of credit rating methodologies including changes of existing methodologies, models, and key rating assumptions; and assessment of credit ratings performance.
>
> (Moody's, 2013b)

Moody's Credit Policy Group is an interesting initiative, because it is the only control unit that reports directly and quarterly to Moody's Corporation (NYSE: MCO)'s board of directors.

Discussion of results

Overall, agencies' pretentions with regard to the quality of their internal audit seems to differ from their daily practice. The information gathered in this chapter supports the conclusion that, given the specificity of rating activity, existing internal audit systems do not seem to provide measurable and accountable, assessment of the quality of the internal audit processes within rating agencies. Further, the existence of an internal audit committee with agencies does not drive whether or not rating quality is assured and whether rating internal quality assessments are conducted, since periodical audit in agencies usually focuses on processes and controls to support employee compliance with regulatory requirements. A smaller proportion of agencies seems to be conducting rating quality assessments and it is not clear whether these conducted internal quality assessments meet standards of best practice for ensuring quality.

The largest agencies do, however, have credit policy groups (CPGs) that are a key part of the control and analytical support framework and seem to be independent of and separate from the ratings teams that are principally responsible for producing credit ratings. Except for Moody's, CPGs do not report to the board of directors and seem therefore to be under management control. Credit policy groups may constitute, to our point of view, a viable solution to credit rating accuracy, if only they are conceded the status of a board standing committee, in the same way as the audit committee. In this manner CPGs will be able to report directly to the board and be submitted to the same rules of responsibilities, composition, etc. Accordingly:

i A CPG's responsibility should primarily be the promotion of rating quality, consistency and transparency.

> Its responsibilities fall into three broad areas: 1) promotion of the consistency and quality of MIS's credit ratings; 2) review and approval of credit rating methodologies including changes of existing methodologies, models, and key rating assumptions; and 3) assessment of credit ratings performance.
>
> (Moody's, 2013b)

ii A CPG should be able to report regularly to the board regarding the execution of its duties and responsibilities, activities, any issues encountered and related to credit rating.

iii The CPG should comprise three or more directors as determined by the board and each member should meet the applicable standards of independence and comply with all rating literacy requirements of the IOSCO Code of Conduct.

Is transparency the answer?

The weaknesses identified in Chapter 8 regarding agencies' boards' inability to effectively ensure rating accuracy, and those identified in this chapter regarding rating internal control breaches, indicate how regulating rating transparency finds all its significance. It is often suggested that transparency can be associated with increasing accuracy of credit ratings for the following reasons:

i Agencies' transparency can help users of credit ratings to compare the processes and performance of credit rating providers and contribute to the protection of issuers/investors, and leads to fair rating markets that are also free from systemic risk (IOSCO, 2013).

ii The opacity of credit ratings is, therefore, likely to impede any successful move to be ventured by small CRAs and any new entrant, for competing with the Big 3, since it prevents them from convincing investors to give them a chance by trusting them at least once (IOSCO, 2013).

iii Transparency may allow small CRAs and any new market entrant to assert comparative and observable competitive advantages, distinguishing them from the Big 3.

iv Conversely, it may also encourage major rating agencies to constantly try updating their internal policies and procedures to improve the quality of credit ratings and maintain credibility with investors and other users.

v The literature also usually suggests that the transparency of financial reporting can have significant benefits for the average investor (Verrecchia, 1982).

vi More importantly, a low/fraudulent public disclosure may motivate more private users to exploit to their advantage information asymmetry, to which they contribute significantly. These more informed

> investors can benefit at the expense of the rest of investors, on the sole basis of their informational advantage. This suggests that some investors can actually benefit from opaque financial reporting than otherwise. Consequently, 'although private information acquisition is costly and beyond the means of many investors, sophisticated investors, such as institutions, likely have significant capital and expertise that they can leverage' (Maffett, 2011).

Agencies were constantly fighting rules that may lead to forcing them to more transparency and secrecy in the name of 'trademark protection'. CRAs' secrecy argument doesn't sell anymore in the regulatory world, and a deep requirement of transparency became recently a fundamental component of all CRA registration and oversight programmes over the world. As discussed in Chapter 7, IOSCO members have implemented laws and regulations that require CRAs to disclose information about their rating methodologies, rating performance, conflicts of interest and other operational matters. The IOSCO principle on CRAs' transparency and timeliness of ratings disclosure, in application in more than 100 countries, requires CRAs to make disclosure and transparency an objective of their ratings activities and deals with:

i the timely reporting of publicly issued ratings decisions;
ii the non-selective disclosure of publicly issued ratings decisions as well as discontinuation of ratings;
iii the disclosure of sufficient information about procedures and methodologies to allow outside parties to understand how a rating was arrived at by a CRA;
iv the disclosure of information about historical default rates within a CRA's rating categories, and the disclosure of whether a rating was unsolicited (IOSCO, 2011).

Although, IOSCO's view of CRAs' transparency does not seem to deal directly with the efficiency and the control of the rating process internal structure, it seems to have gained wide recognition in that many countries have adopted it. The SEC and the EU transparency regulatory programmes are actually containing provisions that promote IOSCO principles of CRAs' transparency. In the US the Dodd–Frank Act directed the SEC to adopt rules to implement a number of provisions requiring transparency froms. Rules 17g-4 to -6, for example, emphasize the need for credit agencies to adhere to written policies and procedures applicable in the determination of credit ratings and in the identification and management of conflicts of interest arising from rating activities, including the prohibition of unfair activities or the exercise of coercive practices. The Big 3 and other NRSROs are already publishing a number of reports required by the monetary authorities as registration requirements, as dicussed in Chapter

7. At the European Union, for instance, a rating agency requesting registration with the European markets authority must publicly disclose its methodology and describe the key assumptions and models used in the assessment of credit ratings, as well as any significant changes they may undergo. A registered credit rating agency must also publicly disclose any conflict of interest, actual or potential, that may affect its judgement on the rated issuer. Rating agencies are also required to publish an annual transparency report, that includes information on the legal structure of the agency, its ownership structure, its internal controls and an internal annual report on compliance with its rating policies and the conduct of its rating analysts (IOSCO, 2013). Appendix 9.1 gives an overview of the other regulatory initiatives illustrating CRAs' transparency provisions in a given jurisdiction's laws and/or regulations. Most countries seem to follow the path set up by IOSCO and require in their regulatory frameworks more transparency from CRAs.

Thank to NRSRO and ESMA requirements and registration processesses, rating agencies appear to have significantly improved the quality of the information made public to users since 2007. One fundamental area seems, however, to be still neglected by regulations, namely rating market concentration. Although agencies currently disclose much information, this information still does not allow the replicability of the ratings, to make sure of their accuracy. S&P (2009), for instance, warns that agencies do not perform an audit in connection with any issuer credit rating and may, on occasion, rely on unaudited financial information. This is, indeed, a sensitive area but issuers (and maybe only issuers) should be given the right to replicate the work done that has led to the ratings they were assigned and eventually challenging it. Even though agencies' efforts are certainly laudable, there are always those who still doubt the ability of this enormous amount of legally required information, to provide a thorough improvement in the understanding of the real reasons behind credit ratings. Agencies recognize that this is only a starting point towards creating a culture of ethical behaviour in the credit rating industry. The right tone at the top carried by business unit managers, throughout the agency is, however, vital to ensure that these values are shared by all rating analysts and staff (PWC website).

Conclusion

The chapter analyses agencies' behaviour regarding internal control and identifies weaknesses in some of the procedures and supervisory controls governing their rating processes. It concludes the following:

i Regarding whether agencies establish an effective internal control structure, there seems to be no specific mandate given to audit committees in rating agencies, with regard to rating integrity.

ii Regarding whether agencies maintain an effective internal control structure, some agencies do not consistently conduct surveillance within the time frames set forth in their procedures.

iii Regarding whether agencies enforce an effective internal control structure, some agencies' model quality review processes were tainted with weaknesses, 'including lack of communication between criteria and model quality review functions and inadequate follow-up on model quality review recommendations and insufficient procedures for rating model validation and testing' (SEC, 2013a).

iv Regarding whether agencies document an effective internal control structure, agencies appear to be maintaining internal records related to credit ratings and internal audit for a reasonable period of time, in accordance with the applicable laws.

v Regarding whether agencies have appropriate mechanisms to prevent the misuse of material, non-public information, some agencies appeared to have weaknesses in procedures and controls governing certain prohibited acts and conflicts of interest, including employee securities ownership.

vi Regarding whether agencies have appropriate mechanisms of enforcing written policies and procedures designed to prevent the inappropriate dissemination of pending credit rating actions, most agencies seem to have policies and procedures reasonably designed to prevent the inappropriate dissemination of pending credit rating actions within and outside agencies before issuing the rating.

vii Regarding whether agencies assess ratings internal quality, except for one exception, agencies do not seem to have formal quality control functions, specifically designed to ratings, that are directly under the direct supervision of the board.

Shortcomings in agencies' internal control were identified, 'including non-compliance with document retention policies, lack of adherence to rating committee guidelines and most significantly, the failure of management to formally review/validate derivatives models prior to posting for general use' (SEC, 2008b). Thanks to regulatory requirements, rating agencies appear to have significantly improved their way of funtioning and may have enhanced the quality of their ratings, but the rating market appears closer than ever.

An effective IA function can have several benefits: it can 'facilitate financial and operational services of companies to achieve key business objectives by bringing a systematic, disciplined approach to evaluating and improving the effectiveness of corporate governance, risk management and internal control processes' (Aksoy and Sezer, 2013).

Appendix 9.1 Other regulatory initiatives

Country	*Initiative*
Argentina	In Argentina, CRAs are required to disclose through the Argentinian Comisión Nacional de Valores' (CNV) website a description of their methodologies to determine credit ratings, internal procedures for managing conflicts of interest and information about the number and qualifications of credit analysts and their supervisors.
Australia	In Australia, each licensed CRA must publish on its home webpage links to (1) the CRA's code of conduct, (2) a description of the methodologies it uses and (3) information about the CRA's historic performance data (including historic default rates and performance of rating opinions).
Brazil	In Brazil, registered CRAs are required to annually file a Reference Form for posting on the Brazilian Comissão de Valores Mobiliários' website, which discloses the CRA's performance measurement statistics for credit ratings since 2002, a description of the methodologies used to determine credit ratings, a description of the CRA's internal control policies and other policies to manage and identify conflicts of interest, and information about the number and qualifications of credit analysts and other employees.
Canada	In Canada, registered CRAs are required to publicly disclose their rating categories' historical default rates, the principal methodology used for each rating, their methodologies and key rating assumptions, and any material modifications thereto.
Chile	In Chile, registered CRAs are required to prepare an annual management report, which includes comparisons with the previous year's rating actions as well as the CRA's administrative structure. In addition, registered CRAs must declare semi-annually that they do not have conflicts of interest with the issuers of securities rated by the CRA.
Hong Kong	In Hong Kong, a licensed CRA must disclose its ratings transition frequency, recordkeeping policy, rating analyst rotation policy, internal control mechanisms, and code of conduct and changes thereto. In addition, licensed CRAs are required to publish historical default rates for their rating categories.
Japan	In Japan, registered CRAs must prepare explanatory documents for each fiscal year and make them available to the public. These documents must include, among other things, the CRA's sales volume, changes in ratings, historical default rates, safeguards against conflicts of interest, policies on confidentiality and compliance policies. Registered CRAs are also required to disclose to the public the description of their rating policies and rating methodologies.
Korea	In Korea, a licensed CRA must make publicly available its credit rating performance report, which includes descriptions of the CRA's future outlook, principal redemption rate of rated securities, changes in ratings, historical default rates, and limits and characteristics of credit ratings. In addition, licensed CRAs must publicly disclose material modifications to rating methodologies and key rating-related policies including the CRA's code of conduct and fee schedule.

continued

Appendix 9.1 Continued

Country	*Initiative*
Mexico	In Mexico, each registered CRA is required to disclose on its website historical information regarding the payment default rates for each of its rating categories, criteria for evaluating credit quality, and its code of conduct and policies for disclosure of ratings. In addition, CRAs are required to prepare an annual report disclosing statistical information about the performance of awarded ratings, information about their legal structure, internal control system, processes related to compliance and rotation policy. Methodologies used to award or modify a rating must be disclosed through press releases.
Taiwan	In Taiwan, each licensed CRA must provide on its website the CRA's business report, which identifies the CRA's issued ratings during the year, information regarding default rates for each rating category, and credit rating methodologies and assumptions, as well as the CRA's organizational structure and financial condition.
Turkey	In Turkey, each listed CRA must make publicly available its ratings, changes to ratings, historical default rates and changes thereto, rating methodologies, assumptions and conflicts of interest that may affect agency decisions. Listed CRAs must also establish a publicly available code of conduct and establish a department to consider received complaints.

Source: adapted from IOSCO's April report to the G20, Appendix A: Member CRA Transparency Provisions, at: www.iosco.org/library/briefing_notes/pdf/IOSCOBN01-13.pdf, retrieved 6 April 2014.

Notes

1 See www.defaultrisk.com/rating_agencies.htm, retrieved 29 October 2013.

2 Some small agencies have exemptions from the requirement to have independent non-executive directors by virtue of the fact that they have fewer than 50 employees, A.M. Best, for example.

References

A.M. Best (2014), 'Code of conduct', at: www.ambest.com/nrsro/code.pdf, retrieved 26 May 2014.

Aksoy, T. and K. Sezer (2013), 'Measuring the internal audit performance: tips for succesful implementation in Turkey', *American International Journal of Contemporary Research*, at: www.aijcrnet.com/journals/Vol_3_No_4_April_2013/8.pdf, retrieved 16 January 2014.

Dominion Bond Rating Service (DBRS) (2013), 'European Union transparency report', at: www.dbrs.com/, retrieved 16 May 2014.

European Securities and Markets Authorithy (ESMA) (2013), 'Annual transparency report', at: www.esma.europa.eu/, retrieved 7 May 2014.

Feldblum, S. (2011), 'Rating agencies', at: www.casact.org/library/studynotes/Feldblum_Rating_Oct%202011.pdf, retrieved 2 March 2014.

Fitch Ratings (n.d.), 'Code of ethics and conduct', at: www.fitchratings.com/web/en/dynamic/about-us/code-of-ethics-and-conduct.jsp, retrieved 26 May 2013.

Fitch Ratings (2013), 'European Union transparency report', at: www.fitchratings.com/web_content/compliance/eu_transparency_report_fiscal_year_2012.pdf, retrieved 2 June 2014.

Institute of Internal Auditors (IIA), (2012), 'Best practices in mplementing, quality assurance & improvement programs', Austin Chapter Research Committee, at: https://na.theiia.org/iiarf/Public%20Documents/2012%20Research%20Report%20-%20Austin%20Chapter.pdf, retrieved 6 April 2014.

Institute of Internal Auditors, IIA Handbook, at: https://global.theiia.org.

International Organization of Securities Commissions (IOSCO) (2004), 'Code of conduct fundamentals for credit ratings agencies', at: www.iosco.org/library/pubdocs/pdf/IOSCOPD271.pdf, retrieved 12 June 2013.

International Organization of Securities Commissions (IOSCO) (2011), 'Regulatory implementation of the statement of principles regarding the activities of credit rating agencies', Final Report, at: www.fsa.go.jp/, retrieved 26 May 2014.

International Organization of Securities Commissions (IOSCO) (2013), Report to the G20, at: www.iosco.org/library/briefing_notes/pdf/IOSCOBN01-13.pdf, retrieved 26 May 2014.

Maffett, M. (2011), *Who benefits from corporate opacity? International evidence from informed trading by institutional investors*. Chapel Hill: University of North Carolina at Chapel Hill.

Moody's (2013a), 'Moody's code of professional conduct', www.moodys.com/Pages/reg001003.aspx, retrieved 16 June 2014.

Moody's, Audit Committee Charter, at: http://ir.moodys.com/GenPage.aspx?IID=108462&GKP=210651, retrieved 2 July 2013.

Moody's Investors Service (2013b), 'European Union transparency report', at: www.moodys.com/Pages/reg001007.aspx, retrieved 6 May 2014.

PricewaterhouseCoopers (PWC) website, at: www.pwc.com/us/en/corporate-governance/publications/board-effectiveness.jhtml, retrieved 20 January 2014.

Securities and Exchange Commission (SEC) (2008a), 'Annual report on nationally recognized statistical rating organizations', at: www.sec.gov, retrieved 13 June 2014.

Securities and Exchange Commission (2008b), 'Summary report of issues identified in the commission staff's examinations of select credit rating agencies', Office of Compliance Inspections and Examinations Division of Trading and Markets and Office of Economic Analysis, United States Securities and Exchange Commission, July.

Securities and Exchange Commission (SEC) (2013a), 'Summary report of the commission staff's examination of each NRSRO', at: www.sec.gov/news/studies/2013/nrsro-summary-report-2013.pdf, retrieved 3 January 2014.

Securities and Exchange Commission (SEC) (2013b), 'Annual report on nationally recognized statistical rating organizations', at: www.sec.gov, retrieved 13 June 2014.

Securities and Exchange Commission (SEC), 'Section 15E(c)(3)(A) of the SEC', at: www.sec.gov, retrieved 12 April 2014.

Standard & Poor's (S&P) (2014), 'S&P code of business ethics for employees', at: http://investor.mhfi.com/phoenix.zhtml?c=96562&p=irol-govcobe, retrieved 25 January 2014.

Standard & Poor's (S&P) (2009), 'Understanding Standard & Poor's rating definitions', at: www.standardandpoors.com/spf/upload/Ratings_EMEA/GeneralCriteriaUnderstandingSandPsRatingDefinitionsJune32009.pdf, retrieved 7 June 2014.

Standard & Poor's (S&P) (2013), 'European Union transparency report', at: www.standardandpoors.com/ratings/european-union-regulatory-disclosures/en/us, retrieved 6 May 2014.

Verrecchia, R. (1982), 'Information acquisition in a noisy rational expectations economy', *Econometrica*, vol. 50, pp. 1415–1430.

10 The Cha6

Shall they present a serious challenge to the Big 3?

Critics of the Big 3 have long voiced concern about legislation and financial regulations that have created institutional frameworks that too abnormally rely on the rating agencies, leaving investors few alternatives and the market with only three major players.[1] Regulations and private contracts referencing credit ratings are considered to be a major contributing factor to lower competition among CRAs. In 2014, however, international agencies, both in the United States and the European Union, and some other countries, have taken serious steps towards ensuring more competitiveness and transparency to the rating industry (SEC, 2012),[2] by eliminating references to credit ratings in regulatory requirements (Shecter, 2012). But are such initiatives capable/sufficient of introducing easier access to the extremely concentrated rating market and are there existing or future rating agencies capable of meeting the challenge of occupying the space that might be freed by the Big 3?

This chapter relates five, although benign, possible breaches to Big 3 credit rating market supremacy to assess their chances of success in taking advantage of this new regulatory era. The second section, following the introduction, indicates why for the sake of better governance, the market dependence on the Big 3 must be reduced; the third section presents a recent regulatory framework aiming at reducing reliance on CRAs for regulatory purposes; the fourth section describes the credit rating market outside the Big 3; the fifth section assesses small agencies' market share; the sixth section considers SmAs and initiatives that can make a difference; the seventh section discusses the situation; the final section concludes the chapter.

Why for the sake of better governance, the market dependence on the Big 3 must be reduced

In 2011, the Big 3 accounted for approximately 98 per cent of the outstanding credit ratings issued by CRAs registered in the United States, including approximately 96 per cent of asset-backed security ratings, 91 per cent of corporate issuer ratings and 99 per cent of government security ratings (SEC Annual Reports). The Big 3 (Moody's, Standard & Poor's and Fitch) have been under intense criticism and scrutiny since the 2007 global financial crisis. They were initially criticized for their favourable pre-crisis ratings of insolvent financial institutions, like Lehman Brothers, as well as the highly risky mortgage-related securities discussed in Chapter 6, and this has significantly contributed to the collapse of the US housing market. The EU has long been convinced that the Big 3 were issuing overly aggressive ratings in the Eurozone financial space. European officials have publicly accused the Big 3 of showing preferential treatment to US issuers. China, on the other hand, does not hide its displeasure with the current global rating system and likes to underline that it is working towards developing an alternative to the American credit rating theories and methodologies and echoes other countries in their search for ways out of the Big 3's grip. Notwithstanding the obvious observed deficiencies of the ratings and the numerous critics, related in many chapters of this book, CRAs have been subject to hardly any formal regulation or supervision, prior to the recent financial crisis. Whereas for other institutions or professions that are comparable or less in their impact on the financial markets, auditors, for example, have had a wealth of legal standards or professional codes. The effects of such monitoring on transparency and conflicts of interest, remain to be seen. Arguments for regulating CRAs were extensively discussed in academic literature.

For a long time CRAs claimed successfully that competition and the need to maintain a good reputation were sufficient to guarantee high professional quality standards in the provision of rating assessments (Theis and Wolgast, 2012). This, however, did not keep concerns from growing and being constantly expressed with respect to the control of the rating market by the Big 3, and the dominant feeling has become that Big 3 oligopoly has to be diminished, first for oligopoly reasons, and also for the damage it is supposed to cause to economic efficiency, and finally for the fact that the informational accuracy of credit ratings has never been reasonably proven without doubt.

The use of ratings by market participants and for regulatory purposes has been a constant credit ratings irritant for their users. Indeed, the mechanistic use of ratings by a large number of market participants seems to present enormous frustrating disadvantages. It was, for instance mentioned that:

i One should not expect market participants using ratings for regulatory purposes to have a big interest in the quality of the ratings, as long as supervisory authorities are satisfied (Theis and Wolgast, 2012). This has led to suggestions that, rather than rely on CRAs' ratings in financial regulation, financial regulators should instead require the use of credit spreads when calculating the risk in their portfolio (Theis and Wolgast, 2012).

- ii Big 3 oligopoly is believed to lead to poor rating quality. Some empirical studies have, for example, documented that yield spreads of corporate bonds start to expand as credit quality deteriorates, but before a rating downgrade, implying that the market often leads a downgrade and this has led to this questioning of the informational value of credit ratings (Kliger and Sarig, 2000; Koresh, 2003): although other studies suggested the reverse. In their view when competition is increased this may result in a reduction in credit rating quality. This was the case, according to Becker and Milbourn (2009b), as Fitch increased its market presence across industries during the 1990s.
- iii There is a risk that the market could be dominated by incompetent CRAs. According to some authors 'CRAs cannot charge higher fees for low rating than for high rating. Under these conditions a rather incompetent CRAs can dominate the market without being worried about potentially more competent entrants' (Jeon and Lovo, 2012a).
- iv Because of the 'privileged' regulatory treatment CRAs were enjoying, they were not concerned or held civilly liable for malfeasance to the same standards of negligence as those applying to other institutions.
- v Rating changes could have highly procyclical effects and trigger major market developments, which could be seen in the course of the rating downgrades (Theis and Wolgast, 2012).

In addition to the issues of concern from the perspective of market participants, there are also important macro-prudential issues of worry, with respect to the effects of ratings on the stability of the financial system as a whole. Here, it has become apparent that market participants and regulators may be subject to conflicting objectives with respect to ratings, and such an issue might prove to be difficult to resolve. On the one hand, it is widely seen as a major advantage of ratings that they aim at stability throughout the cycle and show much less volatility than most other risk measures. At the same time, there is a desire for timely rating adjustments (Theis and Wolgast, 2012).

Overall the idea that excessive reliance on ratings may present the risk of decreasing market heterogeneity, thereby contributing to a less resilient financial system that is more susceptible to the potential effects of conflicts of interest in CRAs, seems to be a commonly shared believe. We learned, for instance, about the American government suing S&P for its inaccurate rating of government securities. There is, however, a risk of an overflow of suits against CRAs especially in US.

Recent regulatory framework aiming reducing reliance on CRAs for regulatory purposes

The much decried reliance on ratings for legislative purposes that has made ratings extended to virtually all financial sectors (banks, insurance companies, securities firms, capital markets, mutual funds and private pensions), is legitimately seen as one the main factor that has kept competition from entering the global rating market. In October 2010 and in face of much criticism, the Financial Stability Board (FSB) endorsed principles summarized in Figure 10.1 (discussed in Chapter 7), to reduce authorities' and financial institutions' reliance on ratings.

In summary the FSB's principles call for removing (or replacing by suitable alternative standards of creditworthiness), wherever possible, references to a credit rating agency. The FSB requires market participants to make their own credit assessments and invites central banks, commercial banks and investors to avoid mechanistic approaches to risk assessment and the creditworthiness of assets and to conduct their own risk analysis. FSB principles have been approved by the G20 and, since then, the Basel Committee on Banking Supervision (BCBS) has also being working on specific policy actions to reduce reliance on ratings in the regulatory framework and has made several recommendations that are supposed to be included in the Basel III rules. The International Organization of Securities Commissions (IOSCO) also published a final report, on 30 July 2013, entitled 'Supervisory colleges for credit rating agencies', which recommends the creation of supervisory colleges for internationally active credit rating agencies. Supervisory colleges were indeed established for the Big 3, i.e.

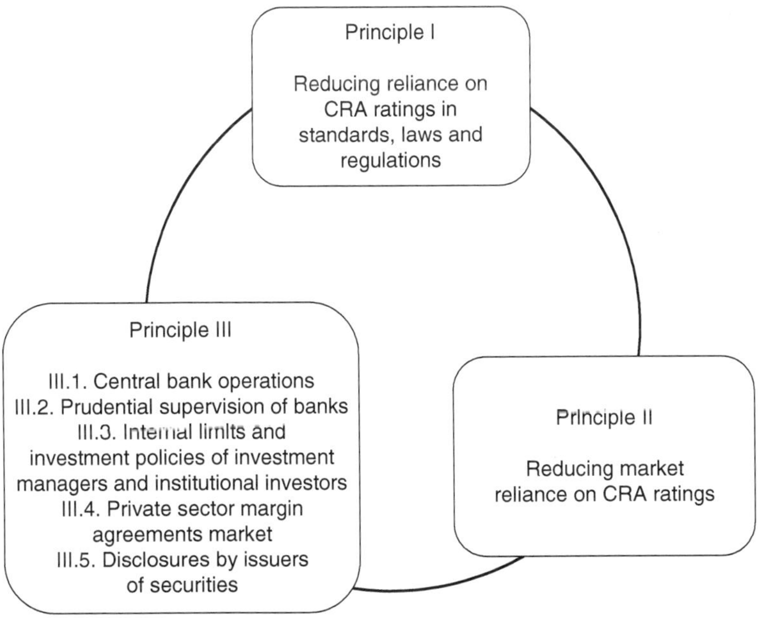

Figure 10.1 FSB's principles for reducing reliance on ratings for regulatory uses (source: adapted from FSBs' Principles for Reducing Reliance on CRA Ratings).

Standard & Poor's Ratings Services, Moody's Investors Service, Inc. and Fitch Ratings, Inc., as discussed in Chapter 8. The Dodd–Frank Act[3] enacted in 2010 required the SEC, since then, to remove any references to credit ratings from its regulations and to substitute such standards of creditworthiness as the SEC determines to be appropriate. On 27 December 2013 (with a compliance date of 7 July 2014), the SEC put the Dodd–Frank Act provisions into practice by adopting amendments to eliminate references to credit ratings by NRSRO in financial acts and rules. Similarly, the new rule EC IP/13/555 of 18 June 2013 imposes stricter rules for credit rating agencies.[4] In line with our G20 commitments, 'European Supervisory Authorities should also avoid references to external credit ratings and are required to review their rules and guidelines and where appropriate, remove credit ratings where they have the potential to create mechanistic effects' (European Commission, 2013).

The credit rating market outside the Big 3

Notwithstanding the Big 3's market dominance, smaller independent CRAs operate in a number of IOSCO member jurisdictions and may focus on niche areas or on issuers not dealt with by the Big 3. Very few small CRAs directly compete with them for some specific rating segments. There are, actually, besides the Big 3, over 150 known credit agencies in the world today (our sample includes 123, listed in Appendix 2.1) but most of them are small agencies, (SmA). Further, Table 10.1 summarizes the total number of registered CRAs located in certain IOSCO member jurisdictions, as well as the number of such CRAs affiliated with Fitch, Moody's or S&P.

Table 10.1 Registered CRAs located in certain IOSCO member jurisdictions, as well as the number of CRAs affiliated with the Big 3

IOSCO member juridiction	*Number of registered CRAs*	*Number of CRAs affiliated with the Big 3*	*IOSCO member juridiction*	*Number of registered CRAs*	*Number of CRAs affiliated with the Big 3*
Argentina	4	3	Japan	7	5
Australia	7	3	Korea	4	2
Brazil	6	3	Mexico	5	3
Canada	4	3	Taiwan	2	2
Chile	4	2	Turkey	6	3
European Union	19	3	United States	10	3
Hong Kong	7	3	Total	85	38

Source: IOSCO, 2013b.

Of the 85 registered agencies with IOSCO member jurisdictions, 38 agencies are affiliated with one of the Big 3, i.e. 45 per cent of all agencies, and this percentage seems to be on thc rise. As of today, Moody's, for instance, is seeking to purchase a majority stake in the Indian rating agency ICRA Ltd. In doing so Moody's will be expanding its existing 28.5 per cent ownership position: it is currently making the offer on the condition it acquires enough to boost its ownership to more than 50 per cent. The percentage of a given country's CRAs affiliated with the Big 3 is, however, not necessarily representative of the Big 3's market share. For example, although the Big 3 own 71 per cent of Japan's registered CRAs, they only possess approximately 55 per cent of the market share of Japanese CRAs, as measured by disclosed sales volumes for credit rating services in 2011. Similarly, although the Big 3 comprise only 30 per cent of the total CRAs registered in the United States, they possess approximately 97 per cent of the total net income reported by all US registered CRAs in 2011 (NRSRO Report). Small rating agencies are, however, hardly ensuring 4 per cent of the world's credit rating activities, and the 96 per cent left is taken care of by the Big 3. Appendix 10.1 lists the credit agencies registered/certified by NRSRO or ESMA (the European equivalent of the US NRSRO). This list does not include the Big 3, nor does it include their affiliate agencies in Europe. It does, however, include agencies registered with FINMA, the Swiss Financial Market Supervisory Authority, a government body responsible for financial regulation.[5] From Appendix 10.1 we can learn a number of important facts:

- i Five small agencies on the list come from the United States, six from Germany, three from Italy and only one agency comes from each advanced economy: Canada, France, Japan, Switzerland and UK. The rest come from other European countries like Cyprus, Slovakia, Greece or Bulgaria.
- ii Most of ESMA's registries, listed in Appendix 10.1, seem to be of a very limited scope and seem to be being pressed to take the opportunity offered to them by the recent implementation of the European registration system.
- iii Of the 26 agencies listed in Appendix 10.1, there are eight agencies registered with the SEC as NRSRO, 21 agencies recognized by the European authority (ESMA) and two agencies with FINMA recognition (all the Big 3 have NRSRO, ESMA and FINMA recognition).
- iv While three NRSROs also have ESMA recognition, namely A.M. Best Company and Kroll Bond Rating Agency (from the USA), the Dominion Bond Rating Service Ltd (from Canada) and the Japan Credit Rating Agency, Ltd, no European ESMA has an NRSRO status and only the Canadian DBRS and the Swiss Fedafin, besides the Big 3, are recognized by FINMA.

v Further, most agencies recognized as NRSRO come from the United States, except for three agencies belonging to NAFTA countries: the Canadian Dominion Bond Rating Service Ltd, the Mexican HR Ratings and the Japan Credit Rating Agency, Ltd.

vi On the other hand only two US small NRSRO, A.M. Best Company and Kroll Bond Rating Agency, have ESMA recognition. The other non-European small NRSRO with ESMA recognition are the Canadian Dominion Bond Rating Service Ltd and the Japan Credit Rating Agency, Ltd.

This distribution in agencies' registration/certification may make us fear some partisanship in the granting of NRSRO and ESMA certifications. Table 10.2 gives a list of small agencies that do not detain NRSRO or ESMA status, despite the fact that some of them may have gained some international reputation, like Dagong Global Credit Rating of China, Global Credit Ratings Co. of South Africa or the Indian ICRA Ltd.[6]

Some SmAs are asking for more openness (less restrictiveness) in the granting of NRSRO or ESMA status. In their view the observed restrictiveness strongly contributes to the de facto Big 3 oligopoly in rating activity and they are calling for mutual and mechanical recognition of agencies registered by NRSRO or ESMA (CPR Portugal).

Assessing small agencies' market share

Although, it is commonly advocated that new agencies will create healthy competition, leading to more accurate ratings, the question of small SmAs' ability to seize the opportunity offered to them, by the new global rating legal environment, is raised. The capacity of SmAs to take the space that might be left to them by the Big 3, due to the implementation of new rules denying them the legal monopoly they used to enjoy, will be assessed on the ground in the analysis of three variables:

i the SmAs' staffing, as measured by the number of analysts employed by SmAs to the number of analysts servicing the Big 3 (AR);

ii the SmAs' outstanding ratings, as expressed by the number of outstanding ratings performed by SmAs to the number of outstanding ratings performed by Big 3 (RR); and

iii the SmAs' market share, as expressed by small agencies' market share to the Big 3's market share (SR).

The number of analysts employed by SmAs to the number of analysts servicing the Big 3 (AR) is given by:

$$AR = SmA_A / Big3_A \tag{10.1}$$

Table 10.2 Agencies without formal recognition

Number	*Agency*	*Citizenship*	*Number*	*Agency*	*Citizenship*
1	Agusto & Co.	Nigeria	8	Muros Ratings	Russia
2	Credit Rating Information and Services Ltd	Bangladesh		NUS Risk Management Institute (not for profit)	Singapore
3	Dagong Global Credit Rating	China	9	RusRating	Russia
4	Expert RA	Russia	10	Public Sector Credit Solutions (not for profit)	USA
5	Global Credit Ratings Co.	South Africa	11	Ontonix	Italy
6	ICRA Ltd	India	12	Veda	Australia
7	Levin and Goldstein	Zambia	13	Wikirating (not for profit)	Switzerland

Where:

> SmA_A represents the number of analysts employed by the SmA;
> $Big3_A$ represents the number of analysts employed by the Big 3 (Fitch, Moody's and S&P).

The number of outstanding ratings performed by SmAs to the number of outstanding rating ratings performed by the Big 3 (RR), is given by:

$$RR = SmA_R / Big3_R \tag{10. 2}$$

Where:

> SmA_R represents the number of outstanding rating of SmAs;
> $Big3_R$ represents the number of outstanding rating of the Big 3 (Fitch, Moody's and S&P).

Finally, the market share of SmA to the market share of the Big 3 (SR), is given by:

$$SR = SmA_M / Big3_M \tag{10. 3}$$

Where:

> SmA_M represents the global market share of SmAs,
> $Big3_M$ represents the global market share of the Big 3 (Fitch, Moody's and (S&P).

Table 10.3 provides the number of rating analysts employed by agencies as of 31 December of each calendar year 2010, 2011 and 2012.

During this period, the number of analysts that were employed by SmAs has increased by 15 per cent [(152/132)−1], compared to 5 per cent for the

Table 10.3 Number of rating analysts employed by agencies as of 31 December of each calendar year

	2010	*2011*	*2012*
Total of rating analysts employed by the Big 3	3,482	3,636	3,651
Total of rating analysts employed by the SmA	283	330	371
Total of rating analysts employed by all agencies	3,765	3,966	4,022
AR (SmA in % of Big 3)	0.08	0.09	0.10

Source: adapted from data contained in NRSRO Forms, Exhibit 8.[1]

Note

1 Since HR Ratings became an NRSRO in November 2012, the relevant information was not reported prior to such date.

Big 3 [(3,651/3,482)−1]. The relative increase in staffing levels has, however, been much greater at DBRS and the overall improvement in staffing in SmAs represents the hiring of 20 new analysts in two years, compared 169 new analysts hired by the Big 3. To summarize the behaviour of analyst hiring at agencies, we computed the analyst ratio (AR), i.e. the number of analysts employed by the SmAs, divided by the number of analysts employed by the Big 3. As indicated in Table 10.3, final row, AR has increased by one percentage point in 2011 and 2012. Indicating a modest improvement in analyst staffing at SmAs.

Table 10.4 provides the number of outstanding credit ratings reported by SmAs and the Big 3 for the calendar year ending 31 December 2012, in each of the five categories: (i) financial institutions, (ii) insurance companies, (iii) corporate issuers, (iv) asset-backed securities and (v) government securities.

As of 31 December 2012, SmAs have issued a modest 4.5 per cent (comparatively, the Big 3 have issued about 96.5 per cent of all the ratings that were reported to be outstanding as of 31 December 2012) and had registered the lowest number of outstanding ratings in each of the rating categories. Their contribution ranged from 30 per cent for insurance companies to around 1 per cent for corporate issuers and government securities. They also count for around 20 per cent of the ratings for the financial institutions category. It appears also in the light of Table 10.4 that on 31 December 2012 DBRS, KBRA and Morningstar are the three agencies that distinguished themselves by scoring the largest number of outstanding credit ratings being reported, after the Big 3. This represents approximately 2 per cent, 1 per cent, and little under 1 per cent respectively of all outstanding ratings. Together these three agencies had issued approximately less than 4 per cent of all the ratings reported to the SEC on 31 December 2012.

Figure 10.2 describes the behaviour of the ratios of the number of outstanding ratings performed by SmAs to the number of outstanding ratings performed by the Big 3 ($RR = SmA_R/Big3_R$). It depicts the rating ratio (RR) in each rating category, based on information reported by the NRSRO as of 31 December 2012.

SmAs have a good number in the insurance rating category, performing 32 per cent of all outstanding ratings in this category: they also have 20 per cent of all outstanding ratings in the financial rating category, 10 per cent for asset-backed securities and 8 per cent for corporate issuers. Figure 10.3, on the other hand, shows that the market share of all credit rating agencies, excluding the Big 3, has oscillated between 5.3 per cent in 2010 and 5.4 per cent in 2012, after topping at 6.0 per cent in 2011. The weight of SmAs to the weight of the Big 3 as given by the ratio SR ($SR = SmA_M/Big3_M$) is around 4.7 per cent.

All together the three performance measures (ratios) show a weak capacity of SmAs to compete significantly with the Big 3 and underline the fact

Table 10.4 Number of reviews of credit ratings by other NRSRO, for the year ended 31 December 2012

NRSRO	*Financial institutions*	*Insurance institutions*	*Corporate issuers*	*Asset-backed securities*	*Government securities*	*Total ratings*
A.M. Best	Not registered	4,610	1,787	55	Not registered	6,452
DBRS	16,222	148	3,736	10,054	15,952	46,112
EJR	109	48	1,004	Not registered	Not registered	1,161
HR Ratings	Not registered	Not registered	Not registered	Not registered	184	184
JCR	159	27	472	Not registered	56	714
KBRA	15,646	50	1,000	352	1,945	18,993
Morningstar	Not registered	Not registered	Not registered	13 935	Not registered	13935
Total other	32,136	4,883	7,999	24,396	18,137	87,551
Total	194,949	19,908	103,276	260,564	1,925,887	2,504,584
Big 3	162,813	15,025	95,277	236,168	1,907,750	2,417,033
Total agencies	194,949	19,908	103,276	260,564	1,925,887	2,504,584

Source: NRSRO Annual Certifications for the year ended 31 December 2012, Item 7A.

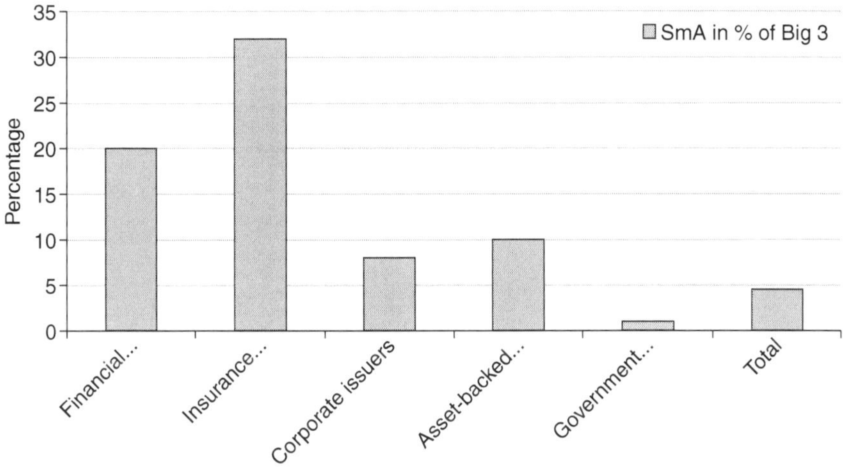

Figure 10.2 Ratings ratio (source: adapted from SEC NRSRO data).

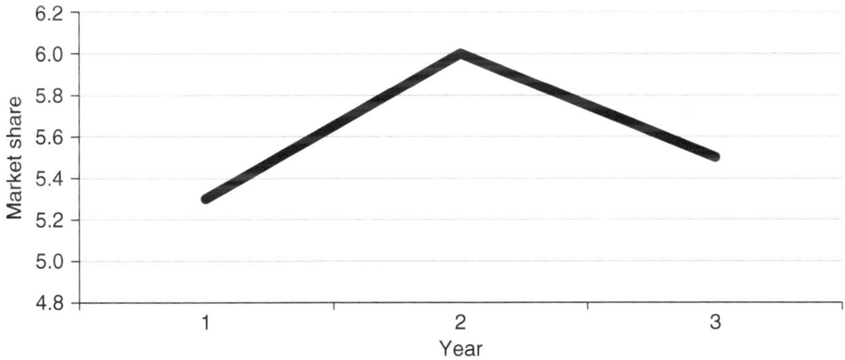

Figure 10.3 Credit rating market share, all agencies, excluding the Big 3, for the period 2010–2012.

that in the foreseeable future, they can represent no serious challenge to the main global agencies. If we concentrate, however, on the commercial mortgage-backed securities (CMBS) market, our conclusion can be slightly tempered. Table 10.5 provides ratings for CMBS issued by NRSRO agencies in the first half of the period 2010–2012.

Some of the smaller agencies have increased their market share in the past few years in structured finance market sector, specifically in the market of CMBS. KBRA and Morningstar, both newer entrants to the CMBS market, have gained market share in the past few years. Morningstar's market share increased from 15 per cent in 2010 to 23 per cent in

Table 10.5 Small rating agencies for CMBS issued in the first half of 2012

Agency	*1H-2012 issuance ($ million)*	*No. of deals*	*1H-2011 issuance ($ million)*	*No. of deals*	*1H-2010 issuance ($ million)*	*No. of deals*
KBRA	8,897.4	10	410	1	n.a.	
DBRS	7,711.4	12	4,991.2	7	2,936.2	3
Morningstar	4,632.4	8	4,516.1	8	2,195.1	5
Total others	21,241.2	30	9,917.3	16	5,131.3	8
Total Big 3	29,618.9	47	33,582.3	34	18,021.5	42
Total all	50,860.1	77	43,499.6	50	23,152.8	50

Source: NRSRO December 2012 Report.

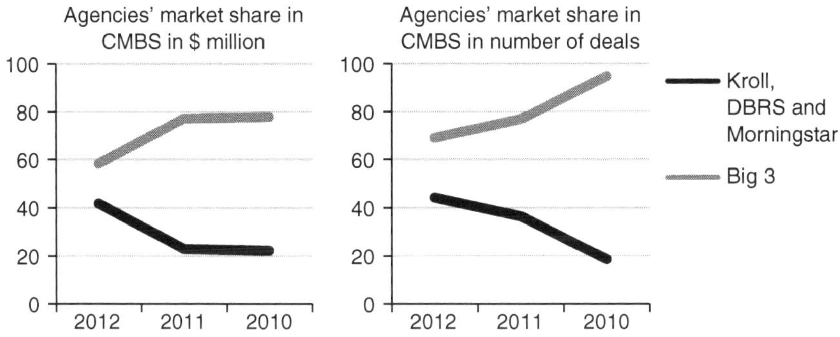

Figure 10.4 Agencies' market share in CMBS ($ millions) and number of deals for the period 2010–2012.

the first half of 2012. KBRA, which first began issuing ratings on CMBS in 2011, had a market share of approximately 44 per cent in the first half of 2012. DBRS, which is not new to the CMBS market but is one of the smaller NRSRO, also increased its market share. DBRS's market share grew from approximately 20 per cent in 2010 to approximately 38 per cent in the first half of 2012 (SEC, 2012b). Figure 10.4 describes the behaviour of Kroll's, DBRS's and Morningstar's market share in CMBS issued for the years 2010, 2011 and 2012.

In 2012, market share in CMBS issues of the three agencies, Kroll, DBRS and Morningstar, expressed in dollars and in number of deals has increased by more than 20 per cent since 2010, at the expense of Big 3 decreasing shares. Although the three largest CRAs continue to dominate the credit rating market, they only reported a decline in their market share of structured finance ratings from approximately 96 per cent in 2008 to approximately 91 per cent in 2011. IOSCO acknowledges that other factors also affect competition in the credit rating industry; new entrants face some specific barriers to entry, including high start-up costs and the difficulty in changing investor preference for ratings determined by the large established CRAs (IOSCO, 2011).

Investors tend to think of various CRAs' ratings as similar, which does not seem really to be the case, although, some small CRAs do have approaches that can distinguish them. Further, some SmAs are focused on specific niches that can give them the starting point for their potential competitiveness and may form the essential route by which new entrants can enter the market. They seem, however, unable to use them as competitive advantage. Consequently, despite some slight improvement, SmAs seem to have made little progress in gaining a greater market share; their income share has not changed, compared to its 2010 level, with the exception of a modest growth of less than 1 per cent in 2011 and which was almost entirely cancelled in 2012.

SmAs and initiatives that can make a difference

This section will discuss the cases of some of the promising SmAs to becoming serious challengers to the Big 3, along with an international initiative that was recently launched by agencies from five emerging economies.

Three American agencies along with three non-American agencies, can present a serious hope of becoming modest challengers to the Big 3. These are:

i the American AM Ratings agency;
ii KBRA;
iii Morningstar;
iv the Canadian DBRS;
v the Japanese Credit Rating Agency; and
vi the Chinese Dagong,

We call these small agencies the six challengers or the Cha6. We think that these six agencies may have the potential of impact in the future of the global rating market and each one for its own reasons. In 2012 Cha6 had around 47,000 outstanding ratings, 46,000 were performed by DBRS. Together, Cha6 represent a very insignificant percentage of the total outstanding ratings of 2.5 million ratings made by NRSRO in 2012. Table 10.6 provides the number of outstanding credit ratings by rating category – Cha6, SmA and Big 3 – for the calendar year ending 31 December 2012.

As of 31 December 2012, Cha6 had a very low number of outstanding ratings in each of the rating categories. Their overall contribution represents 3.44 per cent of the total of outstanding ratings, ranging from 24.29 per cent for insurance companies to around 1 per cent for government securities. They also account for around 16.43 per cent of the ratings for the financial institutions category, 6.77 per cent for corporate ratings and 4.01 per cent for asset-backed securities. A brief description of Cha6 is provided below. The rating agencies that can present some hope of challenging the Big 3 on the global rating market are of three different origins, those coming the US environment, those coming from an environment with strong ties to the US environment and those coming from emerging markets or are product of international initiatives.

The US challengers

The US challengers, included in the Cha6, are A.M. Best, KBRA and Morningstar. Table 10.7 provides the number of outstanding credit ratings by rating category, made by A.M. Best, KBRA and Morningstar for the calendar year ending 31 December 2012 amounting to 39,380 issues, or 1.57 per cent of 2,504,584, the total ratings for all NRSROs. Each one of

Table 10.6 Number of outstanding credit ratings by rating category, Cha6, SmA and Big3 for the calendar year ending December 31, 2012

NRSRO	*Financial institutions*	*Insurance institutions*	*Corporate issuers*	*Asset-backed securities*	*Government securities*	*Total ratings*
Cha6	32,027	4,835	6,995	10,461	17,953	86,206
% Cha6 of the total	16.43	24.29	6.77	4.01	0.93	3.44
Big 3	162,813	15,025	95,277	236,168	1,907,750	2,417,033
% of Big 3	83.52	75.47	92.25	90.64	99.06	96.50
Total agencies	194,949	19,908	103,276	260,564	1,925,887	2,504,584

Source: adapted from NRSRO Annual Certifications for the year ended 31 December 2012, Item 7A.

Table 10.7 Number of outstanding credit ratings by rating category, the three American challengers for the calendar year ending 31 December 2012

NRSRO	*Financial institutions*	*Insurance institutions*	*Corporate issuers*	*Asset-backed securities*	*Government securities*	*Total ratings*
KBRA	15,646	50	1,000	352	*1,945*	18,993
A.M. Best	–	4,610	1,787	55	–	6,452
Morningstar	–	–	–	*13,935*	–	13,935
Total	15,646	4,660	2,787	14,342	1,945	39,380
% of the total	8.03	23.41	2.70	5.50	0.10	1.57
Total agencies	194,949	19,908	103,276	260,564	1,925,887	2,504,584

Source: adapted from SEC, NRSRO Annual Certifications for the year ended 31 December 2012, Item 7A.

these three small American agencies seems to have, however, a competitive advantage in a specific rating category. KBRA, for instance, takes the lead in the financial institutions and government securities categories, insuring 100 per cent of these two categories, A.M. Best, in the insurance institutions category also insuring a little under of 100 per cent of this category and Morningstar, in the asset-backed securities category, also insuring around 97 per cent of the ratings of this category.

The following is brief description of A.M. Best, KBRA, and Morningstar. A.M. Best may be regarded as a relatively serious future challenger to the Big 3, because it 'is a global full-service credit rating agency dedicated to serving the insurance industry. It began its rating activity in 1906, making it the first of today's rating agencies to use symbols to differentiate the relative creditworthiness of companies'.[7] According to NRSRO, A.M. Best issued about 23.2 per cent of the ratings outstanding in insurance category, next to S&P, which issued about 38.2 per cent, and exceeding Fitch and Moody's, which issued about 19.0 per cent and 18.3 per cent, respectively. A.M. Best has consistently been reported as one of the top three issuers of insurance ratings. Nothing can keep A.M. Best from extending its competitive advantage in insurance rating to other rating categories, and this makes it one of the more serious candidates for future expansion.

Kroll Bond Rating Agency (KBRA) was established in 2010 and has created new standards for assessing risk and offered credit ratings with its over 90 professionals. On top of being an NRSRO, KBRA is also recognized by the National Association of Insurance Commissioners (NAIC) as a credit rating provider (CRP). KBRA 'never relying solely on information provided by issuers of bonds; we'll look under the hood to find out what goes into each security' (KBRA website).

Morningstar was founded in 1984 and went public in 2005. It provides ratings on approximately 433,000 investment offerings, along with real-time global market data on nearly ten million equities, indexes, futures, options, commodities and precious metals, in addition to foreign exchange and treasury markets. Morningstar also offers investment management services through its registered investment adviser subsidiaries and has approximately $166 billion in assets under advisement and management as of 30 June 2013. The company has operations in 27 countries. Morningstar is a fast growing agency: it has, since 2003 undertaken numerous corporate acquisitions.[8]

Close to US challengers

In this group we have the Canadian DBRS and the Japan Credit Rating Agency Ltd (JCR). Table 10.8 provides the number of outstanding credit ratings by rating category, of the two non-American challengers (DBRS and JCR) for the calendar year ending 31 December 2012, Together these

Table 10.8 Number of outstanding credit ratings by rating category, the three non-American challengers for the calendar year ending 31 December 2012

NRSRO	*Financial institutions*	*Insurance institutions*	*Corporate issuers*	*Asset-backed securities*	*Government securities*	*Total ratings*
DBRS	16,222	148	3,736	10,054	15,952	46,112
JCR	159	27	472	–	56	714
Total	16,381	175	4,208	10,054	16,008	46,826
% total	8.40	0.88	4.07	3.86	0.83	1.87
Total agencies	194,949	19,908	103,276	260,564	1,925,887	2,504,584

Source: adapted from SEC, NRSRO Annual Certifications for the year ended 31 December 2012, Item 7A.

two agencies have insured the rating of 46,826 issues for a total of 2,504,584, corresponding to 1.87 per cent. DBRS has a competitive advantage in all rating categories. It insures the quasi- totality of the rating in all categories, leaving JCR with insignificant scores. JCR was included in the challengers list not so much for the number of its ratings it makes, but rather for its standing in the global rating market.

The following is brief description DBRS and JCR. DBRS was founded in in 1976. It is the biggest provider of credit ratings after the Big 3, with 46,112 in 2012,[9] for all categories of ratings whether financial institutions, insurance companies, corporate issuers, asset-backed securities or government securities. DBRS enjoys large international recognition and it is registered with both NRSRO and the EC. Currently, DBRS rates more than 1,000 different companies and single-purpose vehicles that issue commercial papers, term debt and preferred shares in the global capital markets. DBRS ratings are distributed publicly at no cost via the Internet. DBRS is a Canadian agency and, as such, it can enjoy easy acceptance both from the Anglo-Saxon business world, but also from emerging economies issuers. Its deep knowledge of the Big 3 rating systems makes an acceptable alternative to Big 3, for all those who are looking for Big 3 reputation, but fearing their 'pretended' impartiality.

The Japan Credit Rating Agency (JCR) was establishment on 1 April 1985, with the main business objective being credit ratings, including medium-term note programmes and asset-backed securities. JCR is one of the key credit rating agencies in Japan. JCR provides a number of services, including rating debt securities of all types, as well as financial market and industry research. JCR also offers political and economic research, and various publications and informational services for its data. Although the majority of JCR's activities concern Japanese institutions, it enjoys a wide international recognition. It is, for instance, registered with both NRSRO and the EC. JCR is the fourth NRSRO in terms of outstanding ratings, with 714 ratings in 2012.[10]

Emerging market initiatives

Two emerging economies' initiatives are worth mentioning here: the Chinese agency Dagong and the international initiative of ARC Ratings.

The People's Bank of China and the former State Economic and Trade Commission jointly founded Dagong in 1994. Currently, it has 34 branches domestically and two abroad, with about 600 employees. Dagong performs the following credit rating activities: (i) sovereign credit rating; (ii) public finance credit rating; (iii) corporate credit rating; (iv) financial institutions credit rating and (v) structural financing rating. Although the impact of Dagong on the global market is still very limited, this agency is advancing very well. It has imposed itself as the defender of global credit market efficiency and it is pleasing to all those who accused the Big 3 of showing preferential treatment to the United States and seeking alternatives to the Big 3 agencies. The Big 3, they say, no longer meet the needs of the new globalized world. Dagong as one of the promoters of the reform of the international credit rating system may have gained an emblematic role at the international level. Dagong is convinced that the existing international credit rating system is the origin of the global credit crisis and that only a new international credit rating system could help the recovery of the world economy. Dagong may have inspired other searches for initiatives. Dagong, although representing a benign competition in the international credit rating sector believes that 'the theories and roadmaps it proposed to reform the international credit rating system have got recognized widely in the international community. The actions of reform now are gradually carrying out' (Dagong president's message). It is argued that 'the independent and impartial rating stance and standard of Dagong have also got recognition around the world' (Dagong president's message). The biggest achieved market stake by Dagong is it registration with the EU, through its European affiliate with headquarters in Milan, Italy, in June 2013, after being turned down by the SEC for NRSRO registration in 2010. In a smart move Dagong Europe is capitalizing on other agencies' former staff. The management is composed of the general manager with an S&P background, the senior credit officer previously worked for 25 years at NatWest, Banka Cabot (Intesa Sanpaolo Group), the head of financial institutions analytical team, former director of financial institutions at Fitch Ratings of Chile, and the head of the corporates analytical team was previously vice president and senior analyst at Moody's Investor Service Ltd (Dagong Europe)

Five credit ratings institutions from five countries that launched a new global agency, ARC Ratings, recently undertook an international initiative. This is a joint venture between CPR of Portugal, CARE Rating of India, GCR of South Africa, MARC of Malaysia and Brazil's SR Rating (Glover, 2014). A brief review of these five founding agencies of ARC is given below.

- CPR of Portugal (Companhia Portuguesa de Rating, SA)[11] was established in 1988, with a private shareholding, as one of the oldest European credit rating agencies. It seems to enjoy a good reputation and credibility in Portugal and has certainly contributed to the expansion of the credit rating market in the country, where the highest number of ratings in Europe is found. CPR is registered with ESMA, allowing it to exercise in the 27 Member States of the European Union; it is also recognized as External Credit Assessment Institution (ECAI) for corporates by the Banco de Portugal.
- CARE Ratings of India,[12] started operations in 1993, with majority shareholding by leading domestic banks and financial institutions in India and later had also attracted many other investors. It has established itself as one the major credit rating agencies in India. With the

rating volume of debt of around Rs45,901 billion (as on 31 December 2012),[13] CARE Ratings has also emerged as the leading agency for covering many rating segments like that for banks, sub-sovereigns and initial public offering grading. CARE Ratings provides the entire spectrum of credit rating. CARE's head office, is located at Mumbai, but has also regional offices at eight other Indian cities and international operation in the Republic of the Maldives.

- The origins of the Global Credit Rating Co. (GCR)[14] of South Africa can be traced back to 1996 when it was established as the African arm of the New York Stock Exchange-listed Duff & Phelps. Very rapid growth followed and within only a short period the group had established itself as the market leader, accounting for the majority of all ratings accorded on the African continent. GCR's African regional headquarters are based in Johannesburg, with its main office, West and East African regional offices established in Harare, Lagos and Nairobi respectively. GCR rates the full spectrum of security classes and accords both international scale and national scale ratings, and, together with its international affiliates, rates almost 3,000 organizations and debt issues – spanning four continents.
- The Malaysian Rating Corporation Berhad (MARC)[15] was incorporated in 1995. MARC's shareholders are the major life and general insurance companies, and investment banks in Malaysia. MARC undertakes ratings of corporates and corporate debt issuers, including Islamic capital market instruments, asset-backed securities, as well as financial strength ratings of financial institutions and insurance companies.
- The Braziliùn SR Ratings[16] was established in 1993, with the objective of classifying the first structured receivables securitization in Brazil, through debentures issue of the Mesbla Trust. SR gained notoriety, being responsible for important ratings for varied types of issues and issuers, a fact that has granted ample experience in rating assignments that include everything from project finance to bonds in the real estate sector, FIDCs, Cédula de Crédito Bancário, certificates, letters and grades, bonds in the agribusiness sector, bank and insurer risks, asset management quality evaluations, and sovereign and sub-sovereign risk.

ARC presents itself as the rating of emerging economies; it feels that these economies are not well deserved by the Big 3. ARC Ratings promises reconfiguring the ratings scales, although it will still grade companies from AAA to D rating. It specially wants to move away from the simple dichotomy of investment grade or non-investment grade (junk). That, it believes, does not help investors to make rational decisions; instead ARC will further split the grades into (i) low risk, (ii) moderate risk, (iii) high risk and (iv) imminent or actual default.

Together, the five ratings agencies forming ARC are currently rating 6,000 clients in their various local markets. It is estimated that around 10 per cent of these are mid- to large-size companies that will be prospective clients on an international level. It is hoped that many more companies would appreciate a choice of ratings agency outside the Big 3. Given the geographies of these countries, ARC Ratings would be well represented across four continents. Further, given that the Portuguese agency has an ESMA licence, operations in Europe could begin right away. All the participating agencies in ARC Ratings are dominant players in their own markets. They do rating assignments for top companies domestically. Many of these companies also source global markets for funds where it is essential to take a rating from one of the established global credit rating agencies. Here the rating of the sovereign as well as the company matters. Today given limited competition, they are perforce going to these agencies and getting two ratings. Given their own strong relationships with these companies for domestic purposes, they could offer them a global rating through ARC, which can be taken along with the rating from one of the other established CRAs. This way it would be possible to scale business and build volume.

Discussion

Despite the new regulatory framework, somehow favourable to small agencies, negative effects of the old regulatory system persist. Small CRAs can, however, still increase their market share by focusing on specific niches or on issuers not rated by the Big 3. New entrants to the ratings market will surely face insurmountable barriers to entry, beginning with high starting costs and the difficulty in changing ingrained tendencies of investors favouring the well-established Big 3 ratings. This chapter shows that the establishment of an appropriate regulatory environment for discouraging the use of credit ratings for regulatory purposes may not be sufficient to introduce real competition to the global rating market. Even if some smaller rating agencies may have begun to make their mark in the rating market, the historical dominance of the Big 3 seems to have no end, or even just register a slight decrease. Agencies operating in the North American environment, DBRS, AM Ratings, KBRA and Morningstar seem to have managed to focus on niches that seem to favour their market shares advances, but their success of competing significantly with the Big 3 depends largely on their ability to convince investors that their ratings are as of high quality, which, in turn, could encourage issuers to hire them. In this regard, transparency can play an important role in enhancing market competition, in a sense that transparency allows investors to compare the practices of CRAs and permits the smaller and the newer to establish observable competitive differences from the Big 3 (FIDC, 2007). IOSCO goes further and asserts that transparency and competition of CRAs can 'promote investor protection; help ensure fair and transparent markets, and contribute to reduction of systemic risk' (IOSCO, 2003). Such an endeavour may prove to be easier for small agencies with North American tradition than for agencies coming from other economic environments. Familiarity with the North American credit rating environment may not, however, be of great help, unless decisions driven by ideological reasons to impede seriously the Big 3's ability to expand are taken by legislators. Unless such restrictive procurement rules are implemented, any new promising existing or new agencies may quickly run the risk of being rapidly annexed by the Big 3. Not everyone, however, is convinced of the efficiency benefit that may result from new agencies coming to the market: 'we find that the entry of a third major rating agency (Fitch) coincides with lower overall quality, as measured by both the levels and informational content of incumbents' ratings', argue Becker and Milbourn (2009a).

Conclusion

Despite the promising future of six small challenger rating agencies, Cha6 presented in this chapter, it will be naive to think of the Big 3 abandoning voluntarily, even an insignificant portion of their market share, despite tremendous efforts undertaken by regulators, and more legal monitoring might be needed. Otherwise, only the best prepared small North American NRSROs (DBRS, EJR, HR Ratings, KBRA and Morningstar) may finally be in position to benefit significantly from the recent international move for eliminating references to credit ratings in regulatory provisions.

Notes

1 Laws, regulations and private contracts referencing credit ratings have been a factor contributing to lower competition among CRAs.

2 On 27 December 2013, with a compliance date of 7 July 2014, the American Securities and Exchange Commission (SEC) adopted amendments to eliminate references to credit ratings by nationally recognized statistical rating organizations (NRSRO) in financial acts and rules.

3 SEC proposes first in series of rule amendments to remove references to credit ratings, 9 February 2011, at: www.sec.gov/rules/proposed/2011/33-9186.pdf, retrieved 2 June 2014.

4 Press release, http://europa.eu/rapid/press-release_IP-13–555_en.htm, retrieved 9 February 2014, Brussels, 18 June 2013.

5 FINMA is the Swiss Financial Market Supervisory Authority, a government body responsible for financial regulation in Switzerland.

6 ICRA Limited (ICRA) is an Indian independent credit ratings agency, established in 1991.

7 See www3.ambest.com/ratings/default.asp, retrieved 26 February 2013.

8 See http://en.wikipedia.org/wiki/Morningstar,_Inc, retrieved 4 July 2014.

9 DBRSs' NRSRO Annual Certifications for the year ended 31 December 2012, Item 7A.

Appendix 10.1 The list of agencies (excluding the Big 3 affiliates) registered or certified by NRSRO, ESMA or FINMA in accordance with Article 18(3) of the Credit Rating Agencies Regulation, on 3 June 2013

No.	*Agency*	*Citizenship*	*SEC recognition*	*ESMA recognition*	*FINMA recognition*
1	A.M. Best Company	USA	NRSRO	ESMA	–
2	ASSEKURATA Assekuranz Rating-Agentur GmbH	Germany	–	ESMA	–
3	Axesor SA	Spain	–	ESMA	–
4	Bulgarian Credit Rating Agency AD	Bulgaria	–	ESMA	–
5	Capital Intelligence (Cyprus) Ltd	Cyprus	–	ESMA	–
6	CERVED Group SpA	Italy	–	ESMA	–
7	Companhia Portuguesa de Rating, SA (CPR)	Portugal	–	ESMA	–
8	Creditreform Rating AG	Germany	–	ESMA	–
9	CRIF SpA	Italy	–	ESMA	–
10	Dagong Europe Credit Rating Srl (Dagong Europe)	Italy	–	ESMA	–
11	Dominion Bond Rating Service Ltd., DBRS	Canada	NRSRO	ESMA	FINMA
12	Egan-Jones Rating Company	USA	NRSRO		
13	Euler Hermes Rating GmbH	Germany		ESMA	
14	European Rating Agency AS	Slovakia		ESMA	
15	Fedafin	Switzerland	–	–	FINMA
16	Feri EuroRating Services AG	Germany	–	ESMA	–
17	GBB-Rating Gesellschaft für Bonitätsbeurteilung mbH	Germany	–	ESMA	–
18	HR Ratings	Mexico	NRSRO	–	–
19	ICAP Group SA	Greece	–	ESMA	–
20	Japan Credit Rating Agency, Ltd	Japan	NRSRO	ESMA	–
21	Kroll Bond Rating Agency	USA	NRSRO	ESMA	–
22	Morningstar, Inc.	USA	NRSRO	–	–
23	Rapid Ratings International	USA	NRSRO	–	–
24	Scope Credit Rating Gmb	Germany	–	ESMA	–
25	Spread Research	France	–	ESMA	–
26	Economist Intelligence Unit, Ltd	UK	–	ESMA	–

Source: adapted from NRSRO Annual Certifications for the year ended 31 December 2012, Item 7A; ESMA publications.

10 JCR's NRSRO Annual Certifications for the year ended 31 December 2012, Item 7A.
11 See www.cprating.pt/, retrieved 24 May 2014.
12 See www.careratings.com/about-us.aspx, retrieved 8 June 2014.
13 On 5 March 2014, US$1 = Rs61,88.
14 See https://globalratings.net/#, retrieved 3 March 2014.
15 See www.marc.com.my/home/index.php?mid=11, retrieved 3 March 2014.
16 See www.srrating.com.br/en/institutional, retrieved 3 March 2014.

Bibliography

Becker, B. and T. Milbourn (2009), 'How did increased competition affect credit ratings?' Harvard Business School Working Paper, No. 09-051.

Becker, B. and T. Milbourn (2009), 'Reputation and competition: evidence from the credit rating industry.' Harvard Business School Working Paper, No. 09-055.

Dodd–Frank Wall Street Reform and Consumer Protection Act, 29 June 2010, at: http://thomas.loc.gov/cgi-bin/bdquery/z?d111:HR04173:@@@L&summ2=m&, retrieved 12 June 2013.

European Commission (2013), 'Stricter rules for credit rating agencies to enter into force', at: http://europa.eu/rapid/press-release_IP-13-555_en.htm?locale=FR, retrieved 23 July 2014.

Federal Deposit Insurance Corporation (FIDC) (2007), 'Supervisory insights, enhancing transparency in the structured finance market', at: www.fdic.gov/regulations/examinations/supervisory/insights/sisum08/article01_transparency.html, retrieved 4 March 2014.

Financial Stability Board (FSB) (2013), 'Credit rating agencies reducing reliance and strengthening oversight', Progress report to the St Petersburg G20 Summit, 29 August.

G20 Seoul Summit Leaders' Declaration (2010), 11–12 November, at: www.g20.org/Documents2010/11/seoulsummit_declaration.pdf, retrieved 12 July 2012.

G20, Toronto G20 Summit Declaration (2010), 26–27 June, at: www.g20.org/Documents/g20_declaration_en.pdf, retrieved 12 June 2010.

Glover, J. (2014), 'ARC ratings seeking to exploit credit grading credibility loss', Bloomberg, 16 January, at: www.bloomberg.com/news/2014-01-16/arc-ratings-seeking-to-exploit-credit-grading-credibility-loss.html, retrieved 23 September 2014.

International Organization of Securities Commissions (IOSCO) (2003), 'Objectives and principles of securities regulation', at: www.cssf.cl/cssf/docs/ti-IOSCOPD154.pdf, retrieved 12 December 2013.

International Organization of Securities Commissions (IOSCO) (2011), 'Regulatory implementation of the statement of principles regarding the activities of credit rating agencies', Final report, at: www.fsa.go.jp/, retrieved 26 May 2014.

International Organization of Securities Commissions (IOSCO) (2013a), 'Re: transparency and competition among credit rating agencies', at: www.iosco.org/ retrieved 12 July 2014.

International Organization of Securities Commissions (IOSCO) (2013b), 'Response to the G20's communiqué resulting from its meeting on November 4–5, 2012: re: transparency and competition among credit rating agencies', 15 April, at: www.iosco.org/, retrieved 12 July 2014.

Jeon, D.-S. and S. Lovo, (2012a), 'Credit rating industry: a helicopter tour of stylized facts and recent theories', *International Journal of Industrial Organization*, Vol. 31, pp. 643–651.

Jeon, D.-S. and S. Lovo (2012b), 'Reputation as an entry barrier in the credit rating industry', Toulouse School of Economics and CEPR, Working Paper.

KBRA website, at: www.krollbondratings.com/, retrieved 30 November 2013.

Kliger, D. and O. Sarig (2000), 'The information value of bond ratings', *Journal of Finance*, December, Vol. 55(6), pp. 2879–2902.

Koresh, G. (2003), 'The quality of corporate credit rating: an empirical investigation', EFMA 2003 Helsinki Meetings, European Financial Management Association.

Reuters (2013), 'The Big 3 credit ratings agencies have a new competitor', 12 November, at: http://business.financialpost.com/2013/11/12/the-big-3-credit-ratings-agencies-have-a-new-competition, retrieved 2 June 2014.

Securities and Exchange Commission (SEC) (2012) 'Summary report of the commission staff's examination of each NRSRO', at: www.sec.gov, retrieved 23 June 2014.

Securities and Exchange Commission (SEC) (2012), 'Annual report on nationally recognized statistical rating organizations', at: www.sec.gov, retrieved 13 June 2014.

Securities and Exchange Commission (SEC) SEC Initiatives under New Regulatory Reform Law, at: www.sec.gov/rules/proposed/2011/33-9186.pdf, retrieved 13 December 2013.

Shecter, B. (2012), 'Canada imposes oversight on credit rating agencies', at: http://business.financialpost.com/author/bshecter/, retrieved 2 May 2014.

Theis, A. and M. Wolgast (2012), 'Regulation and reform of rating agencies in the European Union: an insurance industry perspective', Geneva Papers 37, pp. 47–76, at: www.palgrave-journals.com/gpp/journal/v37/n1/full/gpp.201133a.html, retrieved 20 June 2012.

11 Critical perspective and concluding remarks

Although, most spheres of power in our contemporary society seem to be contributing, more or less consciously and to a certain extent, to the weakening of the best economic and social system ever, the blame was most virulently addressed to rating agencies. 'How badly do the major credit-rating firms have to perform before investors stop using their services?' was the question in a 2008 *Wall Street Journal*, in the aftermath of the crisis and the answer is: can they? Indeed, although most people would agree on the need of supervising CRAs for the sake of improving their governance and decreasing their hegemony on the world credit rating market, most continue desperately to rely on them for credit default assessment, for instance. US regulators, for instance, depend on credit ratings to monitor the safety of $450 billion of bonds held by US insurance. Warning is issued that 'any changes must be carefully assessed and remain cognisant of the important contribution of CRAs to credit assessment in the international financial system' (FSA *et al.*, 2013).

This chapter discusses the dilemma facing the international standard-setter with regard to Big 3 governance and their control over the rating market. Additional to the introduction, the second section discusses the main findings of the book; the third section explains why co-existing with the Big 3 oligopoly would seem inevitable, at least in the short run; the fourth asks if there are alternatives to agencies' credit ratings? The final section concludes the chapter.

The main findings of the book

Credit ratings are supposed to improve the efficiency of the market by reducing the informative asymmetry and its cost; indeed, individuals, firms and institutional investors find it useful to be guided by a rating, when making their investment decisions. Since debt ratings affect coupon rates and issue prices, any positive initial rating decreases the yield needed to sell the debt security, and any rating upgrade may increase its market value and vice versa. Evaluating financial solidity of issuers requires, however, expertise and extensive data. Most agents, and even some regulators, do not have the time, experience or resources of the rating agencies to thoroughly research the financial condition of all issuers. Agencies were expertly feeding such belief and using it as the best defence of their competitive position. Ratings, however, are feared to be a source of a lot of inefficiencies and this book deals with some of them in order to assess their veracity. Its main findings can be summarized in the following: if rationally and accurately developed, CRAs' ratings would represent the best bet and the more efficient way of assessing the default risk of issuers. We can easily imagine a system where each investor and/or issuer has to make its own calculations and convince others about the worthiness of its debt: this certainly would be the most socially costly way of doing things (Chapter 2). So it makes sense and represents a huge economy of time and effort to delegate such information gathering, sifting and dissemination to specialists, so long as one can trust them.

It is believed, however, that credit ratings can have several negative setbacks, on the one hand, not everyone anymore is pleased with the oligopoly they established over the years in the global credit market. Further, the accuracy of credit rating is overtly challenged; on the one hand they can make certain issuers unduly suffer downgrades, while making others abnormally benefiting from positive grades (whether voluntarily or not). Various studies that have compared Moody's and Standard & Poor's ratings, have found a great similarity for investment grade ratings (Cantor and Packer, 1996; Ammer and Packer, 2000). In case of speculative-grade issues, however, they found that Moody's and Standard & Poor's assign divergent ratings much more frequently to sovereign bonds than to corporate bonds. On the other hand, ratings are feared to destabilize financial markets at a systemic level, whenever downgrades and rating triggers result in mass selling and write-downs. CRAs are also believed to lag badly behind events in adjusting ratings in response to subsequent changes in the condition of issuers. Although, it is difficult see how CRAs can 'monitor continuously the unpredictable behaviour of myriads of individual debt issues' (Goodhart, 2008). David Wyss (who was till in July 2011 chief economist at S&P) summarized a certain feeling towards agencies by noting that, 'the credit agencies don't know any more about government budgets than the guy in the street who is reading the newspaper' (Crutsinger and Rexrode, 2011). One can wonder if the need for agencies' ratings was not artificially introduced, since their impact on economic efficiency has never been demonstrated. Many believe this is the case, and that like many similar activities in the financial market, they were extended not that much because of a need, but rather skilfully transformed in special niches for abnormal return production, abusively protected and intelligently expanded. Anyway, analysis of the credit rating market undertaken in this book reveals many other setbacks and weaknesses that are shared here:

i Not only is an excessive level of concentration noted in the global credit market, implying a limited choice of rating providers, but also an increasing market concentration trend can be identified, pointing to the existence of an economic rent for rating agencies, most likely to allow them to price abnormally high their services and set up impassable entry barriers, preventing serious potential newcomers from entering the rating market (Chapter 3).

ii Further, the accuracy of the methodologies used by agencies in assessing debt quality and defaults are overtly questioned (Chapter 4).

iii The default categorization followed by agencies is also subject to criticism, as it is believed to push them to make wrong diagnosis of default, making some issuers pay more than required for their debt, while others pay abnormally less, consequently mingling with market efficiency they are supposed to reinforce (Chapter 5).

iv Numerous instances were identified where agencies have dramatically lacked transparency and demonstrated conflicts of interest and 'it has been suggested that the issuer-pays business model fundamentally compromises the objectivity of the rating process' (World Bank, 2009) (Chapter 6).

v Consequently, many jurisdictions now have rules providing them with guidance on how to discourage reliance on CRAs' ratings for regulatory purposes. Thanks mainly to the well-orchestrated international regulatory initiative, authored by the US, the EU and international standard setters. It is warned, however, that any alternatives to ratings for use in the regulatory framework must meet the test of delivering the desired diversity of information without compromising the accuracy with which exposures of different credit quality can be distinguished (FSA *et al.*, 2013) (Chapter 7).

vi Agencies seem, however, to have substantially improved the integrity of their credit rating processes and the procedures, but much remains to be done, especially at the level of the internal monitoring system of rating accuracy control, board functioning and committees (Chapter 8).

vii Weaknesses are also identified in some audit procedures and supervisory controls governing rating processes (Chapter 9).

viii It is showed that it will be naive to think of the Big 3 abandoning on a voluntary basis, even an insignificant portion of their market share. Consequently, despite the promising future of some small agencies (Cha6), their chance of benefiting significantly from the recent international move for eliminating references to credit ratings in regulatory provisions remains very thin and only very few small North American agencies may finally find themselves in a position to benefit significantly from the recent international move for eliminating references to credit ratings in regulatory provisions (Chapter 10).

ix Overall, and the way the situation is currently evolving, credit rating activity appears to be quasi-exclusively a US activity.

Governance failures of the Big 3 may have been essential in the 'wheel' of the recent financial disaster, but also in many other less publicized financial scandals. Indeed, while agencies' structured finance failures have been their focus of criticism, they actually were blamed for many other ills. Although, 'a crisis of this magnitude cannot be the work of a few bad actors' (FCIC, 2011) but it was recognized that mortgage-related securities at the heart of the structured finance scandal could not have been marketed and sold without agencies' seal of approval that incite investors to rely on them, often blindly. They were, therefore key enablers of the process. In 2006 alone, Moody's put its triple-A seal of approval on 30 mortgage-related securities every working day. 'The results were disastrous: 83 per cent of the mortgage securities rated triple-A that year ultimately was downgraded' (FCIC, 2011). The only reason that can explain the Big 3's longevity, despite multiple failures unearthed by this book, has to do with the rating oligopoly they were enjoying and till recently was enforced by national and international regulatory agencies, through the huge number of promulgated rules requiring the use of ratings. Some central banks, for instance, till very recently, will only accept as collateral securities those rated by the Big 3. Similarly, various international agencies will only invest in development projects of countries that are rated by the Big 3. Market participants and even regulators had in effect 'outsourced' their own risk assessment to the Big 3 and often used ratings without taking their limitations into account (Theis and Wolgast, 2012).

Why co-existing with the Big 3 oligopoly would seem inevitable, at least in the short run

The key lesson that seems to have been learned from the current turmoil seems to be that it is vital for ratings to be able to provide a reliable indication of issuers' creditworthiness in periods of prosperity as in times of crisis and the best way to approach the problem of rating inaccuracy is by making CRAs compete in a market where no one is required to hire them. Reforms have come and gone, but no viable alternative has emerged yet to diminish the Big 3's impact. Recently however, the G20, in the United States, like the European Union, and several other countries (Australia, Japan), regulatory regimes for CRAs were established. One main reason that may have motivated such mass public intervention in credit agencies' affairs appears to be the weakness of their internal oversight mechanisms. CRAs could have therefore eased such regulatory pressure by having efficiently operating internal structures and demonstrating their effective operating.

As discussed in Chapter 7, at the international level, the G20 (initiating a worldwide trend to establish a strict regulatory framework for CRAs) agreed in 2009 on the need to introduce a registration and supervisory regime for CRAs based on the principles of the IOSCO Code. In the United States, for instance, the Credit Rating Agency Reform Act, enacted in 2006, constitutes a fundamental reform of the informal system of 'nationally recognized statistical rating organizations' (NRSRO) and introduced a formal registration regime and charged the SEC with some oversight of CRAs. In the European Union, CRAs' business conduct has been provided by three European Directives: the Market Abuse Directive, the Capital Requirements Directive, which set up the system of recognized External Credit Assessment Institutions (ECAI) as part of Basel II, and the Markets in Financial Instruments Directive. The objectives of all these CRA regulations are very similar, reflecting the internationally accepted principles developed by IOSCO (IOSCO, 2008, 2011). It certainly was to be expected that the erection of a complex new regulatory framework and supervisory practice from scratch would take quite some time to be settled and would be associated with controversial discussions and some readjustment regarding the detailed implementing measures and supervisory standards. However, at the moment it seems unclear when the new system will be fully functional, but one thing was becoming clear following the crisis, the so-called self-disciplining role played by reputation cannot always be relied on and only may function over the long term. Hence, on 27 December 2013, the SEC (and so the European Union) went further by adopting specific amendments eliminating references to credit ratings. Removing, however, the use of CRAs' ratings in regulatory and statutory requirements, is one thing, having them replaced by credible means, is another, and this objective may prove to be very difficult and lengthy to attain.

Although the last international regulatory initiative headed by the FSB under G20 auspices is a perfect example of international coordination, regulation and supervision of CRAs is usually made complex by interdependencies between different national regulatory systems, coming from different international business models of the global CRAs and the global financial markets, in particular as major CRA reforms were enacted in parallel. Although almost everybody would agree that governance in the rating industry should be improved, the quests for better monitoring of CRAs towards such objective may diverge. The US authorities, for instance, and so UK authorities seem to privilege market discipline through transparency and competition over excessive supervision, whereas EU authorities aim to promote CRAs' accountability through more supervision. Generally, it is feared that imposing a new business model on CRAs might be seen as a significant market intervention, which, 'if done without thorough cost benefit analysis, could have severe, unintended consequences for the wider financial system' (FSA *et al.*, 2013). Further, competition within the global market for ratings should be expected to work only slowly and indirectly as successively more information will become available and market participants will learn how to make use of it in their decision-making processes.

Any inability to cooperate at the international level may raise more difficulties in speeding Big 3 reform. The misalignment of rules, inconsistent across nations may help the Big 3 to perpetuate their control over global rating activities. In order to avoid entering into conflicting arrangements with regulators in different countries, a homogeneous global cooperative approach between regulators in the implementation and enforcement of regulations is critical to restore investor confidence in ratings. Also, provisions aiming at increasing market pressure on CRAs for greater transparency will work only slowly and indirectly as successively more information will become available and market participants will learn how to make use of this information in their decision-making. Therefore, at this point, it is not yet possible to assess the full impact of the new regulatory framework for CRAs and in particular whether it will prove sufficient to remedy the shortcomings of the rating market and to ensure an adequate quality of ratings (Doherty *et al.*, 2012).

Eliminating references to the Big 3 in regulatory requirements may not be a determinant incentive for small credit rating agencies to cross the line and join the Big 3. For most small agencies (SmAs), having to observe rules established for the Big 3, may even prove to be penalizing.[1] Indeed, the costs of staying abreast of the legislative developments and adapting to them can be excessive for SmAs, while for the Big 3 these costs can be very marginal. Transposing international rules could be extremely penalizing for SmAs for another reason: the lack of relevant information and historical data will always make them second order agencies. This is can be the reason for ESMA recognition to appear less restrictive than NRSRO. On the other hand, some believe that any international development of SmAs will be seriously impeded if mutual recognition does not occur automatically between the SEC and ESMA. If this is not the case, major issuers will certainly continue to resort exclusively to the Big 3. Practically, however, such mutual recognition is inconceivable at this time.

On the other hand, 'despite extensive debate, there has been limited action on promoting competition in the credit rating industry and revising the issuer-pays model – probably for good reason, because there are no easy solutions' (World Bank, 2009). Competition in the rating market needs to be improved but the question remains how to achieve such improvement without jeopardizing the quality of ratings. In the mind of the United Kingdom authorities, for instance, an impacting reform package should focus only on causes of disturbance within credit ratings. Consequently any proposed rating reform package should require (FSA *et al.*, 2013):

i to be based on comprehensive and careful analysis of where exactly the problem lies;
ii to have undergone full assessment of the potential impact of such changes; and
iii changes should only be envisaged in those areas where it can be verified that problems have occurred.

Besides, agencies usually argued that any strategy that aims to increase competition might actually lower the quality of ratings. 'The reason is that new entrants in an issuer-pays system would probably compete by offering higher ratings or by lowering prices and thus reducing both the level of effort in ratings and their reliability' (Becker and Milbourn 2009). It is argued that there may even be benefits to having a limited number of global credit rating agencies: this may promote greater consistency and uniformity in ratings across markets, making it easier for investors to compare debt securities issued in different countries (World Bank, 2009).

At this point, however, it is not possible to fully assess the impact of the new regulatory framework for CRAs and in particular whether it will prove sufficient to remedy the shortcomings of the rating market and to ensure adequate quality of ratings (Theis and Wolgast, 2012). Reforms are proving to be complicated by the fact that size and market recognition may be higher barriers to entry than regulatory status. In fact, only the smaller North American agencies, most of which have the same standing for regulatory purposes as the major rating agencies, seem to have any chance of gaining market acceptance. Indeed, 'while economic and regulatory barriers to entry continue to exist in the credit ratings industry, the smaller NRSROs have made notable progress in gaining market share in some of the ratings classes' (SEC, 2013).

Therefore, nobody has yet figured out how to solve the problem of the unshared Big 3 control of the global credit market and this makes us wonder if there are really alternatives to Big 3?

Are there alternatives to agencies' credit ratings?

The range of suggested alternatives to Big 3 hegemony is broad and does not always take into account what ratings can achieve and what they cannot: at one end of the spectrum is the idea that CRAs should be left to monitor themselves; at the other end, there are demands for the rating process to be entrusted to the public sector. Between self-regulation and state credit rating agencies lies the model of state regulated private sector of CRAs. While the introduction of state agencies should be excluded simply for the reason that the state would then also have to assume liability for ratings, the other two alternatives remain the subject of heated discussions. For a long time, policy-makers rejected the arguments for state regulated agencies. In Europe, it was only the present financial crisis that led to its reconsideration. There are also those who offer partial solutions to a big problem. There are those who think there is a need for a clear distinction between the rating of structured finance products and traditional debt products and thus many people believe different rating symbols could be used so as to avoid confusion (Mason, 2007). Indeed, despite identical symbols, structured products typically do not have the same risk profile as traditional corporate bonds. Whereas corporate default can be estimated by very few factors related to a single issuer, 'default on structured debt is dependent on hundreds or thousands of individual defaults [underlying mortgage pool] that are estimated given some distribution. They are not the same analysis so they should not be the same ratings' (CFA Institute, 2008). A different rating scale according to the risk profile of the products could be used so as to not mislead investors into buying mis-stated securities (CFA Institute, 2008). The UK financial authorities, for instance, assert that 'CRA ratings have offered reasonably reliable estimates of credit quality, at least amongst corporate issuers', but relying uniquely on CRAs' ratings for risk assessment can be insufficient to reach a well-informed investment decision; there is, therefore, a need for alternatives.

CRAs to monitor themselves

Regulation should never constitute the first choice[2] and agencies should be allowed to escape it, if they can demonstrate that their internal structure can ensure rating accuracy. Continuing to rely on the ability of CRAs to monitor themselves is usually justified on the basis that 'Exchanges are self-regulating and that ratings can be as well' (CFA Institute, 2008). Self-regulation, however, can have different meanings and the first wave of (self-)regulation of CRAs already resulted in substantial efforts by CRAs to improve their business conduct. The major CRAs developed individual codes of conduct that largely incorporated the IOSCO provisions. Significant improvements of standards could be observed in the rating market, for example with respect to transparency of methodology, and CRAs increasingly entered into dialogue with market participants (Theis and Wolgast, 2012). However, shortcomings of the new regulatory framework, which relied entirely on self-regulation and (reputational) market pressure, also emerged soon. Several provisions of the IOSCO Code proved insufficient, and it became clear that there was a need for some form of supervisory guidance on the interpretation of some provisions. The most important shortcoming was the lack of any enforcement mechanism. In cases where reputational pressure by market participants and moral persuasion by supervisory authorities proved to be insufficient to ensure adherence to the minimum regulatory standards, it was like there was no way to induce a CRA to alter its business conduct in the market. The success of any self-regulatory regime stands or falls with the question of control. First, there needs to be effective supervision to reveal deviations from the self-imposed rules. Second, there must be a mechanism to sanction deviations. Self-regulation in the credit rating industry is only an option if it fulfils both requirements.

Use of CRAs' ratings as complementary information

Using CRAs' ratings 'to generate an alternative credit assessment, or as complementary information, would reduce the degree of reliance on external credit ratings' (FSA *et al.*, 2013). A number of alternative metrics can be mentioned; some are market based, others are non-market based. Although, financial institutions have been reluctant to incorporate market-based measures into their internal ratings, these could potentially be useful measures of credit risk, since they do provide an arm's length assessment (FSA *et al.*, 2013). 'This is primarily because movements in market prices are driven by factors other than credit risk – such as the depth and liquidity of the market – and are prone to overshooting (procyclical effects)' (FSA *et al.*, 2013). Non-market-based measures include financial ratios based on accounting data and are subject to issuers' accounting methods and assumptions.

There may be also scope for introducing a so-called dual ratings approach. Such an approach might involve taking the more conservative of a bank's internal rating (produced by a validated model) and the prevailing external rating. Requiring two external ratings may potentially improve the accuracy of some regulatory capital requirement calculations. It might reduce investor demand for some structures if it was not possible to get a second rating. It could also have unintended consequences. These would need to be carefully considered before implementing such a rule. For example, a requirement for two external ratings could constrain issuance and innovation in some markets. It could also hinder efforts to improve competition in the industry, especially if it favours large incumbents that may be more likely to possess the resources to meet the demand for additional ratings. More generally, different CRAs' ratings tend to be very close together (as might be expected if methodologies converge over time). According to a 2006 report by the French AMF, even where ratings for a given issuer differ between CRAs, the difference is typically just one notch. Therefore, the practical effect of mandating multiple ratings may not be material anyway (FSA *et al.*, 2013). The practical effect of mandating multiple ratings may have an unintended perverse effect of contributing to more Big 3 market domination.

The National Association of Insurance Commissioners (NAIC) in the United States in relation to insurance companies has recently adopted the approach of outsourcing (by product class) to non-CRAs that use a tailored approach to assessing credit quality. The NAIC appointed a third party to conduct a credit risk assessment exercise tailored to the capital determination process (FSA *et al.*, 2013).

Public CRAs

Some EU member states raise the possibility of creating a European credit rating agency. This idea does not, however, please everyone. The UK authorities, for instance, are strongly opposed to any issuance of credit ratings by a public European CRA, central banks or public–private partnerships. According to them, the use of such ratings would potentially heighten scope for moral hazard and harm the independence of these institutions and their ability to fulfil other objectives (e.g. price stability). A public agency would also risk crowding out private sector ratings and inevitably stifle competition in the industry.

The UK authorities are firmly of the view that the provision of ratings by any central banks or a European credit rating agency will face serious problems and not necessarily resolve the problems associated with CRAs. These concerns would also apply if other international institutions, such as the IMF expanded, their role to the provision of credit ratings. Several reasons are advanced for such a conclusion (FSA *et al.*, 2013):

1 Conflict of interest: it is feared that involvement in such activities by central banks could create an inherent conflict of interest with their core objective and threaten their independence and credibility – both of which are paramount in the central bank's monetary and financial stability roles.
2 Market acceptance: in the case of a European credit rating agency, appropriate governance processes could conceivably surmount the conflict of interests. However ratings produced by CRAs supported or established by EU or national funding could be viewed as biased by investors. Their use might have to be incentivized in some way, such as granting them some official status in regulations, which could create its own set of problems as set out below.
3 Increased moral hazard: as predictions of future performance, ratings cannot be entirely accurate or stable over time. Therefore, there would be a great deal of moral hazard attached to the production of public sector ratings. The assessments produced by any of the mentioned institutions could be perceived as having 'official status', particularly if the problem of market acceptance was overcome by promoting the use of the ratings.
4 Barrier of entry: the provision of credit ratings by these institutions would be a further barrier to entry for new competitors, since the 'official rating' would be used by investors. Even while considering the benefits of consistent criteria, definitions and procedures that a European credit rating agency would bring, the crowding out of other ratings providers if sponsored by public authorities is a particular concern.
5 Cost, coverage and innovation: it will be extremely costly for any public institution to attract skilled credit analysts and to achieve adequate coverage. There would be a tension between the range of securities and issuers it rates based on its independent funding, and preferred coverage of the providers of funding.
6 Insufficient innovation: there is a concern that the proposals a European credit rating agency would be subject to familiar problems associated with public provision of services, leading to insufficient innovation in credit assessment methodologies. Encouraging the

creation of a European Network of small and medium sized credit rating agencies may prove to be a more efficient solution.

There is a broad consensus that the rating process should not be entrusted to the public sector and that rating methodologies should not be subject to any monitoring activity and several reasons are advanced. First, regulation of this magnitude could result in the state being considered partly responsible for published ratings. Second, given that states themselves are also issuers of debt, a new conflict of interests would arise if the state was in a position to influence the methodologies used for assigning sovereign ratings. Some believe that state credit rating agencies could prevent misjudgements of the kind made before the present financial crisis (*Spiegel-Online*, 2009). For them, a key lesson to be learned from the current turmoil is that it is vital for ratings to be able to provide a reliable indication of a debtor's creditworthiness even in times of crisis. In their view, the present crisis proves that the self-disciplining role played by reputation cannot always be relied on and only functions over the long term. Self-regulation does not work effectively when the pressure of reputation as a controlling power exists only to a limited degree due to a lack of competition (Blaurock, 2007). In addition, the argument goes, a rating does not only buy an issuer's information. It should not be forgotten that ratings also regulate market access. Against this backdrop, CRAs have not managed to demonstrate that they are able under the existing regime to successfully resolve conflicts of interests. State regulation advocates feel that, in the interest of financial market stability, the current market failure justifies state regulation. However, the priority should be given to ensuring robust internal control and risk management within agencies (FSA *et al.*, 2013).

As can be seen there is no easy solution to the credit ratings dilemma, but who is to blame?

Whom to blame?

Credit rating governance failure that brought such financial crisis as the subprime one cannot only be the work of a limited number of players as the Big 3. It must have been the consequence of a general acceptance of fraud and lack of responsibility and a deep worship for easy gain. Many crisis witnesses must have been stingy with critiques, indeed who remain silent consents. For this reason, the blame has to be shared. It goes first to regulators who got rid of their responsibilities by passing them over to agencies. Over the years, indeed, the reputation of ratings has become so unchallenged that regulators began to rely on them to monitor risk-taking by banks, since the 1930s, and such reliance by regulators expanded significantly and increasingly, till 2008, the year of the subprime crisis. Regulators, however, do not seem to have checked the accuracy of the rating they were calling for their use. Instead they were convinced that agencies would never bargain their reputation against higher income, since if agencies were seen as having produced inaccurate ratings nobody would be ready to pay for them. Well regulators seem to have got it all wrong.

Despite the limited assurance regarding their accuracy, regulators have depended extensively on credit ratings in setting regulatory policies in strategic areas like determining capital adequacy requirements for financial institutions or evaluating the credit risk of assets in securitization.

> By incorporating credit ratings into their requirements, regulators effectively outsourced many regulatory functions to rating agencies and made credit ratings essential for issuers and the cornerstone of regulations across a range of financial sectors. As a result, rating agencies now play a critical role as de facto 'capital market gatekeepers' – despite their apparent lack of liability and their reluctance to assume such a responsibility.
>
> (World Bank, 2009)

The blame goes also to investors who rely blindly on agencies' ratings. Attracted by greed, investors fail to look beyond ratings and to develop a greater awareness of the risks they are exposed to. This may also have encouraged the Big 3 not to constantly update their internal policies and procedures in order to improve the quality of their ratings and thus reinforce their credibility (FSB, 2013).

The whole of society is finally to blame. As human beings, we strongly entered an era of intense manipulation of public opinion; the false cannot be distinguished from true anymore, except for the intimate character of their author. We entered what we can call a 'mafia era' and we are surprised to see our organizations keeping the pace. Prosperous new industries were created, whose sole purpose is to deceive under the helpless eyes of governments. Of course regulations are constantly promulgated; but can we regulate every potential misbehaviour? Instead of producing quality services and products, our organizations are busy studying how to render their poor quality unnoticed. All shots are allowed, opacity, management collusion, corruption and so on. As a citizen we value lies in our votes, as consumers, we encourage them by our consumption choices and, as investors, we institutionalize them by our unrealistic returns requirements. We actually contribute significantly to a worst future for coming generations. For this reason, we must collectively accept responsibility for what we permitted to occur in the rating industry and in other sectors and for having embraced systems that gave rise to our present predicament and dilemma.

The road ahead

In the short term, there is an extreme urgency for CRAs to be more transparent and regulatory initiatives towards such an objective should be encouraged to continue. The global credit market needs greater transparency about CRAs' overall rating model: rating assumptions, methodologies but also fee structures, past performance and expressing ratings using numbers. And indeed the SEC and ESMA formerly required registered agencies to fill in a return which goes in that direction. The criteria and data used to produce debt ratings should be transparent and issuers that are rated should be given time to prepare their comments, which should be published before the rating. In the meantime, the monitoring of agencies should be 'given the authority to set standards, monitor and evaluate compliance, and discipline ratings agencies for violations' (Levitt, 2007): to ensure full implementation of such a supervision regime, in order to make sure that CRAs are serving investors, the monitoring authorities should provide themselves with the right tools and personnel. Since, however, the main CRAs all operated internationally, the more suitable forum, to our point of view, would be the International Organisation of Securities Commissions (IOSCO). Under current rules, however, even though we can judge whether or not agencies are complying with internal and international procedures and policies, it is not possible to judge the quality of such compliance. In the long run our suggestions are the following:

i Our first suggestion for improving rating accuracy goes to the implementation of an efficient internal oversight and self-regulation and industry surveillance. When referring to the auditing sector, such industry oversight, implemented with the Sarbanes–Oxley Act, has made a difference in behaviour that may have benefited investors by providing stricter rules on transparency and corporate governance. In Chapter 8 we suggested the introduction of Standing Rating Committees of the Board (SRCB) within agencies, with the primary objective of overseeing rating activities by the board. SRCBs should have the same power as the audit committee with the same reporting obligations. Currently the main agencies do have credit policy groups (CPGs) that are supposed to be a key part of the control and analytical support framework and that can be enhanced to become SRCBs. IOSCO also recommends the creation of supervisory colleges for the largest rating agencies and these have indeed been established for Standard & Poor's, Moody's Investors, Inc. and Fitch Ratings, Inc. The Office of Credit Ratings (OCR) of the United States is ensuring the chairmanship of supervisory colleges of Standard & Poor and Moody's and the ESMA is chairing the supervisory college of Fitch (SEC, 2013). Supervisory colleges seem to politically oriented, and do not deal with the issue of internal control mechanisms. Of the Big 3, only Moody's seems to have a board that can exercise direct monitoring over the credit rating activity of the company through its Moody's Investors Service committee.

ii Our second suggestion is to make CRAs compete in a market where no one is required to hire them. Till recently it is quasi-impossible for any serious player to enter the global credit market and ensure itself a significant share of that market. Statutory requirements for investors to buy only securities rated by regulator sanctioned CRAs are being progressively removed, thanks to the G20, SEC and ESMA. They all seem to rally to the idea of: 'Why not just abolish the agencies' special status and let the market gauge creditworthiness? If the equity market can regulate on its own and grade its securities itself, then why would the debt market be unable to do the same?' (UKEssays, 2010). The entry to the market of newcomers should be encouraged, as competition from new agencies might create a healthy diversity of opinion, leading to more accurate assessments of debt issuers' default. In fact, despite the predominance of Moody's and Standard & Poor's, and, to a lesser extent, Fitch, there are an estimated 150 CRAs to be found around the world. Since, thus far, the SEC has only given official status (NRSRO) to seven of these agencies, there seems to be a lot of room for growth in terms of competitiveness in the credit rating industry. Laing (2011) indicates that the SEC can help to increase competition in the industry by speeding up the process of approving new agencies. In fact, despite the predominance of Moody's and Standard & Poor's, and, to a lesser extent, Fitch, there are an estimated 150 CRAs to be found around the world and there seems to be a lot of room for growth in terms of competitiveness in the credit rating industry. However, according to some authors 'increasing competition in the ratings industry involves the risk of impairing the reputational mechanism that underlies the provision of good quality ratings' (Becker and Milbourn, 2009). It seems that a higher level of competition in this specific case reduces future economic rents and increases the short terms gains and incentives to cheating.

iii Our third suggestion has to do with CRAs' remuneration model: it would be wise, like in other sectors to separate rating activities from consulting and require all issuers to pay for advice/analysis separately from the rating. This may have also the other advantage of preventing some issuers asking several CRAs for their ratings assessment, and then only paying the agency offering the most optimistic rating.

iv Inaccurate ratings should be associated with legal sanction and therefore credit ratings should be denied the pretended First Amendment protection and the 'not subject to underwriter's liabilities'. They must be held liable for any significant wrongdoing. Many lawsuits have been filed against CRAs, in some cases, by rated institutions, in others by investors. Plaintiffs have not been successful in either event. The American government is, however, taking the lead and opening the door by suing S&P. As mentioned before, in its civil lawsuit against Standard & Poor's the American government is seeking $5 billion, accusing the agency of having defrauding investors.

> The United States said S&P inflated ratings and understated risks associated with mortgage securities, driven by a desire to gain more business from the investment banks that issued those securities. S&P committed fraud by falsely claiming its ratings were objective, the lawsuit said.
>
> (Viswanatha and Lacarpa (Reuters), 2013)

CRAs usually minimize their role, which they advocate remains limited to producing a rating opinion and informing the investing public. This, however, underestimates their fundamental role in rating structured finance products that they helped create. Such a move on the part of the American government is commendable and determining, but there is the need for a global strategy for imposing liability on credit CRAs to ensure appropriate (both public and private) accountability. Particularly that misconduct may be difficult to prove. Liability should be dependent on the negligent breach of a pre-determined set of duties (and revisable in the course of time). In fact, why not submit faulty CRAs to an international arbitration? Convicted agencies should be sanctioned including the revocation of the NRSRO/ESMA status and all the privileges that it implies.

Competition can best be enhanced by reducing the mechanistic reliance on ratings; enforcing transparency and disclosure that enables the comparability of different CRAs; and removing unnecessary barriers to entry. Transparency and disclosure are also key reforms particularly whenever a product is surrounded with much complexity and opacity. However, among the previous suggestions, increasing agencies' liability may prove to be the more efficient tool of improving rating accuracy and decreasing conflicts of interest. Fairness should, however, prevail, in order to avoid CRAs being used as scapegoats for a more collective endeavour, by making sure all major financial market players are submitted to the same liability requirements.

Conclusion

The global rating market has been displaying signs of disarray for some time now, and reducing the mechanistic and simplistic dependence on credit ratings for regulatory purposes remains an important accomplishment and can help to solve a number of other issues raised in this book; it cannot, however, solve all the problems, like, for instance, when a security gets downgraded below the investment grade threshold, managers have to liquidate their positions in huge quantity, thus causing unneeded sudden volatility and possible portfolio losses. Transparency required from the Big 3 may also play an important role in the introduction of more competition in the global rating market. Investors should be encouraged to compare practices of ratings among agencies and allow smaller rating agencies and newcomers to the rating market to build brands with observable differences compared to the Big 3 and thus be able to compete. It seems that only very few small agencies, mainly North American NRSRO (DBRS, EJR, HR Ratings, KBRA and Morningstar), because of their long term cohabitation and familiarization with the Big 3's systems and strategies, may finally be the only agencies in a position to benefit significantly from the recent SEC amendments aiming to eliminate references to credit ratings in rules and acts. So unless the Big 3, aware of being watched from everywhere, concede to some openness, or the SEC (or the EU) venturing into the rating marshland, mingling with market laws, small agencies may never catch up, or for some of them even escape extinction.

The global credit rating market appears to be North American and it is expected to stay that way for the foreseeable future, and the solution to credit agencies' issues, if any, can only emanate from the United States.

Notes

1 Comments of CPR Portugal within the scope of the public consultation on the Proposed Regulatory Framework for Credit Rating Agencies submitted by the Committee of European Securities Regulators (CESR).

2 Some European experts are already arguing that the recent European legislation (Rule CE no. 1060/2009), given its ambitious objective, has had little effect on the way to interpret data or to deal with the potential conflict of interests that may be created by the complex contractual arrangements between credit rating agencies and their clients (Firzli *et al.*, 2011).

Bibliography

Ammer, J. and F. Packer (2000), 'How consistent are credit ratings? A geographic and sectorial analysis of default risk', Board of Governors of the Federal Reserve System, International Finance Discussion Papers, No. 668, June.

Becker, B. and T. Milbourn (2009), 'How did increased competition affect credit ratings?' Harvard Business School Working Paper, No. 09-051.

Blaurock, U. (2007), 'Control and responsibility of credit rating agencies', at: www.ejcl.org/113/article113-16.pdf, retrieved 2 July 2014.

Cantor, R. and F. Packer (1996), 'Determinants and impact of sovereign credit ratings', *Economic Policy Review*, Vol. 2(2) , pp. 37–54.

CFA Institute (2008), 'CFA institute member opinion poll confirms support for CRA reform', 7 July, at: www.cfainstitute.org/aboutus/press/release/08releases/20080707_01.html, retrieved 20 November 2013.

Crutsinger, M. and C. Rexrode (2011), 'Fitch Ratings keeps its rating on long-term U.S. debt at the highest grade of AAA', at: www.WPTV.com, retrieved 19 October 2011.

Doherty, N.A, V.A. Kartasheva and R.D. Phillips (2012), 'Information effect of entry into credit ratings market: the case of insurers' ratings', *Journal of Financial Economics*, November, Vol. 106(2), pp. 308–330.

Feldblum, S. (2011), 'Rating agencies', at: www.casact.org/library/studynotes/Feldblum_Rating_Oct%202011.pdf, retrieved 2 March 2014.

Financial Crisis Inquiry Commission (FCIC) (2011), 'Financial Crisis Inquiry Commission report: final report of the National Commission on the causes of the financial and economic crisis in the United States', ISBN 978-0-16-087727-8.

Financial Stability Board (FSB) (2013), 'Credit rating agencies reducing reliance and strengthening oversight: progress report to the St Petersburg G20 Summit', 29 August.

Firzli, J., M. Nicolas and V. Bazi (2011), 'Infrastructure investments in an age of austerity: the pension and sovereign funds perspective', *Revue Analyse Financière*, Vol. 41 (Q4), pp. 19–22.

FSA, HM Treasury and Bank of England (2013), 'The United Kingdom authorities response to the European Commission internal market and services consultation document on credit rating agencies', at: https://circabc.europa.eu/d/d/workspace/SpacesStore/0d1ea101-b6d0–470b-b8b3-e28e4c1cba30/BoE-FSA-Treasury_EN.pdf, retrieved 2 July 2014.

Goodhart, C.A.E. (2008), 'How, if at all, should credit ratings agencies (CRAs) be regulated?' Special Paper LES Finance Market Group Paper Series, June.

International Organization of Securities Commissions (IOSCO) (2008), 'Revised code of conduct fundamentals for credit rating agencies', at: www.cmvm.pt/CMVM/Cooperacao%20Internacional/Docs%20Iosco/Documents/CodCondutaIOSCOCRA.pdf, retrieved 26 May 2014.

International Organization of Securities Commissions (IOSCO) (2011), 'Regulatory implementation of the statement of principles regarding the activities of credit rating agencies', Final Report, at: www.fsa.go.jp/, retrieved 26 May 2014.

International Organization of Securities Commissions (IOSCO) (2013), 'Supervisory colleges for credit rating agencies', at: www.iosco.org/about/, retrieved 2 December 2013.

Levitt, A. (2007), 'Conflicts and the credit crunch', at: http://online.wsj.com/news/articles/SB118912606193520154, retrieved 2 October 2014.

Laing, J. (2011), 'Pillar 3 disclosures', at: www.laing.com/what-we-do/asset-management/john_laing_capital_management/pillar_3_disclosures.html, retrieved 2 October 2014.

Mason, J.R. (2007), 'Hearing on the role of credit rating agencies in the structured finance market', at: www.gpo.gov/fdsys/pkg/CHRG-110hhrg39541/html/CHRG-110hhrg39541.htm, retrieved 28 April 2014.

Ropes & Gray LLP (2014), 'SEC removes reference to NRSRO credit ratings in rule 5b-3 and forms N-1A, N-2 and N-3', at: www.lexology.com/library/detail.aspx?g=d960acc0-adfa-4a16-b28b-4c15cc70fd3b, retrieved 21 February 2014.

Securities and Exchange Commission (SEC) (2013), 'Annual report on nationally recognized statistical rating organizations', at: www.sec.gov, retrieved 13 June 2014.

Spiegel-Online (2009), at: www.spiegel.de/flash/0,,24236,00.html, retrieved 4 July 2014.

Testimony of John C. Coffee, Jr, Adolf A. Berle Professor of Law, Columbia University Law School before the Senate Banking Committee on 26 September 2007, 'The role and impact of credit rating agencies on the subprime credit markets', at: www.banking.senate.gov/public/index.cfm?FuseAction=Files.View&FileStore_id=d1c0419e-d84a-4b43-b02d-4e246e2dbec7, retrieved 2 October 2014.

Theis, A. and M. Wolgast (2012), 'Regulation and reform of rating agencies in the European Union: an insurance industry perspective', Geneva Papers 37, pp. 47–76, at: www.palgrave-journals.com/gpp/journal/v37/n1/full/gpp.201133a.html, retrieved 20 June 2012.

UKEssays (2010), 'Problems of the credit rating agencies', at: www.ukessays.com/dissertations/economics/problems-of-the-credit-rating-agencies.php, retrieved 30 September 2013.

Viswanatha, A. and L.T. Lacarpa (2013), 'U.S. government slams S&P with $5 billion fraud lawsuit'. Reuters, 5 February.

Wall Street Journal (2008), 'A first amendment defense for the rating agencies?' 21 April.

World Bank (2009), 'Credit rating agencies, no easy regulatory solution', at: http://siteresources.worldbank.org/EXTFINANCIALSECTOR/Resources/282884-1303327122200/Note8.pdf, retrieved 2 July 2014.

Index